How Slavoj Became Žižek

THE DIGITAL MAKING OF
A PUBLIC INTELLECTUAL

+ + + + + + + + + + + + + +

ELIRAN BAR-EL

THE UNIVERSITY OF CHICAGO PRESS
CHICAGO AND LONDON

The University of Chicago Press, Chicago 60637
The University of Chicago Press, Ltd., London
© 2023 by The University of Chicago
All rights reserved. No part of this book may be used or reproduced in any manner whatsoever without written permission, except in the case of brief quotations in critical articles and reviews. For more information, contact the University of Chicago Press, 1427 E. 60th St., Chicago, IL 60637.
Published 2023
Printed in the United States of America

32 31 30 29 28 27 26 25 24 23   1 2 3 4 5

ISBN-13: 978-0-226-82350-8 (cloth)
ISBN-13: 978-0-226-82352-2 (paper)
ISBN-13: 978-0-226-82351-5 (e-book)
DOI: https://doi.org/10.7208/chicago/9780226823515.001.0001

Library of Congress Cataloging-in-Publication Data

Names: Bar-El, Eliran, author.
Title: How Slavoj became Žižek : the digital making of a public intellectual / Eliran Bar-El.
Description: Chicago : University of Chicago Press, 2023. | Includes bibliographical references and index.
Identifiers: LCCN 2022020466 | ISBN 9780226823508 (cloth) | ISBN 9780226823522 (paperback) | ISBN 9780226823515 (ebook)
Subjects: LCSH: Žižek, Slavoj. | Philosophers—Slovenia—Biography. | BISAC: SOCIAL SCIENCE / Media Studies | PHILOSOPHY / Individual Philosophers
Classification: LCC B4870.Z594 B37 2023 | DDC 199/4973.—dc23/eng/20220615
LC record available at https://lccn.loc.gov/2022020466

♾ This paper meets the requirements of ANSI/NISO Z39.48-1992 (Permanence of Paper).

HOW SLAVOJ BECAME ŽIŽEK

The particular is for the most part of too trifling a value as compared with the general: Individuals are sacrificed and abandoned.

G. W. F. HEGEL

The philosopher is inscribed in the discourse of the master. He plays the role of the fool within it. . . . The court fool has a role: that of being the replacement of the truth.

J. LACAN

Contents

List of Figures ix

Introduction 1

1 Slovenia between East and West: The Origin of Superpositioning 25

2 If at First You Don't Succeed: The Emergence of Hegelacanese 66

3 Going Global: Narrating the (Traumatic) Present 103

4 The End of Žižek: Performing the Sacrificial Intellectual 145

Conclusion 175

Acknowledgments 191
Notes 193
Index 235

Figures

0.1 The Sociological Study of Intellectuals *10*
0.2 Model of the Movement of Intellectual Intervention (in the Humanities) *21*
1.1 Yugoslavia/Slovenia Timeline *26*
1.2 Žižek's Early Period Timeline *35*
1.3 Razprave (Discussion) issue of *Problemi*, 1979 *43*
1.4 Parts of pages 3–4 from the censored *Punk Problemi* issue, 1982 *48*
2.1 Žižek's Formative Intellectual Interventions, 1989–2000 *69*
3.1 Žižek's Mentions in English Books, 1982–2008 *119*
3.2 Žižek in *The Reality of the Virtual* *130*
3.3 Žižek in *The Pervert's Guide to Cinema* *130*
3.4 Žižek in *Žižek!* *131*
3.5 Žižek's Digital Interest over Region, 2004–2019 *134*
3.6 Comics of Žižek and the 2008 Financial Crisis *140*
3.7 Žižek's Interest over Time, 2004–2019 *141*
4.1 "The Collected Jokes of Slavoj Žižek" *147*
4.2 Žižek in *The Pervert's Guide to Ideology* *149*
4.3 Visual Rendition of the Žižek-Chomsky Controversy, 2013 *155*

4.4 Anti-Žižek Flyer circulated in the Left Forum in New York City on May 22, 2016 *168*
4.5 Žižek's Citations per Year, 1996–2018 *169*
4.6 Žižek's Public Media Interventions in English, 1999–2018 *170*

Introduction

Not many intellectuals can claim a nightclub or a fashion collection to their name.[1] The very idea of it seems odd, as if the ivory tower of isolated intellectuals—working alone to candlelight in their room—shattered onto the streets of the beating masses. Even within the confines of the tower, most intellectuals could only dream that their work would inspire a journal and conference dedicated to their studies or a dictionary devoted to their conceptual armory, let alone a professional impressionist video clip with millions of views.[2] Slavoj Žižek has all of these, and more. In this sense of oddity, the object—or rather, the subject—of this book is somewhat exceptional. As I will try to establish, Žižek might just be a new breed of public intellectuals.

Since the beginning of the twenty-first century, Žižek has been positioned as both a militant academic and a public figure. One of the most prolific, renowned, and controversial thinkers alive, his public interventions have made him an intellectual celebrity with the status of cultural star. Along the way, he has made enemies and attracted critics too, mainly because of the way he combines theory and practice: by associating German idealism with French theory in English, Žižek became both famous and infamous from the inception of his global academic career.[3]

Slavoj Žižek was born in 1949 in Ljubljana, the capital of Slovenia, which was then part of Yugoslavia and the Eastern bloc.[4] He enrolled at the University of Ljubljana in 1968 and studied sociology and philosophy. After earning his bachelor of arts in 1971, he was able to publish his graduation paper, on Heidegger and Derrida, in a Slovenian-language book entitled *The Pain of Difference*. During his undergraduate studies, he had traveled to France in 1969 and established academic connections that would influence his later thinking and intellectual trajectory. His master's degree, earned in 1975 in Slovenia, was completed with a thesis on French theory: "Sign, Signifier and Writing." This led to his pursuit of two doctorates, one in philosophy from Slovenia and the other in psychoanalysis from France. The latter, defended in 1982 and entitled "Philosophy between the Symptom and Fantasy," marks the beginning of Žižek's official intellectual recognition, and it is the departure point of this book.[5]

Although coming from a rather humble familial and institutional background, far from the limelight of Harvard, Oxford, or the Sorbonne, Žižek managed to burst onto the global intellectual scene and become one of its most significant representatives. He has since never looked back. As indicated on one his book covers, "Žižek was born, writes books, and will die." His level of prolificacy and rate of interventions are unparalleled in the academic world. He has around one hundred English books and dozens more in at least ten other languages, published with approximately twenty publishers at a rate of two books a year. Moreover, between 1982 and 2018, Žižek's intellectual interventions include around 100 academic articles and 400 public media articles (of which 288 were in English), with more than fifteen different outlets, a total of thirteen languages, and an average of at least once a month for over twenty years. Besides this staggering amount of academic writing, Žižek is unique for his engagement with popular culture, and particularly cinema.

Žižek's engagement with the public moves beyond words on a page and is embodied in person. In addition to media interviews and academic lectures, he has appeared in films—including as the main protagonist—a dozen times. These performances began in Slovenia during the 1980s, when he frequently engaged in public affairs, contributed to numerous journals, formed the Ljubljana School for Theoretical Psychoanalysis, and even ran for public office. Since then, he has made hundreds of public appearances in dozens of countries, including the United States, United Kingdom, China, Russia, India, and Palestine, and today his publicity has reached an international scale. Every public appearance of his resembles a rock concert, with flocking crowds and people sitting on corridor floors. In fact, "Žižek always feels more like a show than like a person. It is as if he cannot simply be Žižek, but must always perform Žižek as if he himself were a role not a person."[6] Perhaps for this reason the *Chronicle of Higher Education* called him "the Elvis of cultural theory"; for the *Guardian*, he is "the Borat of philosophy."[7] This unusual range of intellectual interventions has also gained Žižek triple access to *Foreign Policy*'s list Top 100 Global Thinkers, as well as the title "most dangerous philosopher in the west" according to the *New Republic*.[8]

This odd conjuncture could be a part of the world we live in, alongside Žižek: a world of opposing claims, shifting positions, and blurred boundaries—all indicators of the new digital public sphere. Many of Žižek's appearances, lectures, and interviews are recorded, uploaded, and circulated online by faithful followers, enhancing his international recognition in this mediatized public domain. This is true not only in geographical terms but also disciplinary ones. His span of intellectual activity is immense, encompassing hard-core philosophical issues like being and truth, psychoanalytical issues like sex and subjectivity, political and economic issues like capitalism and communism, artistic issues like Wagner and *The Matrix*, scientific issues like quantum physics and neurobiology or ecology, and so on.

This sketchy description already begins attesting to the scope of the phenomenon called "Žižek," which I describe and explain in this book. Of course, many books have been written about Žižek.[9] Nonetheless, most deal with either his philosophical ideas or his political arguments. The common literature, for the most part, engages with his intellectual *products*. Rarely do we find a systemic evaluation of Žižek's production *process*, and that is the perspective I adopt in this book. Specifically, this book is about the emergence, development, and reception of Žižek, as well as—but not confined to—his intellectual products and interventions. Only recently do we find a performative gaze at the Žižekian phenomenon.[10] Yet even this evaluation is not sociological or empirical, but mostly artistic and theoretical. In contrast, the primary goal of this book is to explicate systematically and practically the Žižekian phenomenon. It does so by building upon the sociology of intellectual interventions toward elucidating the *positioning process* that accounts for the becoming of Žižek as a global public intellectual.

This kind of inquiry relates Žižek's theory and practice to the timing of his global emergence.[11] Thus, the book analyzes various social aspects that provide the contexts for the production of the Žižekian phenomenon and its celebritization, digitalization, and even cancellation. It is developed along different stages from inception through reception to rejection: first, his early career in Slovenia with its changing political, cultural, and intellectual atmosphere; then, his engagement with France and French theory followed by his success in English; and then his explosion in the United States and the global arena. Particularly, I adopt a dramaturgical approach, which links performativity, rhetoric, and dialectic, to examine Žižek's intellectual interventions in all their various forms, from the book to the blog, and to show how they position Žižek differentially.[12] As these interventions and the positioning they bring about are relational in nature, Žižek's teams and networks of colleagues, critics, commentators, and publishers will reveal their key role in the spreading of the phenomenon.

By now we have a sense of who Žižek is, what he does, and what makes him a unique phenomenon. Yet we have a lesser sense of *how* Žižek does it or *how* he should be studied sociologically. To answer this, we have to examine Žižek within the lineage of public intellectuals and the latest digitalization of the public sphere.

Intellectuals from the Cave to the Digital Public Sphere

In every society there are some individuals whose social position, function, role, or value is defined chiefly by their capacity to perform intellectual activity, whether it is writing, speaking, or thinking. In fact, throughout its history, the term "intellectual" has positioned its holder not only with relation to knowledge, insight, or expertise but also to the ethical, social, and political duty to intervene in the public sphere with regard to public affairs on behalf of the public good.[13]

This interventional relation to the public (sphere, affairs, and good) makes the intellectual a natural candidate to be a "public intellectual"—for now defined tentatively as "a person concerned with symbols and ideas who comments publicly on the social condition with the objective of influencing or guiding its future."[14] Importantly, this singularity of "the public" should not divert us from its inherent multiplicity, referring at once to various actual publics, such as, in Žižek's case, the Slovenian, French, English, and American, as well as to their externality vis-à-vis the self-regulated and relatively autonomous academy. In this diversified sense, the "general" public is the space, whether physical or virtual, in which different publics and public agents engage in public affairs.

Nonetheless, the relationship between the intellectual and the public has been somewhat problematic from the very beginning. In the Allegory of the Cave from Plato's *Politeia*, and in Socrates's trial from *The Apology*, this problematic of the philosopher-intellectual is as clear as it is perilous.[15] The philosopher was supposed to bring truth to people (or vice versa), at all costs. One such cost has been the accusation of corruption. And just as in Socrates's ancient case, Žižek too is often accused of corrupting today's youth—a crucial point to which I shall return.

Historically, the public intellectual was understood as one who occupies an external, general, and independent position regarding the given, particular society or any of its private groups. This understanding led to the characterization of the free-floating, a-topos, placeless intellectual. One image in particular propagated this external position and independent role of intellectuals. According to it, "public intellectuals were seen as burdened with a mission: to introduce society to a universal set of norms sanctioned by a higher authority, like the biblical prophet who speaks divine truth to earthly powers."[16] From Plato's philosopher through to the biblical prophet and the modern author, there is a great sense of vocational calling related to the public intellectual.[17]

This intellectual position, and the interventional call of duty or mission accompanying it, have changed in modern secular times, oscillating between affirmative and negative connotations. During the Enlightenment era, the notion of the homme de lettres was used to denote writers in equivalence with the notion of intellectuals, as those who performed rational rather than emotional thinking. More recently, the notion of intellectuals still bears witness to the problematic position of those carrying it. In the French Dreyfus affair of the 1890s, the term was used by his supporters to adopt the truth of his innocence. But it was also used by his accusers who delegitimized the former abstract thinkers for lacking concrete legal training. Thus, in modern times the (external, general, and independent) "intellectual" is attributed two additional characteristics: the writer, as opposed to the speaker, and the professional, as opposed to the layperson.[18]

Clearly, the trope of "public intellectual" is context dependent.[19] The convoluted relation of the intellectual and the public (as both nouns and adjectives) arise because of their various contextual definitions and consequential roles. For instance, in his 1928 *The Treason of the Intellectuals*, Julian Benda provided an affirmative definition of intellectuals as "all those whose activity essentially is not the pursuit of practical aims, all those who seek their joy in the practice of an art or a science or a metaphysical speculation, in short in the possession of non-material advantages."[20] Against this affirmative definition, he also termed intellectuals "clerks," negatively defined as "all those who speak to the world in a transcendental manner,"[21] that is, who bring earthly power under the guise of transcendental truth. Stressing the importance of culture, Jeffery Alexander proposed that "intellectuals are actors who can exercise judgment because they themselves are free-floating, independent of any particular commitments. . . . In theoretical terms, 'intellectuals' and 'public' are concepts that go hand-in-hand, . . . being a public intellectual is symbolic action, a matter of becoming . . . 'a representative man.'"[22] However popular this intellectual position might be, it rests on some dichotomies that restrict our understanding of intellectual phenomena, such as private versus public, internal versus external, speaker versus writer, passive versus active, and layperson versus expert.

These dichotomies still play a significant role in the study of intellectual activity, which is commonly understood through the normative function associated with it. This "missionary" association leads to the following recurrent question about the relationship between truth and power: can the one *speak* to the other? Practically, this translates into studying intellectuals along a dual trajectory defined by the level and type of their interventions: intellectuals could basically follow Benjamin Disraeli, Woodrow Wilson, or Václav Havel, and intervene in politics, supposedly bringing truth to power; or, alternatively, they could follow Zola and Gandhi, who abstained from power in the name of truth.

However attractive they may be, these two ways may still be incomplete since, as Gil Eyal concisely put it: "What exactly is *done* by adding the qualifier 'public'? The answer is *boundary work*. The addition of 'public' redraws the boundary between who is, and who is not, a 'true' intellectual in a very specific way, excluding from the category of academics and especially experts who are understood to be confined to narrow technical pursuits."[23] Working diligently on that boundary, this book utilizes positioning theory, and specifically the concepts of performativity and intervention, to overcome such restricting dichotomies, thus challenging even the idea that intellectuals are (or should be?) either on the side of power or on the side of truth, a dichotomy that betrays Žižek's unique mode of intellectual intervention. In that sense, it follows a conception of intellectuals as "a class of hybrid beings standing with one foot in the contemplative world and the other in the political."[24]

Moreover, it is also today's digital public sphere, despite its challenges, that forms Žižek's interventional *locus intellectus*. Recent technological changes generate new conditions for intellectual activity. Fewer restrictions result in mass access to, and popularization of, knowledge, leading to an information inflation. This is added to more social changes or transformations of intellectual life: the widespread emergence of the social sciences from the 1960s onward, the blurring boundaries between experts and nonexperts, the weakening influence of "big" philosophical systems, and consequently, the decline of the "authoritative" intellectual alongside the declining intellectual authority.[25] Together, such changes play a crucial role in Žižek's public and global emergence.[26]

These recent developments touch upon intellectual substantiation, as the legitimization of intellectual interventions in our present knowledge societies. They entail not only the intellectuals working under today's unprecedented social, political, economic, and technological conditions, but also the institutions in which they work such as universities,[27] as well as the space where they perform, the new digital public sphere. Before the internet, the basic political economy of what is conventionally called mass communication media was mostly controlled by elites, which greatly restricted the public access to knowledge. In this environment, as Keren and Hawkins explain, "achieving the social status of public intellectual might seem like the product of a Faustian bargain between the purveyor of ideas and the purveyors of media."[28] In fact, this is how "media intellectuals" were born. According to Jacobs and Townsley, these are politicians, journalists, experts, and other high-status intellectuals who act as "professional communicators" or narrators and use the news media's formats "as a staging ground to gather and debate the issues of the day."[29] However, in today's "post-codex era,"[30] when intellectual work is no longer done solely on paper by experts but also on screen by nonexperts, the technologically mediated public sphere is characterized by abundance, not scarcity: "Ours is an era defined by an expanding diversity of open and interactive communication media to which a majority of the world's population now has access. Apparently in stark contrast to the rise of the traditional mass media, which first fascinated critical theorists in the 1930s, never before has the potential been greater for more individuals to communicate more directly with others in a greater variety of ways and, superficially at least, with fewer, and lower, entry barriers and less restriction and oversight."[31] In these conditions of the Wikipedia age and the elevated importance of the sound bite, the blog, or the tweet—what is the becoming status of the intellectual (as substance and style)? If the decline of the "authoritative intellectual" is accompanied by a decline of "intellectual authority," what can intellectuals do?[32] With the rise of digital communication and new social media, today's "technology intellectuals work in attention economy. . . . [T]hey succeed if they attract enough attention to themselves and their message that they can make a living from it."[33] This new world of what Farrell called "technology intellectualism" has some clear benefits: it connects the world of ideas to a broader public than in the time of the traditional public intellectual. It also facilitates the elevation of thinkers who would never have succeeded in traditional academic settings. However, as Henry Farrell also noted, the new technology intellectualism has some drawbacks. Mainly, he argues that it ignores the social conflicts and inequalities that shape politics, economy, and culture. This is why the challenging task at hand, for contemporary intellectuals and therefore for this book, is "figuring out how genuinely contrary and interesting intellectuals can support themselves in a tacit economy that seems geared either to co-opt them or turn them into professional controversialists."[34] Another issue with digital media is noted by Jodi Dean in her *Blog Theory*, namely "the turbulence of networked communications: that is, the rapidity of innovation, adoption, adaptation, and obsolescence."[35] It is part of what she calls "communicative capitalism," as the convergence of democracy and capitalism by networked communications and entertainment media. It is here, as Beller remarked in his investigation into attention economy and the society of the spectacle, that the "cinematic organization of attention yields a situation in which attention . . . is that necessary cybernetic relation to the *socius*—the totality of the social—for the production of value for late capital."[36]

In this precise sense, intellectual substantiation, as a positioning process of ideas and knowledge production based on intellectual epistemology and legitimacy, is a site of intersection between public life (pressing matters of the present, daily public affairs and debates), and intellectual life (involved in producing and disseminating ideas, knowledge, and so on). Substantiation is "what underpins the credibility of those who appear in nominally public intellectual roles, as well as the validity of their statements and the quality of their insights."[37] But today, "the fruits of academic investigation must now compete in a new information 'ether' in which many of the traditional knowledge hierarchies have become confused, it is much harder for intellectuals to substantiate their claims, as uniquely intellectual."[38]

The internet paves the way for crucial challenges regarding issues of access, both academic and public, to knowledge, which change the public sphere as we experience it. Whereas traditionally defined as "the milieu in which the institutions and practices of social and political governance interact with the general population engaged in everyday life," the public today, more than ever, is determined by "who grants access to the media, with the content and nature of the speech itself being forged by this power relationship."[39] This development also generates a phantom and a phantasm. The phantasm is best captured by the motto "We're all public intellectuals,"[40] premised on the opportunities in a public sphere that is now more open. Because the internet is supposed to allow access, "the tendency is to argue either that this openness is a product of democratic social forces—a dubious historical assumption—or, worse, that public affairs as conducted in this sphere will adopt similarly open characteristics—a dubious technological as well as political assumption."[41] Indeed, claims Pirnie, the efficacy of intellectuals' effort to convey messages intended to spur social change thus depends in part on the specific technologies of communication they adopt.[42] An early example of this recognition is Søren Kierkegaard's 1864 essay *The Present Age*, which mounts a scathing critique of "the Press" and its constitutive role in creating and sustaining an illusory phantom, "the public,"[43] as an imagined whole and passive receiver of knowledge.

The challenges of democratization (in quantity) and popularization (in quality) of knowledge also affect the performative role of public intellectuals in today's digital public sphere as they relate to knowledge, truth, and power. In the digital cave appearances are ever-more omnipresent and sophisticated, which poses drastically different conditions for the intellectual as well as the public. In light of these developments, I am concerned more with what determines the legitimacy of intellectuals who intervene in the public sphere and seek to influence contemporary issues with knowledge and ideas, and less with typologies and definitions of intellectuals.[44] The aim here is to go beyond long-lasting debates about the nature of intellectuals. By studying the *how* of "Žižek," this book also offers a reflection on the implications of the "free-access" digital agora on intellectual interventions at large.

The Sociological Study of Intellectuals

The sheer volume of Žižek's output over the past forty years, and the multifaceted critique it provoked, as eloquently expressed by Oltarzewska, "render the task of appraisal (let alone introduction) unusually delicate; anxiety besets the researcher confronted with an already monumental yet ever-expanding, tentacular corpus whose compass and ambition appear boundless."[45] To clear some of this anxiety, it is necessary to look at how sociologists have approached questions regarding intellectuals, ideas, and knowledge. Such inquiries ask: What is an intellectual? What makes one publicly successful? And, how are public intellectuals to be studied sociologically?[46] By looking at such recent developments (fig. 0.1), it will become clear why positioning theory is apt for the task at hand.

Recently, sociologists such as Michèle Lamont, Charles Camic, and Neil Gross have developed an empirical approach to the sociological study of intellectual production;[47] this has sometimes been referred to as the "New Sociology of Ideas."[48] In Camic and Gross's view, earlier incarnations of the sociology of knowledge tended to be speculative. For example, in the early work of Karl Mannheim, who founded the sociology of knowledge, we find the idea that one's position in society determines one's worldview by way of imputation. In his inaugural *Ideology and Utopia* from 1929, he tried to expand Marx's notions of class and ideology to include any particular worldview derived from various social positions (e.g., a group, a tribe, a generation). He distinguished ideology from utopia through asserting that only the latter aims at changing, rather than reproducing, the status quo. Mannheim then used this approach to analyze how various classes across Europe have used their position to impute their worldview, whether conservative, fascist, liberal, or communist, to individuals.

In contrast, detailed empirical studies were employed in the "new sociology of ideas," which explored knowledge production within specific sociocultural and institutional contexts. This type of research has taken different forms. For instance, Lamont inquired how Derrida's deconstructive ideas gained acceptance "in the land of empiricism." She analyzed the reception

Sociology of Ideas
- Camic & Gross (1990s): Institution and Self
- Bourdieu (1988, 1991): Field-Capital-Habitus
- Collins (1998): Networks and Mentors
- Lamont (2009): Justified Adaptability

Cultural Sociology
- Alexander's Strong Program (2004, 2011): Performative Turn & Cultural Pragmatics

Sociology of Intellectual Interventions
- Baert (2015, 2017): Positioning Theory of Intellectuals
- Eyal (2010, 2013): Sociology of Public Interventions

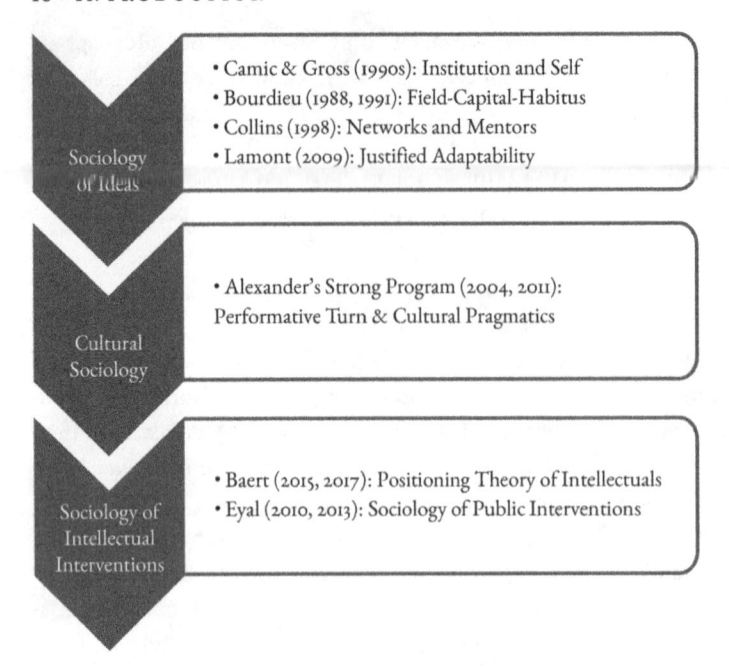

Figure 0.1: The sociological study of intellectuals.

and legitimation of his work by comparing the US and France, and the literary and philosophical fields, respectively.[49] Similarly, by exploring the specific institutional setting at Harvard in the 1930s, Camic provided an explanation for Parsons's surprising choice to align himself during that period with relatively obscure European thinkers like Weber and Durkheim, rather than with the better-known paradigm of institutionalism. In a similar vein, Gross retraced Richard Rorty's intellectual trajectory with the help of the notion of self-concept.[50] Given Rorty's parental activist and literary background, he developed a unique sense of intellectual selfhood, which would eventually guide him in the direction of American pragmatism and away from the more established analytical philosophy.

Two other major contributors to the development of the sociology of ideas are Pierre Bourdieu and Randall Collins. With their own theories of intellectual practice they expand our understanding regarding the study of intellectuals. Bourdieu's *Homo Academicus* (1988) is an exposé of the French intellectual field as a multifaceted space. In it, agents are logically allocated different kinds and degrees of capital that determine their respective habitual positions within that field, as they are drawn to controversies and argumentations that pertain to their professional trajectory. Thus, "Bourdieu's own forays into the sociology of ideas aim, accordingly, to examine sociologically neglected aspects of the knowledge production process—e.g., the historical conditions under which the French intellectual field attained relative autonomy, or cross-national knowledge transfer in the age of globalization."[51]

Bourdieu's sociology of intellectual life, and of intellectuals, is largely shaped by his own social trajectory. In his reflexive terms: "as a body . . . I am not *a-topos*, placeless, as Plato said of Socrates, nor 'rootless and free-floating' as was rather too casually put by . . . Karl Mannheim."[52] Moreover, his trajectory—growing up poor and reaching higher Parisian echelons—led Bourdieu to occupy an ambivalent position regarding the academic field. As the basis for his experience of an "internal-outsider," his ambivalent relationship with intellectual life was the driving force of Bourdieu's vast theorizations.[53] By analyzing art, education, the state, and indeed, intellectuals, "the desire to understand the social relations of intellectual life played an animating role in Bourdieu's sociology."[54] Particularly, with his conceptual triad of field-capital-habitus he analyzed spaces of intellectual production.

Bourdieu's field theory, as elaborated in *The Rules of Art* and *The Field of Cultural Production*, has been specifically useful in analyzing the relationality of agents and their particular choices based on their position in a field.[55] For this reason, field theory seems promising in its capacity to explain Žižek's positioning. However, it suffers from some issues that make it less appropriate to our case. First, "fields" are not distinct by clear-cut and predefined borders as in Bourdieu's opposition between the economic and the cultural, which leads to methodological "disinterest in the unrestricted and undifferentiated production of mass or popular culture."[56] Given Žižek's intense engagement with popular culture, field theory may be too restrictive. Second, Bourdieu's conception of intellectual authority "is not particularly well suited to analyzing those whose power, privilege, and influence rest on an act of blurring the boundaries of intellectual fields."[57] This is particularly problematic for studying the Žižekian phenomenon, as articulated on the dust jacket of his 2017 *Incontinence of the Void*, "if the most interesting theoretical interventions emerge today from the interspaces between fields, then the foremost interspaceman is Slavoj Žižek."

Žižek's case, his performative mode, merits a less restrictive concept for analysis than that of "field." This means focusing more on the production process—as the enunciation and denunciation of positions in- and outside the intellectual arena—than on the product of such a process, which might be termed "habitus." "Habitus" harbors the risk of becoming a catchall concept, and consequently obfuscating and fixating its own practical production process that relates to the positioning in and across fields. As King noted, this association of habitus with field theory "is at odds with [Bourdieu's] formal definition of the habitus,"[58] when it comes to individual freedom doubly and circularly determined by the habitus and the (position in) the field. Also, it may be too restrictive in grasping the multiplicity of publics crucial to Žižek's emergence. As these publics are diverse, compounding them into a unified "habitus" (say, of "Žižek readers") may not do justice to the complexity of the phenomenon.[59]

Attempting to answer more the "how" than the "why" intellectuals act, Collins's network approach and encompassing theory are utilized to explain intellectuals, their commitments, and productions. In his *Sociology of Philosophies*, he describes a general theory of intellectual change across three centuries.[60] With particular interest in the changes within the philosophical discipline, he relates interaction rituals with the specificities of intellectual activity. Accordingly, he uses the notion of intellectual attention-space, arguing for the law of small numbers, which allocates attention to only three to six intellectual groups at a given space-time. This rivalry driven and motivational dynamic then shapes the intellectual institutional space over time. To become an important figure in a field, one is in need of energy, capital, mentors, and networks. Collins's approach is a useful tool to integrate both subjective and objective factors that affect intellectual actions and reactions. Such are his notions of emotional energy and cultural capital, which are what facilitate the intellectually creative process. According to Collins, the process of intellectual creativity, production, and reproduction is dependent on the interpersonal relations—or networks—of face-to-face interactions. This alerts us that ideas should not be taken as individual products, for they are constituted in and through networks of intellectuals.

It is undeniable that the new sociology of ideas, including Bourdieu and Collins, put forward a compelling research program, which presented a necessary corrective to previous accounts of knowledge making. Based on empirical research, the new sociology of ideas rightly drew attention to the importance of institutional and cultural contexts for understanding the choices that intellectuals make (or indeed fail to make).[61] While I applaud this contextual approach and adopt a similar outlook, I would like to supplement it with a detailed analysis of the performative dimensions of the intellectual scene as "the role of public intellectuals must also be performed."[62] In this regard, I am particularly attuned to the practical dynamics of intellectual positioning, moving away from both structural and psychological reductionisms.

In addition to the new sociology of ideas, this book engages with sociological research of the celebrity phenomenon, including celebrity intellectuals.[63] Admittedly, this phenomenon is not entirely new. It was identified and analyzed by sociologists already in the 1960s and 1970s. A striking example of this is Lewis Coser's essay "The Intellectual as Celebrity" from 1973. As Walsh and Lehmann note, this essay was published in *Dissent* magazine, which is significant because *Dissent* "was in a position, like the *New York Review of Books* from the early sixties, to set the tone for the city's literary firmament as gatekeeper to literary celebrity status."[64]

Coser's astute analysis captured and framed the transitional time in which intellectuals became more publicly exposed and attained celebrity status. He classified the old academic intellectual and the new celebrity intellectual on the basis of their audiences and performances. The former, academic intellectual makes contribution to and seeks audience among fellow intellectuals. Or, in the terms of positioning theory, she or he acts within the confines of the intraintellectual sphere, namely academia. This is why academic intellectuals care very little about what others, nonacademics or even academics from other disciplines, think of their work. In this view, judgment and critique are internal to academia and are kept within its walls, in the professional hands of colleagues and peers.

However, celebrity intellectuals do not aim for a specific audience of expert academics. They address general and amorphous, more or less "attentive" publics—to use Gabriel Almond's term—which make no claim to expert knowledge. Bursting out of the confines of a specific, intraintellectual audience, celebrity intellectuals, who intervene in the public or extraintellectual arena, are judged by what Coser called "appeal qualities" such as novelty and brilliance. These, Coser has argued, are "the hallmarks of the celebrity intellectual."[65]

To explain the transition from the old academic to the new celebrity intellectual, Coser mentioned three contributing factors: mass higher education, mass media, and the golden standard of popularity ratings. In the postwar years higher education was no longer a privilege of a small and exclusive segment of society, but, gradually and steadily, it expanded into other societal segments such as the new middle class. In this process the long-lasting cultural homogeneity of the educated class was replaced with a growing heterogeneity. Consequently, instead of a genuine and comprehensive cultural acquisition, there rose the "need" for a quicker and easier way to be "in the know."

The mass media met this condition posed by the new and educated middle class perfectly. Because the unidentifiable yet educated publics lack shared cultural standards or evaluative expertise, the audience of celebrity intellectuals relies on cosmetic criteria such as surface characteristics of style and presentation aimed to startle and shock, rather than on substantive criteria such as content or truth. The more academics turned to the public eye for recognition and reverence, the more they changed the conservative academic neophobia with the timely neophilia. The popularity rating, which replaced the intraintellectual judgment criteria, fundamentally changed the nature of the intellectual. According to Coser, celebrity intellectuals tend to publish in frantic pace, compress a lot in very little, repeat themselves, and parodize themselves as fools "in the effort to grab the mike."[66]

Like performers, celebrity intellectuals compete in the attention economy of viewers and refer more to other performers than to other intellectuals. Whereas charismatic and brilliant personality once was a means for producing valuable intellectual work, nowadays, in the personality market, it seems to be an end in itself. Indeed, as put by Richard Lanham, in an attention economy of the information age, substance and style have changed places.[67] This dialectical transformation is indicated by Coser with another reversal: from Hegel's romantic conception of blaming the public for not "getting" the genius, to accusing the genius of not delivering enough brilliance to the public, for which they must be vanished, or in today's terms, canceled. Celebrity intellectuals are thus seemingly caught between old and new standards, where the new means playing "the fool on demand ... stranded between two worlds, able to sacrifice neither."[68]

A considerable amount of sociological research into celebrities focuses on the distinctive nature of celebrity culture and the extent to which this requires us to talk about a new field involving new types of resources. As Driessens has suggested, "mediatization can be considered both a prerequisite and a possible catalyst for celebritization."[69] In this context, for example, he suggested expanding Bourdieu's four forms of capital (economic, cultural, social, and symbolic) and adding a fifth kind, called "celebrity capital."[70] He argued that this capital, as accumulated media visibility and recognizability, explains how some individuals convert their success from one field to another. With celebrity capital, this approach focuses on the field, be it academic or public, and on the capital flows and accumulations that make one a celebrity.

While there is undoubtedly merit in this Bourdieusian approach, and I most definitely acknowledge the unique features of celebrity culture requiring different resources to compete, my line of inquiry is different in that it draws particular attention to the dramaturgical dimensions that accompany this phenomenon. The dramaturgical dimensions allow for a more pragmatic account of the processes by which intellectuals achieve a public status within specific sociopolitical arenas. I argue that this perspective is particularly fruitful in a context when celebrities, including intellectual celebrities, are seen as cultural icons, symbolically representing a set of values and practices. Jeffery Alexander's cultural pragmatics has been particularly adroit in describing the performances and rituals that make some intellectuals iconic.[71] Particularly, he proposed the perspective of totemism to better understand the current celebrity phenomenon.[72] Drawing on Durkheim and arguing against the view that sees modernity as eradicating irrationality, Alexander points out that cultural idols and icons are like modern totems. Cultural icons such as celebrities create a collective representation by enacting an iconoclastic dichotomy between surface and depth: the former is the profane aesthetic signifier, and the latter is the sacred ethical signified. The individual's identification with such cultural icons leads, according to Alexander, to subjectification as one's own bodily appearance and behavior change in accordance with the icon, which in turn is seen through idealization and objectification. As he puts it, intellectual "persons become iconic, condensed, simplified, and charismatic collective representations of the transformational models they themselves propose—contemporarily, in real time, or retrospectively, in memory."[73]

This book shares Alexander's focus on performativity and his attention to the sacred dimension of contemporary society, yet it does not draw as explicitly on the distinction between surface and depth, and it is less concerned with uncovering hidden societal meanings behind intellectual interventions. Rather, it pays more attention to how Žižek's performances positioned him in a particular fashion within the relevant social contexts and how those forms of positioning were particularly effective in promoting his persona. As concisely put by the anthropologist of Slovenian society Gretchen Bakke, the surface-depth performative model relies on an internal, hidden subjectivity, whereas Žižek "is all surface, all performance."[74] Of specific interest is the more recent context of the celebritization of academic life: whereas previously academic culture had been relatively immune to the external pressures of the market, increasingly economic principles and mass media have started to play a role in legitimizing and making academic careers.[75] So while Bourdieu's depiction of the academic realm as relatively autonomous was pertinent in the context of the mid-twentieth century, it is more difficult to maintain this portrayal in the context of societal shifts over the past few decades. It is in this new context of mass media and new social media that Žižek's performance of the fool, or the sacrificial intellectual, was able to become a hot, viral commodity.[76] In short, he became a phenomenon.

Positioning theory's main contribution is filling the void in the current literature of the sociology of knowledge, ideas, and intellectuals by shifting from *position*, as a state of affairs, to *positioning* as a process.[77] This emphasis on the processual nature of intellectual interventions is consistent with Eyal and Buchholz's plea for a sociology of interventions. Like Eyal and Buchholz are, this book is particularly interested in the intersection between the academic and public domain and is sensitive to the significance of what they call "the interstitial space of expertise, where the borders between these domains are fuzzy."[78] Also guided by Michel de Certeau's anticipation of digital practice, we shall see how in such a context Žižek plays on (and contributes to) the blurring of conventional social borders and knowledge hierarchies.[79]

Camic and Gross's work has proved constructive in highlighting the importance of (institutional and familial) context when studying intellectuals, but their undertheorized research program is at times unclear in explaining the decisions intellectuals take. In both of their exemplars, Parsons and Rorty, lurks a risk of reductionism to individualistic account like the self-concept or unconscious motivations.[80] In addition to the static self-concept and the noncritical approach to self-conceptions, this reductionist tendency—individual rather than social—is also found in Bourdieu's own words, when, in outlining the positions and oppositions of the French intellectual field, he admits, "We have prepared this outline of a sociology of French sociology, which aims at uncovering unconscious affinities."[81] Moreover, Bourdieu's and Collins's perspectives, albeit differently, are somewhat limited in the analysis of interactions *between* different fields and networks, which may result in isolating the intellectual from the wider sociopolitical context. They in practice fall short when accounting for why at a certain point in time and space specific intellectuals or ideas, rather than others, gain wider public recognition. Therefore, this book on Žižek locates the contexts in which he is acting, in geographical and institutional senses, along with his networks of colleagues and critics, and his intellectual or public performances.[82] Such recent theoretical developments present the role of intellectuals as originators, facilitators, and mediators of ideas. They point toward the upcoming focus on interventions, which is crucial for studying Žižek's positioning.

Positioning theory elucidates a number of key concepts in the study of intellectuals, and those help to explain the effectiveness of public intellectuals. "Positioning" indicates the process by which certain features are attributed to an individual or a group or some other entity. It designates a course of action that involves the assignation of meaning performed by an individual or a collective subject capable of judgment and recognition in relation to others. "Intellectuals" are understood as creative individuals who produce relatively innovative intellectual goods, like scientific articles or philosophical books, which are circulated and evaluated by others in the intellectual arena. The "intraintellectual arena" is defined as a relationally constructed space in which professional intellectuals address mainly other professional intellectuals by a self-regulating validation process, that is, "academic peer review, not public accessibility, acceptance and popularity."[83] It is distinguished from the public "extraintellectual arena," where the nonprofessional, general audience is addressed and consumers of knowledge, as well as producers, are admitted a degree of validation. So although a matter of degree, the distinctions between intellectual and nonintellectual, or between the intra- and extraintellectual arenas, are not entirely clear-cut.

For example, not all intellectuals operate in the intellectual arena. Critics and journalists tend to intervene in outlets that have a relatively wider circulation than the restricted communication channels of professional intellectuals, which makes them indispensable for the transmission—fusion or diffusion—of ideas and intellectuals from the intra- to the extraintellectual arena. Moreover, although epitomized by the ideal of the (Humboldtian) academic university, the intraintellectual arena is not conflated with it, as it may also include writers who do not operate within the confines of the university but still produce for a relatively limited group of other specialized producers. To avoid a misunderstanding, although some agents, such as postgraduates, are harder to situate fully and clearly between the extra- and intraintellectual arenas, it is clear that not all agents contribute actively to the intellectual field to the same degree. This is not to say that either side is "more" valuable; on the contrary, it shows the dynamic interrelation between both arenas and their respective agents. Also, this does not unify the extraintellectual arena, where many diverse publics, which will be empirically detailed later, from university students to general readers, engage one another. In the case of Žižek's interventions, these analytic distinctions are useful in discerning how his positioning as an intellectual was facilitated by other intellectuals before he was positioned by nonacademics as a public intellectual with global relevance.

Generally, "intellectual intervention" refers to any contribution to the intellectual arena, whether it is in the form of a book, an article, a video, a speech, or indeed any part of these (say, a passage or a sentence). Therefore, the book analyzes how Žižek's varied interventions have positioned him within the complex intellectual and political landscape in which he has found himself along with others. For instance, we shall see how Ernesto Laclau's preface to Žižek's *The Sublime Object of Ideology* (1989) presented his work as an innovative contribution to post-Marxist social theory. Pragmatically, "performative tools" are material and symbolic means, such as labels or meta-arguments, which enable an effective intervention. This is all the more important because "digital cultures are performative cultures."[84] Indeed, as digital technologies take a significant part in "the making of culture . . . investigations of social, economic, and political processes conducted in and across other disciplines have to reckon with the performativity of digital devices and algorithmic organizing."[85] Thus, intellectual products are performative and rely on the multiple material and symbolic props and devices that help to bring about effectively the interventional positioning. Particular attention is given to "narratives," which can be conceived of as relatively coherent stories that accompany and make possible effective positioning. "Argumentation" constitutes a discursive process oriented toward the presentation and elaboration of reasons invoked in order to justify a stance, belief, conviction, opinion, or narrative. Relationally, "intellectual networks" comprise a large number of agents who engage with an intellectual and confirm his or her positioning, even if they disagree or are overtly hostile. Similar to other webs, sects, or circles of social relations, intellectual networks—since they are generated and sustained by various agents—are in a constant state of flux and potentially complex.[86] "Intellectual teams" are more confined than networks, in that their members actively cooperate in positioning themselves, for instance, by grouping around a school of thought or a research program, often using a label that makes their work and agenda recognizable. Notwithstanding the importance of network and teamwork, "intellectual individualization" refers to the process by which intellectuals distinguish themselves from other intellectuals.

With this array of concepts, the performative approach adopted by this book adds a necessary pragmatic dimension to the study of contemporary intellectual life. Specifically, Žižek's focus on popular culture, which started in Slovenia and was subsequently extended, was of paramount importance to his global success. In this sense, the performative approach does not exclude or replace but rather complements the contextual, institutional, structural, and cultural approaches to public intellectuals, as put forth by the new sociology of ideas. The advantages of positioning theory, its performative approach and dramaturgical framework, will be made clear in the analysis of key paratextual elements from Žižek's career, as well as his numerous and relational performative interventions.

Positioning Žižek

As positioning theory is the theoretical pillar of this study, it guides the practical rationale of the book. For example, in examining Žižek's case, it first directs the reader to the various (kinds of) contexts of this case, for example, the Slovenian context, among others. Second, it points to the performativity of Žižek's interventions, as they appear in different contexts and draw varied reactions. Third, positioning theory focuses on the relationality of Žižek's case: his team of colleagues and network of collaborators, and other social relations, play a critical role in his emergence.

Throughout all stages of this book, the interplay between theory and practice, thought and empirics, forms the explanatory narrative presented in the following chapters. For that, the book utilizes a selection of field- and nonfield methods in data gathering and analysis. This is then put to work in order to articulate and answer the following questions:

1. What are the particular properties of the positioning processes that have allowed Žižek to intervene and acquire his position inside and outside the intellectual arena, to such an extent that he became so publicly known and globally effective in conveying his ideas?
2. How do these positioning processes reflect on the social role and place of intellectuals in today's predicament, and more generally about this predicament itself?

To start answering these questions in a condensed manner, I propose five concrete hypotheses:

1. Žižek employs what I term "superpositioning" as a specific mode of positioning (which is the creation of a "third" position out of an existing opposition) by taking psychoanalysis outside of the clinic and applying it philosophically to cultural and political phenomena, thus constantly repositioning himself along their interstitial border. Through superpositioning high theory and pop culture, Žižek creates a performance that attracts supporters from various, possibly opposing publics, but satisfying none of them as he reaches beyond their existing opposition.
2. In writings and other performances, Žižek is able to spread his ideas effectively because they are packaged and labeled in a coherent intellectual language which I term "Hegelacanese." As a recognizable style of thinking and talking, his language circulates his ideas through his team and network relations while using varied mediums and communication channels in a manner that resonates with wider cultural sentiments and antagonisms.
3. Žižek became globally renowned and recognized as a public intellectual after 9/11, when his interventions succeeded in making new sense of the global cultural trauma. This was achieved by a performance that challenged mainstream public discourse while still attracting many to engage with it, relating past figures to current affairs and to future visions, and

positioning Žižek as "social compass" that effectively provided a sense of direction and meaning.
4. By repetitively using rhetorical questions, jokes, and examples of popular culture as integral to and indicative of his performative repertoire, Žižek is able to relate high-minded theory to common, everyday experience that encourages many readers/viewers to engage in theorizing their practice. His position of "social compass" affords him the role of making sense of today's global context of the senseless postmodern (post-1989).
5. Žižek signals a certain type of public intellectual, which I term the "sacrificial intellectual." Unlike the "authoritative," "expert," and "embedded" intellectuals who enjoy their authentic position, this kind of intellectual sacrifices his or her intraintellectual position to gain a public one. This performative self-positioning renders the intellectual's ideas more accessible, while exemplifying them in a tangible way that carries and attracts a politico-ethical engagement.

Following the above theses, I also put forward two complementing general, contextual arguments that will underpin the following chapters and their respective, more specific arguments. First, I argue, in today's mediatized mode of knowledge production (i.e., the digitalization of the public sphere, the democratization and popularization of knowledge), while all other factors (e.g., gender, race, class, ethnicity, seniority) are controlled, there is a potential for a media-academia trade-off associated with spatiotemporal intellectual interventions: if an intellectual who is still active professionally intervenes in the public, extraintellectual arena, especially in contemporary ethics and politics, then he or she runs the risk of undermining their professional legitimacy or credibility. Second, this mediatized knowledge production facilitates the linguistic relativization of truth and propagates a sociosemiotic tendency for (a) the intellectual sender to disengage politically with the general public, (b) the intellectual message or intervention to be taken locally and relatively, and (c) the public receiver to become a priori cynical toward intellectual universal generalizations.

In addition to these questions, theses, and arguments, Žižek's intellectual positioning is modeled and prescribed by a three-stage process (fig. 0.2). This spatiotemporal dynamic model links both the (academic) intra- and (public) extraintellectual arenas, through the movement of intervention. As exemplified by Žižek's case, such a movement is based on past references (e.g., people; events; other interventions, such as analysis of current affairs, including economy, politics, and science) and an opening of the future (to a new vision, for example). The model is a formalization of the intellectual-becoming-

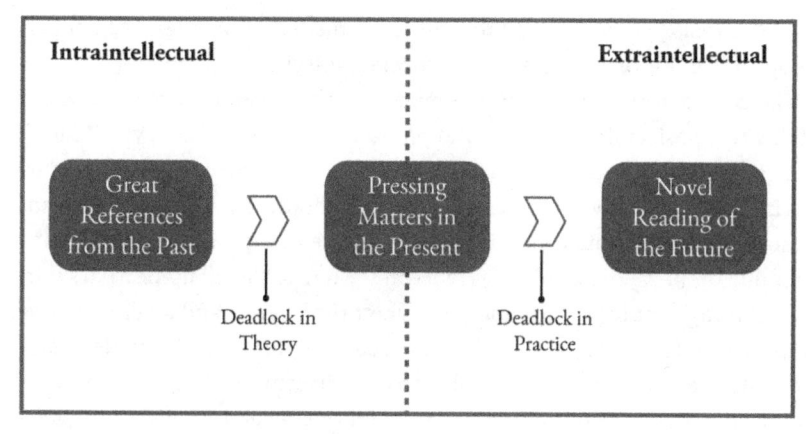

```
Intraintellectual                                    Extraintellectual

    Great              Pressing              Novel
 References           Matters in          Reading of
 from the Past        the Present         the Future

                  Deadlock in         Deadlock in
                    Theory              Practice
```

Figure 0.2: Model of the movement of intellectual intervention (in the humanities).

public: while performing an intervention in the intellectual arena, which relies on positioning around a theoretical deadlock, the movement toward the extraintellectual arena and its multiplicity of publics (of nonacademics) involves a positioning around a practical deadlock central to public concern.

The three-stage model attempts to pragmatically think about intellectual positioning along topological lines. It is conceptualized not as a definitive or restrictive theoretical doctrine but as a schematic guiding principle for the movement—in time and space—of intellectual interventions. It is there to spatially present nonspatial (but temporal) processes in a synthetic fashion, providing an abstract frame to concrete mechanisms of the positioning process and its various specifications. Accepting Jacques Rancière's formulation according to which "time is nothing other than intervention," the model further explains the movement of Žižek's intellectual intervention.[87] It will be shown that his various interventions, albeit differently (depending on the positioning process), correspond to that general form. While performed in different contexts, with or against different agents, this positioning is achieved by creating and maintaining a narrative that temporally links past and future to the present, and spatially extends its relevance outside academia. In that regard, this model is within the third wave of media theories. While the first wave has seen media as representative of a neutral, objective reporting of facts addressing the rational individual, the second wave, from (the Chicago School's) Robert Park to (the Frankfurt School's) Jürgen Habermas, has shifted the focus to small groups and social movements' use of rational deliberation. However, the third sociocultural wave challenged this common appeal to rationality and is more "attentive to the ways that opinion authors unfold dramas," emphasizing "how different media formats tend to encourage specific kinds of speakers and performative styles."[88]

The general form depicted by the model may be generalized to analyze any intellectual positioning, not just that of Žižek's or the sacrificial type.[89] Along that generalizability, the "sacrificial intellectual" position can be occupied by any intellectual, notwithstanding that most choose not to occupy it—not because of their assumed "habitus" but because of a possible loss of legitimacy due to the media-academia trade-off.[90] The sacrificial intellectual's self-undermining, ironic performance, as a rhetorical device and a performative strategy, is unique because the other three contemporary intellectual types—authoritative, expert, and dialogical—do not perform in this way.[91] Therefore, the specific intellectual "sacrificial type" and the general "model of intellectual intervention" provide for an integrative analysis of Žižek, or other intellectuals in the past, present, or future.

Methodologically, this book is based on my archive of Žižek's numerous and diverse intellectual interventions; these include 250 books, 500 videos, and 496 articles.[92] I analyzed these interventions and conducted three semi-structured extended interviews with Žižek and his close collaborators, the philosophers Mladen Dolar and Alenka Zupančič. Each interview lasted between two and three hours. In addition, as part of a digital ethnography of the new social media, I conducted a questionnaire during January 2018, among the main three Facebook groups related to Žižek: Žižek and the Slovenian School, Žižek Studies, and Slavoj Žižek Dank Meme & Discussion Stash. These groups provide an online platform for exchange of texts, videos, comments, and the like.[93] When the poll was made, the number of members in these groups was, respectively, 8,340; 23,663; and 48,711—for a total of 80,714 people.[94] Moreover, and in more traditional ethnographical terms, I participated in Žižek's public lectures in two countries on five different occasions.[95] In addition to interviews and observations the study also shows more objective rather than subjective understanding of Žižek's positioning, utilizing digitally quantitative measures to triangulate the gathered data. By using Google tools such as Scholar's Citations Index, Google Trends, and Ngram Viewer, it is possible to show and monitor the wider scale of the Žižek effect as part of broader intellectual fashions.

The book runs across three overlapping shifts: from local to global, from printed to digital, and from production to consumption. Without succumbing to either extreme of a purely historiographical-chronological or biographical-thematic analysis, the book discusses these shifts in intellectual contextuality, performativity, and relationality. We will see how Žižek and his ideas became public in Slovenia before turning into a worldwide phenomenon. This shift is accompanied by a changing focus toward a greater and deeper engagement with consumers of his ideas, beyond their production process.[96] And last, this will involve more and more, as the book progresses, the digital public sphere.

Structurally, this book has four chapters. Each chapter covers a period of roughly a decade, yet the book suggests a sociohistorical narrative, which, only when taken as a causal whole, effectively explains the multifaceted parts that constitute Žižek's phenomenon. The first chapter discusses Slovenia's (relative) exceptional position within the Socialist Federal Republic of Yugoslavia. Slovenia's intellectual, cultural, and political contexts during the 1980s are described as Žižek's conditions of possibility. These include Tito's opposition to Stalin that created a space in between the communist East and the capitalist West. Thus, Yugoslav republics and intellectuals, including Žižek, started to develop—mostly through journals—their own specific variations of Marxism to be positioned against Stalinism. This in-between space became a fertile ground for new ideas imported from nearby Western countries, such as France and Germany. Moreover, after Tito's death in 1980, Slovenian civil society and alternative culture emerged against the disintegration of what became the ancien régime. Amid this drastic and traumatic change, Slovenian intellectuals positioned themselves in relation to changing social conditions. This process was the basis for Žižek to create a "superposition" for his repetitive performance and repertoire. Maneuvering between institutional constraints and political restraints, Žižek founded the Ljubljana School, made connections with French intellectuals, formed a party that lost the elections, and together with his teammates established himself as local public intellectual.

Chapter 2 turns to the period of the 1990s, actually beginning in 1989 with Žižek's first English intervention. Before this English inauguration, Žižek's first global attempt in French failed to resonate with the French intellectual (and) public. As contexts change, so does the positioning: Žižek's second attempt was made in different contextual circumstances, both intellectual and public, and yielded very different results. With the right kind of intellectual vouching, Žižek's *The Sublime Object of Ideology* was performed as a reaction to the theoretical and practical deadlocks of the time, namely language and power. Once positioned by another established intellectual, Ernesto Laclau, Žižek developed his intellectual individualization in a series of collaborative and independent interventions, performed in various mediums. This, in addition to the unique performative style and rhetorical repertoire, coined as Žižek's language of "Hegelacanese," facilitated Žižek's positioning as a global intellectual.

24 INTRODUCTION

Chapter 3 focuses on Žižek's global *public* emergence during the first decade of the 2000s. The reactions to Žižek's intellectual interventions—in films, books, and articles—ranged from reception to rejection and reproduced (parts of) his performance in other performances, such as readers, guides, reviews, and critiques. Then, particularly after 9/11, Žižek emerged globally and publicly. Drawing on insights from cultural trauma theory, it is shown that Žižek's intellectual intervention in this context positioned him as a prominent global public intellectual by constructing a meaningful narrative to that global event, using past references and future consequences. As a result of this intervention, Žižek's global popularization was carried out through the "media-academia trade-off"; the more he was positioned as a media phenomenon, the less he was taken seriously in academia, and he thus assumed the "sacrificial intellectual" position. Using his popularization, Žižek continued to expand his performances and relations by narrating other such global traumatic events as the financial crisis of 2008 and the Arab Spring of 2011.

Chapter 4 traces the period after 2011. In this chapter, Žižek's highest and lowest moments as a global public intellectual are studied. Firmly established outside academia given his pedagogical style, Žižek produced well-received intellectual interventions, including a (second) magnum opus and a joke book. During this same period, the lowest moments are indicated by fierce debates with prominent intellectuals—such as Noam Chomsky, who positioned Žižek as a jokester—as well as by the growing critique of Žižek's position on facts, race, sex, and refugees. The effects of the increasing public disinterest in Žižek are seen through the perspective of his own superpositioning of philosophy and antiphilosophy. The public sacrifice of his intellectual position and self-questioning of his role as a philosopher rendered digitally the Socratic gesture of corrupting the youth and its costly punishment. Thus, despite Žižek's current marginalization, his dictionary-worthy Hegelacanese still leaves its effective marks on the future generations of the Ljubljana School.

The conclusion synthesizes the arguments made so far in a brushstroke, painting a general yet textured picture. It explains how Žižek reacted to the new intellectual conditions of our knowledge societies—greater access and low longevity of information—by adapting his performance in both form and content, so as to effectively convey his ideas. Žižek's (in)famous repetitive self-plagiarism is thus read via a digital lens of mash-up that informs his theory and practice. This suggests a different, blurred mode of intellectual production and consumption, as in reading, writing, and viewing, where a short attention span encourages visual rather than textual performativity. By partially succumbing to such post-codex conditions of intellectual work, Žižek's position may have been sacrificed, but his ideas carry on.

1 *Slovenia between East and West: The Origin of Superpositioning*

To explain how Slavoj Žižek's became a global public intellectual at the beginning of the twenty-first century, I begin by examining the complex trajectory of Slovenia during Yugoslavia's disintegration, as it transitioned from communism to capitalism. Indeed, Žižek's theoretical work is sometimes represented "*as if* it were universally applicable, when, in actuality, it is both grounded in and reflective of a very specific cultural context."[1] Focusing mainly but not solely on the period 1982–1991, I show how this pivotal period provided the initial setting for Žižek's local—intellectual, cultural, and political—interventions (fig. 1.1). This also explains why it was more likely for a regional and then global intellectual to emerge from Slovenia rather than its neighbors.

The legendary leader Josip Broz Tito died in 1980, during the political and cultural blossoming of Slovenia. It was during this period too that Žižek received his (second) PhD and the Društvo za Teoretsko Psihoanalizo, the Society for Theoretical Psychoanalysis (or the Ljubljana School as it would later be known), was founded in 1982.[2] In this chapter I thus turn to the empirical context of Žižek's local emergence and elaborate on how the disintegrating political reality of perestroika significantly modified cultural and intellectual arenas while changing existing lines of division. These lines shaped the space in which Žižek operated and to which he reacted. As noted by Parker: "How we make sense of this, and how we position ourselves to applaud or bemoan the rise and fall of Tito, self-management socialism, nationalist resistance and the new free-market moral majorities, will influence how we read Žižek and his attempt to make sense of the process."[3] Without understanding the complex context of (Slovenia within) Yugoslavia, and its relation to the West in reinventing Eastern European capitalism, we cannot explain Žižek's performance and later rise to prominence.

As part of Žižek's social conditions of possibility, I discuss how this context

26 CHAPTER ONE

```
1960
Bled Congress
Break with                          1984
1945        dialectical    1962              1990
(second)    materialism as Problemi  1966    NSK           First democratic
Formation of 'state        journal   OHO Group formation   elections in
Yugoslavia  philosophy'    launch   formation and Alternative Slovenia
                                             Culture
```

```
1948           1961          1964          1980    1985          1991
Tito-Stalin Split Non-Aligned Praxis Group  Tito's  Analecta book Formal
Beginning of   Movement      formation      Death   series launch Disintegration
independent    Founded by Tito and journal launch                 of Yugoslavia
economy                                                           Slovenian
                                                                  Independence
```

● Intellectual   ▲ Political   ■ Cultural

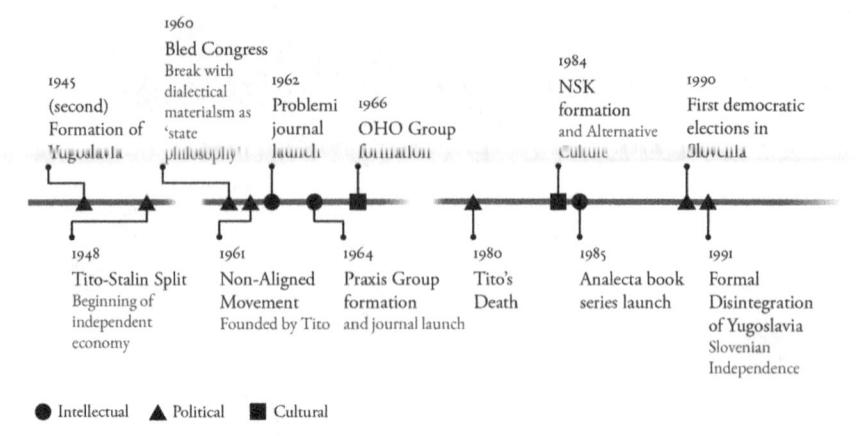

Figure 1.1: Yugoslavia and Slovenia historical timeline.

significantly challenged the Slovenian public, culturally and intellectually, as the communist reality began to change, gradually becoming more capitalist in nature. This dramatic and drastic—to some even traumatic—change forced public figures to redefine their historically rooted positions with respect to long-standing questions about society and its values. While most of the public and intellectuals effectively embraced the change or were co-opted by it, some tried to move beyond it.[4] The rise of civil society also paved the way for an even more radical opposition of alternative culture, assembled by artists, students, and intellectuals. This rift between those who embraced "Western" change and those who did not would dictate, albeit in different ways, the future formation of the intellectual arena and public sphere.[5]

After describing Yugoslavia's space of positioning, I examine the Slovenian space *within* it. I address the political, cultural, and intellectual arenas as they were shaped by and reacting to the shifting reality. The oppositions in each arena affect Yugoslavia's conditions of impossibility, and thus they play out as Žižek's conditions of possibility. I show how these positions compose a "semiotic binarism [which] is isomorphic with what Durkheim called the sacred and profane."[6] In each arena, then, a major social antagonism is located around which opposing positions emerge. I elaborate on how Žižek's positioning process is performed in each of these arenas, stressing its common feature of superpositioning (as creating a third new position out of two or more existing oppositions). The understanding of how this intellectual superpositioning emerged from a concrete political context, while reacting to cultural tensions, will elucidate the Žižekian phenomenon first locally and then globally. This "third" superposition would become "Hegelacanese," and consequently a trademark of Žižek's performativity. Importantly, to appreciate the (emergence of the) "third" we must pass through the (deadlock of the) existing two. These binary positions created three key tensions: a political tension between East and West, a cultural tension between civil society and the alternative, and an intellectual tension between Marx and Heidegger.

At the Beginning: Tito (against Stalin)

The Socialist Federal Republic of Yugoslavia was formed in 1945 as part of the Eastern bloc and an allied state of the Soviet Socialist republics. Soon thereafter, following the Tito-Stalin split of 1948, Yugoslavia became a founding member of the Non-Aligned Movement, officially established in 1961. This torn positioning between East and West remained until Tito's death in 1980, when the regime started to collapse more rapidly. All this time, Slovenia was ruled by the Zveza Komunistov Slovenije (League of Communists of Slovenia), which was the Slovenian branch of the League of Communists of Yugoslavia—the sole party in power from 1945 to 1989. With no real replacement for Tito after 1980, growing nationalism and calls for substates' independence resulted in the official dissolution of Yugoslavia in 1991, the same year of Slovenia's renewed independence prior to the eruption of the Balkan Wars.[7] This disintegration process meant, primarily, that following the major regime change, already-held positions had to be rethought and even redefined. Namely, normative positions, such as left and right, pro and against, were drastically changed.

In the best (or worst) tradition of centralized regimes, to understand the nation is to understand the leader. And at the beginning of Yugoslavia, there was Tito. The influential commander and politician, founder of the Socialist Federal Republic of Yugoslavia, is the one to understand if we are to make any sense of the intellectual and cultural arenas of Slovenia.[8] What he built, and the way he built it, left a mark on the Slovenian predicament with which Žižek was confronted. Early after World War II, Tito started to take a more independent and significant role with regard to both eastern and western powers. Politically, Tito sought to expand his connections to Europe, a move that was disapproved by Stalin. Economically, Tito developed and pushed his own version of an open, democratic form of self-management socialism—the basis for the Yugoslav economic plan—against the more bureaucratic Stalinist tradition. This break with Stalin and Stalinism was made clearer with the foundation of the Non-Aligned Movement in 1961, which positioned Yugoslavia as buffer zone between East and West. Intellectually, this distance from Stalinism also meant adopting—from 1960—a different kind of state philosophy, a different kind of Marxism from the one held and propagated by Stalin.

As Mladen Dolar, one of Žižek's teammates and cofounder of the Ljubljana School, recalls:

> It was a huge historical momentum, and part of that momentum, being a student of philosophy, was on the one hand the Frankfurt School. And my professors were basically Marxists, although with a sort of, roughly, Frankfurt School persuasion. Hegel and Marx, there was a lot of readings of them, and that connection [to] Lukács, Korsch, and Adorno. Those were the big heroes. So the kind of Marxism—it was a Marxist country, so a Marxist philosophy—and the best education we got was of that kind. But this was an absolutely anti-Stalinist Marxism. From beginning to end, there was a very harsh anti-Stalinist stance.[9]

During the early 1950s and 1960s, Yugoslavia was enjoying a period of economic growth and relatively significant political freedom due to "the system of self-management, which differed from the Soviet model of central planning and state ownership of industry, [and] endured through its first decade with reasonable success."[10] Moreover, as the Yugoslav economy also profited from its political position between the two sides of the Iron Curtain, it was "able to export its produce to and establish good economic cooperation with countries from both sides."[11] Nonetheless, both internal and external factors—mainly regarding the inherent tension between liberalized corporations and state-supported firms—led to the end of that prosperity by the mid-1960s. Consequently, two major issues arose with long-lasting effects on Yugoslav society: the rise of ethno-nationalism and the growing economic crisis. From a young philosopher's perspective, Dolar brings to light the momentum of that period in the Slovenian context:

> "May '68"—it's somehow the shorthand for a very politically highly charged era. The whole thing is that Tito's Yugoslavia was not part of the East; in this sense, we had absolute access to the West, we could travel to the West, we did travel to the West, and in '69 I also traveled to Paris for the first time. And Slovenia, being close to the borders of France and Austria, relatedly there was no problem with that. This was absolutely exceptional. It was not an Eastern European country. It is usually seen as a communist country, but the conditions of the exchange with the West were such that we were—my generation was completely aware of the developments in the West. These things I've mentioned, yes, plus the big rock thing, rock music, which was an overarching thing at that time. But '69 was the year of an opening: intellectually, culturally, politically.[12]

As Dolar links global events to the local context, he discerns a timing of opening. Leading to this opening, the Bled congress of 1960 was of both political and intellectual importance. In the Slovenian lake city of Bled, a group (later called Praxis) of young sociologists and philosophers from Zagreb, Belgrade, and Sarajevo, met and decided on the early, humanist Marx as the dominant form of Yugoslav Marxism. It signaled the end of the uniform rule of dialectical materialism as "official philosophy" for all communist countries. Then, as Žižek recalls, gradually, "a very strange situation emerged, where Yugoslavia was already getting more and more decentralized, so in every republic you did have some philosophical orientation which was close to the official Party line, and some main form of intellectual oppositions. But they were not the same in different republics."[13] For these reasons, Slovenia in the 1970s and 1980s was a somewhat distinctive place to be. Its political constellation had created major challenges but also opportunities for the public and intellectuals alike. Even before the last decade of Tito's Yugoslavia, Slovenia had an exceptional position within it; citizens were allowed a certain degree of cultural and intellectual freedom, much unlike other countries of the Eastern bloc that were separated by the Iron Curtain. As Žižek also explains:

> What I think made it possible for us, socially, to work the way we did, was that the regime was still a communist regime. We didn't have any illusions that it's the true socialism or whatever. But at the same time there was certain openness, I mean, borders were so open that in the late '60s, people who lived close to Italy or Austria went every afternoon just across the border for a cappuccino and so on; it was better in Italy at that point. So, we were not [closed] like in East European countries, where "oh, what are the new books?" We were all the time going to London, Paris, or Frankfurt or Munich to buy books. We were totally in contact.[14]

Clearly, Slovenia's position within the global geopolitical landscape affected Žižek's own positioning. The flow of information, such as texts and ideas from the West, had dramatic effects on the reactions that Žižek and other Slovenian intellectuals developed once the Yugoslavian state disintegrated: "Because the West was open to us, the fall of communism was not this big discovery, 'oh, now we are free,' and so on. We were in this *ideal position in the middle*, where we were skeptical towards both from the very beginning."[15] This interstitial "middle" position would become the drive for Žižek's superpositioning. While Yugoslavia was officially communist, it had been already exposed to capitalism, as in Western thought, from relatively early. In this paradoxical political positioning we can see the seeds of Žižek's later intellectual (super)positions. Particularly, Yugoslavia's position in between the Soviet Union and the West exposed Žižek to the obscene, dark side of political discourse and ideology.

Following this economic and political distance from Stalin(ism), new intellectual currents emerged. Specifically, the self-irony and cynicism of the regime, which was officially critical even toward itself, revealed the necessarily illusory status of political, but also intellectual and cultural, appearances.[16] As Parker notes apropos of this self-positioning, "In Slovenia, the northernmost republic in the Yugoslav Federation, Žižek was one of those who noticed that the regime required its population to take a cynical distance from the claims made about democracy in order for it to function."[17] Being inside the communist ideology but also critical toward it, while being exposed to the West and also critical toward it, Žižek was in a position to evaluate the very opposition and to create a third superposition.

The break with Stalin and Stalinist Marxism made it easier for Tito to try to provide an umbrella for other countries that were caught in between, and thus he formed the Non-Aligned Movement in 1961. As there was no unifying system of thought across the Yugoslav nations, each came up with its own intellectual tendency, creating different intellectual positions and oppositions.[18] As part of the journal form of opposition, *Praxis*—one of the most influential Yugoslav journals—was launched at that time, setting the stage for major intellectual and artistic interventions with great political consequences. Published between 1964 and 1974 in both Serbo-Croatian and foreign languages, it was positioned, according to Dolar, as a journal and a group, and "a kind of, broadly, a Frankfurt School thing. They had Petrovic, and Milan Kangrga there, all these guys, with some standing, but they were basically Frankfurt School–based, in a broad sense."[19] Besides publishing articles with a humanist-Marxist orientation, *Praxis* also operated as the main hub for (mostly Western) European critical thinkers to meet and make connections with one another. Dolar explains how since 1964 *Praxis* facilitated a main stage for intellectual networking in the Croatian island of Korčula: "Korčula is very important for intellectual context. It's an island in the Adriatic, and so *Praxis* organized summer school in Korčula every year. Marcuse came, Angela Davis came, Ernst Bloch came, I mean, people of great standing, everybody. Habermas came, who else? Lefebvre came. So, people of great intellectual standing, came every year to Korčula and met on this island. From here, Ljubljana, I was never there, for different reasons, but Slavoj was there. So people from Ljubljana, students would go, professors would go to Korčula. This was in the late '60s."[20] Indeed, a main idea of this book is that "when we are dealing with great movements of ideas, their nodal points are often difficult to detect—it might be a text, a debate, an idea, or a phrase. It might also be a journal overshadowed by more popular 'masterpieces.'"[21] Directing Žižek's words toward his own movement of the Ljubljana School, there is little doubt that one of its nodal points is *Problemi* (1962–). Published in Slovenian, this journal stands for all the political, intellectual, and cultural tensions of Slovenian society and is usually overshadowed by a definite masterpiece like *The Sublime Object of Ideology*. Although the latter is the most common reference point to the emergence of "the Slovenian Lacan," this emergence is determined by preceding developments that started long before 1989 and are related to the Žižekian crux of theory and practice.

The journal provided a site for different intellectual currents to compete over the right to narrate, articulate, and interpret current events. The interventions in the journal tried to incorporate new intellectual traditions, such as structuralism and psychoanalysis, with concrete political analysis of the Slovenian predicament. Bedrock to proactive thinking, *Problemi* was a sort of melting pot and testing ground for ideas. The moment that Žižek and Dolar gained editorial control, around 1980, was decisive for the formalization of the Ljubljana School. Their support of the alternative culture, embodied in the special punk issues between 1981 and 1983, provided a cultural reading that opened up a new way for a political engagement outside the confines of the more co-opted academia and civil society.[22] The journal also integrated cutting-edge translations of French and other scholars, making them both accessible and relevant for the local public before they could be translated in book form.[23] In his description of that time, Dolar also described the oppositional relations between the various factions of intellectuals dealing with journal publishing:

> *Problemi* existed since 1962 or so, and there were different groups which fought each other within this journal. Some of them were Heideggerians, a lot of poets and writers, also avant-garde and whatever, but it was a time of battles, wars within *Problemi*. Because it was an intellectually open journal, various groups tried to get space in it. And ours was one of the groups. . . . So it was first influential in this avant-garde sense, of gathering artists and some Western-inspired intellectuals. Then in the '70s and '80s it was influential in a different kind because our group tried to pursue a very persistent policy following this structuralism, applying it to a number of hot topics, agendas, and making it not a philosophical current but a sort of cultural positioning.[24]

By the time *Problemi* was founded, Slovenia had already witnessed a surge of intellectual journals. Actually, *Problemi* was the fifth to appear locally, after other journals had been shut down by the government. For example, *Beseda* (Word) operated only six years before it was closed in 1957; the same year *Revija 57* (Review 57) appeared, if only for a single year. Then *Perspektive* (Perspectives) was founded between 1957 and 1960, and for nine years it held a strong existentialist position, focusing mostly on Heidegger and Sartre. Finally, the *Praxis Group* was formed in Zagreb in 1964, as explained earlier.

In the period between 1968 and 1980, one can find the early signs of Yugoslavia's disintegration. Not because of any "official" periodization, but because in this period one can detect more or less dormant signs of the later, more intense dissolution between Tito's death in 1980 and the state's breakdown in 1991. The 1970s were the years of students. More than politicians, perhaps, being a student meant being exposed to a greater variety of intellectual ideas and political activities. Dolar felt that "there was the sense, not just about philosophy but of the whole generation: we are the opening, the beginning of something. That all these events carried such a potential: we are the torchbearers for these things."[25]

Especially after May 1968, all across Europe student movements were enveloped in revolutionary spirit. It was around this time that Dolar and Žižek enrolled at the University of Ljubljana, in 1967 and 1969, respectively. Žižek's positioning, being a function of contextuality, relationality, and performativity, was very much affected by these surrounding developments. The changing political condition of his home country of Slovenia, the intellectual condition of university departments, and the cultural sentiments of the public—all these were "the conditions of impossibility of Yugoslavia that made it possible for Republic of Slovenia to appear, and so the conceptual conditions for Žižek to appear as he did."[26] It was not just the fact that Yugoslavia was a buffer zone, an enclave or lacuna between East and West that affected Žižek's positioning, but it was also Slovenia's particular position from within Yugoslavia.[27] As Stalin developed his version of Marxism via his writings on "dialectical" materialism, Tito, as well as Yugoslav intellectuals, developed an alternative way to ground their version of self-management socialism on "historical" materialism. So besides *Praxis*'s tendency toward the Frankfurt School and the humanist Marx, a common feature among the diverged opposition groups that emerged in Yugoslavia was the reckoning—in Belgrade and Zagreb but also in Ljubljana—that words are dangerous things, that is, dangerous for the regime. The hypersensitivity to words, images, and other appearances signaled to intellectuals across Yugoslavia that in actuality there was a gap between the presented (as the nation's essence) and the represented (as its appearance). The political economy of self-management socialism also raised issues of the split self and the superego, facilitating greater interest in the works of Freud and Lacan regarding subjectivity as trauma, and in those of Foucault and Derrida regarding society as symbolic—all the while Marx and thereby Hegel were still lurking in the background, awaiting to be reassociated with the changing political context and the growing public interest in subjectivity.

Structuralism beyond Marx versus Heidegger

As the Yugoslav regime disintegrated, intellectual and political oppositions diversified and intensified. Because the League of Communists of Yugoslavia ("the party") had affiliations with Marxism, there was an intellectual-political tension between Marxists (on the side of the State) and Heideggerians (on the side of the opposition). For Žižek the crucial question became, How does one criticize a (self-)critical regime? Like every intellectual, he was expected to argue his position whether for or against the change, that is, the transformation from communism to capitalism. This became an Archimedean point in Žižek's superpositioning, when he developed his intellectual individualization in the Slovenian political situation, relating publicly known cultural references with yet unknown intellectual sources.

Given that Yugoslavia was (identified as) a part of the Eastern communist world, the relationship between Slovenian intellectuals and politics was more explicit than in the West. "Communism" was taken both as an intellectual doctrine originated in Marx and Hegel, and as a political program materialized in the Eastern bloc. For example, the state itself acquired a certain Marxist perspective as an unquestionable position. Thus, to criticize the regime, one had to be critical toward Marx. In this context, the political positions are interwoven into the intellectual ones, as the latter influence and guide certain practices. However, unlike the Soviet "dialectical" materialism that played a unifying role in the Eastern world and especially in the Soviet Union, Yugoslavia's lack thereof resulted in various formations of intellectual-political positions. Žižek's own mapping of these various positions is revealing, as it serves a self-positioning maneuver on his part, situating others in a space by claiming that "in every [Yugoslav] republic you did have some philosophical orientation which was close to the official Party line, and some main form of intellectual oppositions."[28] Thus, according to Žižek, relations between the party's orientation and the intellectual opposition were not the same in all Yugoslav republics.

Slovenia was influenced by Frankfurt School Marxism, and particularly by

Habermas, who had visited the party. This influence was not as strong as in other places, such as Croatia, but it was enough to direct a party line. In the 1960s and 1970s, the opposition of dissidents was Heideggerian. In nearby Croatia, Heideggerians were closer to the official party line, whereas Marxists were the opposition. This is because in Croatia Marxism was dominated by the influential *Praxis* group, which was affiliated and associated with a more critical, Western Marxism. In Serbia it was analytic philosophical Marxism that was closest to the official party line, under the presumption that language games pose no political danger. Žižek summarizes these variable conditions: "The idea is, even if you are a Marxist, you never know when you will become critical and so on."[29]

In stressing this difference between the Yugoslav republics, Žižek practically explains that, as actually happened a couple of times, "for the same book . . . you were almost sent to prison in Croatia but you got a state prize in Slovenia and so on. But this, I'm not saying this as a critical point, but almost as opening a certain space for freedom, you know. Orthodoxy was broken."[30] Slovenia's uniqueness in that context is the lack of both a strong philosophical orientation and a strong clinical psychoanalytical establishment to challenge Žižek's teamwork and position on controversial subjects: "I was lucky in the sense that precisely because Slovenia wasn't a strong international philosophical presence (in other republics, such as Croatia and Serbia, there was, in the guise of this *Praxis* School of Humanist Marxism, more of an international presence), there existed representatives of all the other predominant orientations of philosophy. We had the Frankfurt School Marxists, we had the Heideggerians, analytical philosophers, and so on. So I was lucky enough to have been exposed to all the predominant orientations."[31] Previously it was shown that Slovenia's openness to the West facilitated such an expedited exposure to and transmission of ideas. Hence, the lack of existing Slovenian intellectual tradition and the exposure to new intellectual ideas were the background against which Žižek individuated by performing his superpositioning.

As Žižek continues his intellectual mapping, he lays the foundations for this superpositioning: "In Slovenia, the big opposition was Frankfurt School Marxists versus Heideggerians. And what shocked us the young generation, we were then students, was how, when confronted with this new explosion of [Structuralist] thinking, both sides—Heideggerians and Marxists—adopted the same language, brutally attacking it."[32] Following this explosion, Žižek was among the first to recognize and emphasize the valence of (Lacanian) structuralism, not only as a novel theoretical current but also as a means for rearticulating the political situation. In his performative interventions of

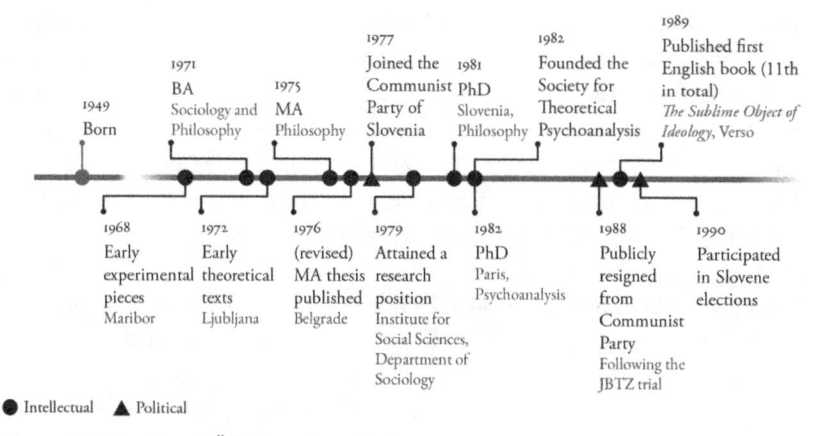

Figure 1.2: Timeline of Žižek's early period.

Intellectual (●) events:
- 1949 Born
- 1971 BA Sociology and Philosophy
- 1975 MA Philosophy
- 1977 Joined the Communist Party of Slovenia
- 1981 PhD Slovenia, Philosophy
- 1982 Founded the Society for Theoretical Psychoanalysis
- 1989 Published first English book (11th in total) *The Sublime Object of Ideology*, Verso

Political (▲) events:
- 1968 Early experimental pieces Maribor
- 1972 Early theoretical texts Ljubljana
- 1976 (revised) MA thesis published Belgrade
- 1979 Attained a research position Institute for Social Sciences, Department of Sociology
- 1982 PhD Paris, Psychoanalysis
- 1988 Publicly resigned from Communist Party Following the JBTZ trial
- 1990 Participated in Slovene elections

this early period leading to the 1980s (fig. 1.2), he was related to both the Slovenian intellectual arena and the communist political one.

Žižek, his teammates, and his colleagues had to react to the changing political situation, along with its shifting intellectual positions. Articulating such an intellectual position is possible only through a relational, differential performance that at once positions the performing agent as well as others—friends and foes—in that context. As such, this articulation comes with material effects and emotional affects. This mapping of different intellectual and political positions is not done solely for descriptive reasons. Rather, it is performed as a theoretical intervention in the situation. Žižek traced the common Marxists' and Heideggerians' reaction to structuralism as a sign for their intellectual compliance and political weakness. Both the regime and the opposition had something (new) in common that they tried to avoid and suppress; the mapping of intellectual and political positions reveals just that.

Once Marxism lost its exclusivity among Slovenian intellectuals, other ideas were sought after to make new sense of the situation. Here, Žižek's application and circulation of structuralism were effective in publicly articulating this condition while supporting his emergence as a (local) public intellectual. Importantly, several political polemics found expression precisely in the intellectual and literary fields of social life. These include interventions in the radio (Radio Študent), weekly news journals like *Mladina* (Youth), science and art journals (*Casopis za Kritiko Znanosti, Domisljijo in Novo Antropologijo*—Journal for the Critique of Science, Imagination and the New Anthropology); and psychoanalytical journals (*Razpol: The Journal of the Freudian Field*).[33]

Besides tense personal relations, what also pulled the Ljubljana School to structuralism was a push from the Heideggerian oppositional camp. Importantly, and given the history and public legitimacy of Yugoslav journals as sites for debates, the Slovenian *Nova Revija* (New Review) was launched in 1982. In contrast to *Problemi*, *Nova Revija* bore a strong Heideggerian tendency, also calling for a multiparty system and an independent critique of Yugoslav socialism. Dolar, who since 1971 had been the chief editor of the student newspaper *Tribuna*, links these intellectual and political developments:

> It was only in the '80s that we took over the journal [*Problemi*]. Because the Heideggerian group got most of the new journals established, like *Nova Revija*, they basically pulled out of these struggles [against us], and had a new journal which was very successful in the eighties. But we stayed with *Problemi* and we're still staying with *Problemi*, which is still being published five issues per year . . . it was influential already in the late '60s, because it was the home ground to the avant-garde. And the first piece that Slavoj ever published, which I think was called *Let's Spend the Night Together*, was in '68 in a very controversial issue of *Problemi*, which caused a lot of scandal.[34]

Despite working together on *Problemi*, Žižek notes that, during this time, Dolar was a member of a critical Marxist group, whereas he was much closer to Heideggerians: Dolar "did have a job at philosophy department. He was their professor [now] for thirty-forty years."[35] Žižek's own intellectual interventions, as well as his material conditions, were largely affected by his positioning, which was somewhat fluid at this formative time—reading the standard Marxist classics at age fifteen, moving to Heidegger at twenty (influenced by *Praxis*), to Derrida at twenty-five (following his French connections), and then to Lacan and Hegel at thirty.[36] Significantly, after the political problems with his MA thesis on structuralist Marxism, and a (first) PhD dissertation on Heidegger, between 1973 and 1977, he was unemployed.

Then, in 1979, after a couple of years working for the Communist Party in speech writing and minutes taking, while still being blocked from a university position, Žižek was placed in a research post at the Department of Sociology in the Institute for Social Sciences in Ljubljana. Nonetheless, "at the time, Žižek thought that this was an intellectual *cul-de-sac* in which the communist regime placed those who were inconvenient to them. As it transpired, however, this job, which would be the envy of most academics, meant Žižek was able to pursue his research interests free from the pressures of teaching and bureaucracy."[37] This freedom, along with the general openness of Slovenia to the West, incentivized Žižek to embark on a second PhD in France under the supervision of Lacan's son-in-law Jacques-Alain Miller, and to establish a French connection, which would be vital for his global emergence in the 1990s: "The first connection was Slavoj, and then there was Rastko [Močnik]. And Rastko actually introduced Slavoj to Derrida. Slavoj and Derrida met in the beginning of the '70s, because Derrida was Rastko's teacher there. So, there were also immediate personal connections."[38] While one local Slovenian intellectual network started to expand, this encounter with Derrida shifted Žižek's intellectual position away from Heidegger to Lacan:

> I should just add that while my doctoral thesis is on Heidegger, my first book—published when I was 22 [in 1972]—wasn't my thesis, it was my graduation paper. It was a mixture of Heidegger and Derrida with a very embarrassing title: *The Pain of the Difference*. I think that without Derrida I would probably have ended up as a Heideggerian. It was Derrida who provided this first impetus to move away from Heidegger. What I was looking for in Derrida was how to break away from Heidegger. It was only with my second doctoral thesis in the late 1970s that a clear Lacanian orientation emerged.[39]

As noted before, this intellectual threat was related contextually to the political positioning of Slovenia within Yugoslavia, and with regard to the West: "Because we were seen as being in danger [of invasion, like Hungary in 1956 and Czechoslovakia in 1958], and the West would not back us up, so we would have to fight on our own, . . . so, in some distant parallel to Israel, we were seen as surrounded by enemies, and there was a militarized society because of that."[40] Crucially, the intellectual relation to the political regime in Eastern Europe transpired as both bureaucrats and dissidents had a relationship with politics. Without a relation to politics it was impossible to become public. When asked why this phenomenon has disappeared in the West, where there is no apparent dialogue between power and knowledge, Žižek explained:

> For me what was partially so attractive, so sympathetic about real socialism, despite being a corrupt, cynical system, was the belief in the power of the spoken word. Some twenty years ago, I was editor of a small art-theoretical journal with a circulation of 3,400. Once we published a small, obscure poem, incomprehensibly modern, but between the lines there was a dissident message. If the power would have ignored the poem, nothing would have happened. But there was an extraordinary session of the Cen-

tral Committee. Okay, this is repression, but what I like about it is that the communist power took the potential, detonating force of the spoken word very seriously. They were always interested in arguing with intellectuals.[41]

The Soviet political sensitivity to the spoken and written word facilitated a relation to the intellectual establishment, but more importantly it served as an early lesson for Žižek on the maintenance of appearances and its significance for political regimes. To understand this experience, he created a link between the Lacanian "logic of the signifier" and the Hegelian "dialectic." With this link, another form of intellectual engagement was articulated, based on a different, more dialectical and symbolic view of authority. Identifying a certain "messianic complex" among intellectuals and seeking to avoid both the wrong engagement and the wrong disengagement, Žižek recalls: "Our influence, beginning in the mid-eighties, was at that time incredibly large, especially the philosophers, sociologists, literary theoreticians. But this was a very limited conjunction. There is a messianic complex with intellectuals in Eastern Europe. Nothing against it, but it was extremely dangerous in Slovenia when this messianic vision of intellectuals was combined with a vulgar anti-Americanism, which is a very popular political attitude of right wingers. This combination of nationalist writers, whose obsession is to retain national identity, and an anti-capitalist right-wing movement is very dangerous."[42] From a more personal perspective, Žižek developed his (Hegelian) structuralist variation of the Marxist position by referring to common subjective experiences, such as serving in the military and working for the party, so as to accessibly demonstrate an intellectual mapping of the State's space of positioning and its deadlock. This approach addressed the challenge of articulating a critical discourse in a postideological age, when isms have lost their desirability and subjectivity becomes cynical toward general ideologies. While maintaining some relations to Marx (as the critique of political economy) and to Heidegger (as the study of being), Žižek provided a synthesized, attractive lesson—condensed in a revisited, psychoanalytical concept of ideology—that would become integral to his intellectual repertoire: ideology works even if no individual believes in it; overidentification with ideology is dangerous for both the regime and the individual; and cynicism or irony is not effective in performing a critique of ideology. He elaborates on these lines as follows:

> For example, being unemployed, I had to work as a lower clerk at Central Committee for two years, just writing minutes of different marginal commissions. There, I knew two young people who sincerely believed in

Yugoslav self-management socialism—they lost their jobs! Because the bureaucracy knew it very well, if you believe too much in the ruling ideology, you are potentially dangerous. So, this was the first thing, how belief is materialized in practice, you don't have to believe . . . and we also already developed at that point the whole notion of cynicism, how cynical distance is not critical. It makes a system function perfectly. This was one insight from our daily life; the second insight was this obscene underside. How ideology is not just the explicit text, but all the series of obscene rituals and so on.[43]

This personal perspective, focused on Žižek's interventions and his consequent positioning, traces back to his MA thesis of 1975 and its relation between Marxism and structuralism. Since the 1960s, Žižek and Dolar, among other intellectuals of the young generation, had been translating key texts of French structuralism in the journal *Problemi*. Yet the first authoritative book in Slovenian to account comprehensively for the structuralist movement— *Strukturalizem: Poskus Filozofske Kritike* (Structuralism: An Attempt at Philosophical Criticism)—was published in 1971 by Žižek's MA supervisor, Boris Majer. Žižek's MA thesis contained an implicit critique of Majer's reading of structuralism. As a recently appointed professor in the Philosophy Department at the University of Ljubljana, Majer was concerned the thesis would position him problematically regarding the officials. He had political aspirations as well, later becoming the president of the Marxist Centre in Ljubljana and an influential member of the League of Communists of Slovenia. Majer, being on Žižek's committee, blocked the thesis's approval and by extension Žižek's career for its problematic relationship to Marxism. An elaboration was requested and submitted in the form of an additional chapter entitled "Teorija Pisanja: Materijalistička Teorija 'Produkcije Ljudi'" (Theory of Writing: The Materialist Theory of the "Production of People").[44] In it, Žižek linked the structuralist signifying process to Engels's concept of the "production of people." With this additional chapter, Majer lifted his objection and allowed the thesis to pass. According to Žižek, "the entire drama of refusing the degree and requiring the additional chapter on Marxism was purely a proverbial insurance policy for Majer, such that he would be politically absolved if things got heated later."[45]

Facing these contextual intellectual challenges, Dolar admits that when he "started as a philosopher and jumped quite enthusiastically on that wagon of structuralism . . . Slavoj was very much instrumental in this."[46] Importantly, while there was some uncertainty as to the exact meaning of this "wagon" called structuralism, their engagement with it proved fruitful. Structuralism resonated with many intellectual disciplines at once and allowed for a rethinking of the changing politics and culture: "So it was a complete misunderstanding. It was imposed by the press, by opinion-makers. This is not a question of self-naming; they wouldn't label themselves as being structuralists."[47] The uncertainty about structuralism was derived from the disciplinarian disparity between the many intellectuals—including Lévi-Strauss, Lacan, Foucault, Derrida, Althusser, Barthes, Deleuze—compounded, from the outside, under that label.[48] But this ambiguity also led to a loose and dynamic use of that label by Slovenian intellectuals, relating it to many intellectual positions, including Marxism and Hegelianism.

As Slovenia lacked a strong intellectual foothold (like the one *Praxis* had in Croatia), its intellectual arena was ripe for experimentation with new ideas like structuralism. Once introduced, it challenged the hegemony of Marxism and produced the intellectual question of the time: how to position oneself in relation to these challenging intellectual developments such as structuralism? The Slovenian intellectual faced, precisely, the question whether to give up Marxism or Heideggerianism and become "a structuralist." As Dolar put it, structuralism was seen as a pander of May 1968, an attractive and momentous "intellectual aroma," which became an intellectual revolution very much related to political and cultural upheavals: "So, jumping on this wagon entailed reading a lot of texts, and going back to Marx also, going back to Hegel, going back to classics, but reading very attentively Adorno, who died in 1970."[49] Žižek's own superpositioning does not only replace the existing two positions; it actually also preserves them as such. Therefore, unlike the vehement rejection of Hegel and German idealism by French structuralists (given the French-German rivalry), Slovenian intellectuals did not share this deep-seated resentment, or the need to abolish Hegel. On the contrary, they made a connection between structuralism and Hegel, and on the way between psychoanalysis and Marxism. In Dolar's description of this opposition, we find the intellectual tension also materialized in their team and networks:

> We didn't see a necessity to choose between Marxism and structuralism. All these structuralists, they were obviously the May '68 thing. They were strongly positioned in the left. It was Marxism of a peculiar kind, like Althusser's . . . but the difficult decision rather was, if I take now up this name of Hegel—this was really the dividing line between Frankfurt School and structuralism. Because [the] Frankfurt School basically depended on a certain reading of Marx as a critic of Hegel, of the material turn of the Hegelian dialectics . . . and seeing negativity, the negative dia-

lectic . . . as a benchmark, as something we should show fidelity to, something we should insist upon; whereas all the structuralists, basically, saw Hegel as their major opponent.[50]

Slovenia, as part of the Eastern bloc, did not share the same "natural" political and intellectual resentment toward Hegel as was present in France. Thus Hegel emerged as a point through which it was possible to adopt, and criticize, both Eastern Marxism and Western structuralism. Dolar and Žižek were the "face" of this relational move, making it a trademark of the Ljubljana School:

> Now, this comes to our very particular position, in being true to certain insights of Frankfurt School which concerned the Hegelian legacy, which we wanted to show fidelity to. Because we always thought that Hegel was somehow the guy with whom to think. And combine this with insights of structuralism, take insights from structuralism in such a way of seeing their anti-Hegel stance as their blind spot. They didn't see how actually what they were doing was, in our sense, in our reading of Hegel, actually, deeply Hegelian. But they never read the Frankfurt School, they didn't have any relation to this.[51]

The readiness to accept, even if only partially, various intellectual currents and to read them together, testifies to a positional openness of using as many resources as possible to make sense of their situation. This positioning, still, came at a political and intellectual price.[52] Although not sharing the same anti-Hegelian atmosphere as in Paris, being openly Hegelian in Ljubljana did pose some risks given the Marxist (reversal of the Hegelian) tradition.[53] Nonetheless, members of the Ljubljana School tried to find a gateway for these tensions and deadlocks:

> Lacan was a way out, in a way, to see how things go together. We draw on the Structuralist tradition and we draw on a certain Hegelian legacy which was for us a certain basis for Marx. . . . We couldn't put it in so many words at the time, but Hegel was for us more important than Marx. And at the time it would seem kind of dangerous to say this, that one would be labeled as an idealist or possibly anti-Marxist, saying that the crucial insights come from Hegel and that Marx was a Hegelian. Brilliant, extremely interesting, but unthinkable. We took it as something completely different than all this. I never denied my Marxism, I'm profoundly with him, but Hegel was more important for us.[54]

How did Žižek articulate his position, linking structuralism with German idealism, Marxism and psychoanalysis? The answer is found in the formative years of the Ljubljana School and its relation to Russian formalism, the intellectual "vanishing mediator" between Eastern Marxism and Western structuralism, which crucially contributed to the emergence of the school. Using Russian formalism as a segue to French structuralism, the school still enjoyed a degree of loyalty to the Soviet intellectual arena while it also developed a Hegelian critique of Marxism. In this way, the school was intellectually unique but still recognizable: unique because it shifted toward (Lacanian) psychoanalysis, and recognizable because it was related to many other schools of thought, such as Hegelianism, formalism, and Marxism. As relations between the Ljubljana School and the *Tel Quel* (*as is*)[55] cooled down from the mid-70s following a growing critique of Kristeva's semiotics and Derrida's deconstruction and a shift toward Lacan's psychoanalysis, Žižek notes apropos of the Slovenian intellectual opposition that "the younger generation, precisely as a third option—to be a dissident but not a Heideggerian—we were a reaction to both of these."[56] Superpositioning himself in reaction and relation to both sides of the intellectual opposition, Žižek articulated another position as a third way: "after a further quasi-religious revelation, finally we made the choice: Lacan."[57] This choice of Lacan is described religiously by Žižek as his "road to Damascus,"[58] that is, a crucial turning point that facilitated his unique appeal both to Marxists and Heideggerians in a fresh, relevant intellectual language of Hegelian-Lacanian structuralism.

To critically confront such a paradoxical (political-intellectual) situation, Žižek and the Ljubljana School performed a superpositioning that allowed them to evade the false criticality of the regime and its pseudo-oppositional intellectuals. Significant in this respect was Dolar's 1979 essay "O Nekaterih Stranpoteh Semiotične Analize" (On Certain Deviations of Semiotic Analysis), published as part of the *Problemi* section "'Umetnost' in Rob" ("Art" and the Margin; fig. 1.3). In that very year Dolar followed Žižek and traveled to study in Paris after winning the Best French Essay contest by the Alliance Française. The argument Dolar presented in this French article (which was part of his BA thesis in French literature) marks two critical moments in the intellectual development of the Ljubljana School, distinguishing its followers' unique positioning from all other positions available in Slovenia, Yugoslavia, and (Western) Europe: (1) rejection of Kristeva's category of the semiotic and Foucault's notion of discourse, and (2) formulation of the inherently inconsistent nature of the symbolic Law.[59] Together, this position, according to which "the fundamental difference between the semiotic and the symbolic

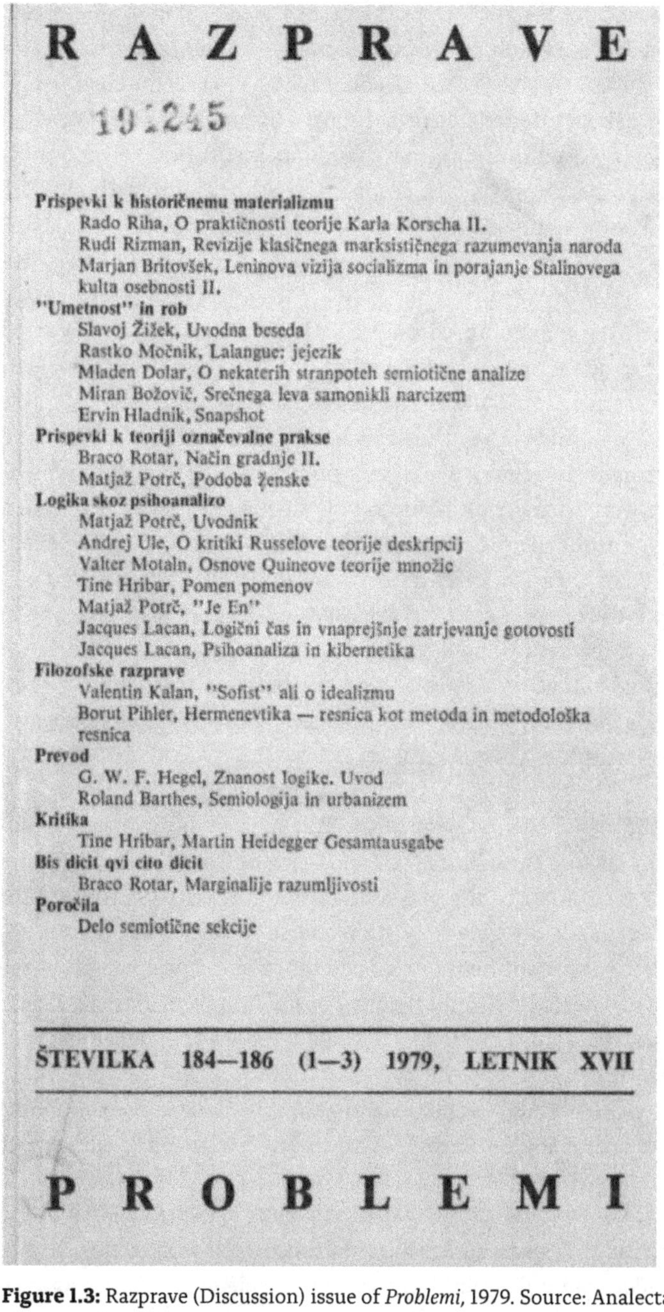

RAZPRAVE

191245

Prispevki k historičnemu materializmu
    Rado Riha, O praktičnosti teorije Karla Korscha II.
    Rudi Rizman, Revizije klasičnega marksističnega razumevanja naroda
    Marjan Britovšek, Leninova vizija socializma in porajanje Stalinovega kulta osebnosti II.

"Umetnost" in rob
    Slavoj Žižek, Uvodna beseda
    Rastko Močnik, Lalangue: jejezik
    Mladen Dolar, O nekaterih stranpoteh semiotične analize
    Miran Božovič, Srečnega leva samonikli narcizem
    Ervin Hladnik, Snapshot

Prispevki k teoriji označevalne prakse
    Braco Rotar, Način gradnje II.
    Matjaž Potrč, Podoba ženske

Logika skoz psihoanalizo
    Matjaž Potrč, Uvodnik
    Andrej Ule, O kritiki Russelove teorije deskripcij
    Valter Motaln, Osnove Quineove teorije množic
    Tine Hribar, Pomen pomenov
    Matjaž Potrč, "Je En"
    Jacques Lacan, Logični čas in vnaprejšnje zatrjevanje gotovosti
    Jacques Lacan, Psihoanaliza in kibernetika

Filozofske razprave
    Valentin Kalan, "Sofist" ali o idealizmu
    Borut Pihler, Hermenevtika — resnica kot metoda in metodološka resnica

Prevod
    G. W. F. Hegel, Znanost logike. Uvod
    Roland Barthes, Semiologija in urbanizem

Kritika
    Tine Hribar, Martin Heidegger Gesamtausgabe

Bis dicit qvi cito dicit
    Braco Rotar, Marginalije razumljivosti

Poročila
    Delo semiotične sekcije

ŠTEVILKA 184—186 (1—3) 1979, LETNIK XVII

PROBLEMI

Figure 1.3: Razprave (Discussion) issue of *Problemi*, 1979. Source: Analecta, Society for Theoretical Psychoanalysis.

is itself only symbolic,"[60] signals the priority of the Lacanian symbolic and thus the break with the French *Tel Quel* structuralism.[61] When asked why Paris, and especially the Université Paris 8, become such a critical site for the Ljubljana School, Žižek mentioned two reasons: first, his progress was blocked in Slovenia, being employed in a marginal dissidents institution with no prospects or jobs at proper departments; second, the School's ultraorthodox Lacanian position, which allowed him to establish ties with J. A. Miller. Žižek recalls:

> We organized a big colloquium through a little bit of cheating, and by some miracle we got some money for it. I think the title was "Psychoanalysis and Culture," something like that (we had to have culture in the title). We invited J. A. Miller and some other Lacanians, such as Gerard Miller and Alain Grosrichard, and it was like a great public event. There was tremendous enthusiasm, with people standing outside in the corridors to listen to the presentations. It was a kind of mystical/mythical founding event of the Slovenian Lacanian orientation. Subsequently, Miller offered one of us the post of Foreign Assistant at Paris 8—each year they have one or two posts for foreigners—and he offered this post to me. I stayed there for a year and then I stayed a couple of further times, for one semester, once even again for the whole year in Paris. And that's where I got my Lacanian training for a couple of years or so.[62]

This followed the initial distanciation of the Ljubljana School from other Slovenian positions such as those of Marx, Heidegger, or Derrida. The blending of these positions together (while preserving some core issues of them) with structuralism was made possible only via recourse to Lacan, who became—along with Hegel—the identifier of Žižek and his school. It was the first time that such an articulated complex intellectual position appeared, with Franco-German and East-West combinations. This could not have happened without Slovenia's unique positioning in the Yugoslav context, as well as the school's insistence on not-choosing, a superposition that would become the motto of Žižek's politics, drawing on Bartleby's affirmative negation "I would prefer not to."

It was in these years of the early 1980s that Žižek's Ljubljana School or the Society for Theoretical Psychoanalysis was formed. In his recollection of that event, Žižek links the intellectual impetus (e.g., academic condition, atmosphere), with the political situation (involving bureaucracy, censorship, and so on)—a crux embodied in the very naming of the school:

The main reason we founded it was because we were excluded from academia—at least the Lacanian orientation was. As a Society, we had the right to organize lectures and courses, which we did to propagate the theory. But these were still communist times and you could not organize spontaneously; you had to have some institutional coverage. That was one reason. The other reason was to secure the autonomy of our publications, because again, as a Society, we had the right to publish things. But establishing the Society was very complicated, and this was reflected in its rather strange title: Society for Theoretical Psychoanalysis. The way it was done was that proposals for new societies had to be sent to certain umbrella socialist organizations which would then ask other similar societies—in this instance, the philosophical, sociological and psychological societies—whether a new society was needed. This was a very tense moment for us. We were lucky in that the philosophers and sociologists didn't block us. The problem lay with the psychologists, and especially the psychiatrists, who were concerned that we would be competing with them. So it was a condition for establishing the society that we add the word "theoretical" to the title: in other words, nothing practical, no clinics. This was purely a pragmatic matter.[63]

These theoretical and practical efforts of the school to differentiate and individuate itself, not for the sake of being unique but as "a way out" of its deadlocks, led it to superposition what was thought as totally opposed, creating the school's singular position. In this context we can understand the recent opening statement of "The Slovene Re-actualization of Hegel's Philosophy" issue of *Filozofija i Društvo* (Philosophy and Society),[64] which claims the "Ljubljana School of Psychoanalysis is undoubtedly the most prominent event in the history of Slovene philosophy: it put our small country on the map of local philosophy."[65] Yet this was possible only through Žižek's utilization of the Lacanian and Hegelian tools to analyze the Yugoslav breakdown which put *him* on the map of *world intellectuals*.[66] Although still limited to intellectual and academic circles, Žižek was noticed as the one who could explain the (Eastern) other in the terms of the (Western) self:

> I think there was partly perfect timing. Because the downfall of the Iron Curtain, the moment it came, Slavoj's success, some of the major emergence of the East. Everybody was waiting for a message from the East. There is this big "East," which we don't know anything about, one day, suddenly. And there emerges, amazingly, a guy who is extremely knowledgeable and can make more sense about structuralism and post-structuralism

than anybody could at the time in the West. And who, amazingly, there is, suddenly, this East which talks back. Which is not like, "to be taught our Western ways," but which actually talks back, and knows better than the rest of us. So, there was a perfect historical timing, because the idea of Eastern Europe was very much an ambiguous imagination. Like, "what are this people, who are they, what do they have in their minds?" And this also connects to Žižek's singularity, as it were, his real talent for showmanship—to combine showmanship with serious conceptual work.[67]

Žižek's ability to speak (and write) structuralism *while* insisting on Hegelian philosophy created a parlance or dialect at once recognizable yet not fully intelligible to the Western intellectual ear. And, related to the political changing context of Europe, the Soviet Union, and the world, Žižek's position was at once supportive and critical of the change. This blend of East-West and French-German ideas allowed Žižek to communicate and collaborate with most intellectual currents of the time—to varying degrees—while signaling and maintaining his unique position on paper and in real life. Hence, Žižek's analysis of Yugoslavia's disintegration is the first indication for his emergence as a global intellectual.[68] In Parker's own words: "The conceptual architecture of Yugoslav society was able to sustain these various ideological trends, but as the state started to disintegrate the fault lines in the texture of life under the bureaucracy started to become lines of battle. And it is then that we see the conditions of impossibility for the Yugoslav state also start to operate as conditions of possibility for Žižek's combination of Hegel, Lacan and Marx to become effective, not only as legitimation but also as critique."[69]

Civil Society and Alternative Culture: From Punk to NSK

Following the political and intellectual tensions, the main tension in the Slovenian cultural arena of the 1980s was the one between the emerging civil society and the more radical alternative culture, which, through its provocative and innovative performances has shaken Slovenian society, causing heated debates over the page and the street. Just like the political arena, and much for the same reasons, even culturally "Yugoslavia under Tito was not like other Eastern Bloc countries."[70] It enjoyed a vibrant and diverse public discourse, drawing from various intellectual sources of both East and West.

The main actors in the Slovenian cultural arena were groups of poets, writers, visual artists, stage performers, musicians, and painters, and they were usually organized into collectives and movements (or less often, parties).[71] Žižek's intellectual-cultural interventions positioned him as part of the alternative culture. His early public interventions can be found in parallel to the development of cultural-cum-intellectual avant-garde collectives such as the OHO Group (1966–1971). Named after the astonishment effect ("oh!") of uncovering the essence of things, the group's artists experimented with new forms and collaborated with several intellectuals, some of them still in the making. For example, in 1969, during his undergraduate studies, Žižek published two experimental pieces in the "OHO-Katalog" edition of *Problemi*. Later, in his texts from the 1980s he linked concepts such as overidentification with the performances of various artistic groups, thus loading them with new and provocative meanings and substantiating a link between new social movements (NSMs) and scientific/intellectual movements (SIMs).[72] It should be noted, though, that it was not a linear process from politics to intellectuals to culture; these loci and processes are interwoven and only analytically distinct precisely to explain their synthetic relations. In different Yugoslav countries, intellectuals adopted distinct positions in particular periods as the social and political changes occurred.[73] Irwin and Motoh observe that the intellectual journals of the time were also "active in the next great wave of alternative culture movements of the early 1980s, which can be systematically divided into *three interconnected trends*: the punk movement, FV 112/15 and Laibach/NSK."[74]

The punk movement was the first NSM in Slovenia, and when it emerged in the 1970s it was a youth subculture. Influenced by British punk bands, the band *Panktri* (Bastards) was formed by Slovenian youth in 1977. Punk innovated cultural codes, and it "not only introduced the concept of an independent social life, but proved that it was possible and created elements for the formation of a new social and political language."[75] Following some openly critical songs—like "Comrades, I Don't Believe You" and "Total Revolution (. . . Is Not a Solution)"—the authorities started to censor, ban, repress, and even prosecute figures of the movement. A major event that Dolar and Žižek were part of was the 1981 "Nazi-punk affair," as a young group was arrested for allegedly forming a national-socialist party.[76] At this time, a close link was made between the *Problemi* group and the punk group. In fact, even before this incident, Dolar was already working on this topic of Nazism and fascism while it was being widely debated across the intellectual arena. After writing his BA thesis, "Contradictions and Alternatives in Marxist Analyses of Fascism," he first published on that topic in *Problemi* in 1978. This was then expanded into a book, *The Structure of the Fascist Domination*, published in 1982.[77]

Two years later, the Sigmund Freud School in Ljubljana organized a seminar that later was compiled into the book *Filozofija skozi Psihoanalizo* (Philosophy through Psychoanalysis), which included Žižek's chapter "Ideologija,

Figure 1.4: Parts of pages 3–4 from the censored *Punk Problemi*, 1982. Source: Helena Motoh, "Punk Is a Symptom," *Synthesis Philosophica* 54, no. 2 (January 2012): 290, https://hrcak.srce.hr/101721.

Cinizem, Punk" (Ideology, Cynicism, Punk). In it he supplemented Dolar's interpretation of fascism (from 1978) while shifting emphasis to the self-management system. For Žižek it operated as the background and the target of the critique against the punk movement and later the art collective NSK. Contextually, "in 1981, the very year of the 'Nazi-punk scandal,' the new movement was given space to present themselves in a special edition of the journal *Problemi*, called *Punk Problemi*, being followed by two consecutive editions in the next two years. The second of these, issued in 1982, caused a particular upheaval when the issue's editors refused to quietly censor parts of punk bands' lyrics that were printed in the journal, but instead published pages with black rectangles marking the censored parts" (fig. 1.4).[78] As a result, Dolar, the journal's editor, was accused of facilitating the publication of pornographic material (exposed body parts) and was forced to pay a fine.[79]

As Phil Cohen has rightly pointed out, subcultures have a latent social function, namely to express and resolve, "albeit magically," the hidden or unresolved contradictions in the parent culture.[80] While the (NSM of the) punk subculture did form an alternative network in the mid-1980s, it remained mostly underground, as most of its actors were younger than eighteen years old. Students and intellectuals hardly participated at that stage, except for those in the younger generation, like Žižek, who played an important role and refuted the ideologically political attacks on the alternative, thus preserving an open space for other actors to emerge. Only a number of the most able intellectuals (shunt from university posts for being "morally-politically inappropriate") actively engaged with the alternative scene. The positional purge that started in the 1970s by persons away from the party line did not stop Žižek and his school from intervening in the public sphere, disseminating their ideas via other, independent media outlets.[81] Thus, following the official media's collapse in the mid-1980s, even intellectuals of the middle generation started to take part in the formation of civil society.

With police repression failing to suppress public debates and discussions, and backed or joined by some intellectuals, the civil opposition expanded. Hence the second trend that marked the spreading of civil and cultural opposition was Group FV 112/15. Taking its name from the random choice of page 112, line 15, of the *France Verbine* loanword dictionary, this art group was represented mostly by students, not youth. While rock music was the big thing in the 1960s and 1970s, as Dolar noted, this group experimented with genres like punk and new wave. They took over a Ljubljana disco and engaged in mixing music and video productions, becoming a locus of new alternative groups and ideas. As a result, "Disco FV and its activities also provided a space for development of new art genres, specific for this generation of artists: they introduced video art and graffiti art, while also exploring the relation between art and pornography and introducing pornographic material into art forms."[82] The group collaborated with other NSMs on topics such as gay rights, until, "in the mid-1980s, the first independent demonstrations were organized, numerous petitions, open letters and public statements were written, a number of seminars were held, feminists appeared in public, and, in 1984, the first week of gay culture was organized in Ljubljana by homosexuals."[83]

The third cultural trend, maybe the most publicly influential and definitely the most related to Žižek, was the new art collective NSK. Announced in 1984, it composed of the new music and cross-media group Laibach (significantly, "Ljubljana" in German), the painters' collective IRWIN, and the Scipion Nasice Sisters Theatre (plus several departments). The NSK was considered the most dangerous by the regime because it purposefully used Nazi symbolism and violated the total prohibition of the same in postwar Yugoslavia. Even its name—Laibach, the first of these groups to appear in 1980—is an irritating reminder of the German occupation during World War II. While previous trends—including punk and FV 112/15—were subversive for their mass popularity, youth rebelliousness, form of performances, choice of genres, use of pornographic material, and affiliation with gay movements, Laibach and then NSK were "questioning the interlacing of art and ideology: they played with the old symbols in completely new contexts, thus inventing the alleged new art movement, called 'retrogradism.'"[84] This group attracted the fiercest and widest critique—even the prohibition of its public performances—as the Slovenian public found it intuitively difficult to relate to the seemingly obscene use of Nazi insignia. Yet mediated by intellectuals' interpretations, the group's status remained a vital part of alternative culture.

In the following years of 1986–1989, several legal and cultural events produced even greater challenges to the disintegrating political system. Particularly, the Slovenian youth had shaken two sacred pillars of the Yugoslav state: the honor related to serving in Tito's Yugoslav People's Army, and the participation—supposed to demonstrate Tito's "brotherhood and unity" motto—in the yearly Relay of Youth race (1945–1988). Noteworthy is the destruction of a clog with a saw in the center of Ljubljana, and the poster scandal, through which the Slovenian youth performed a "symbolic protest and demanded abolition of the relay race and the introduction of civilian forms of national service."[85] By wittingly imitating the aesthetics of the Nazi artist Richard Klein, replacing the Nazi and Yugoslav flags and the German eagle with a dove, an illusory, critical resemblance between Hitler and Tito was created. As the designers touched upon an open nerve in Slovenian society, and with threats from the police, the poster was banned as was the *Mladina*'s issue of it.

In the same year of 1987, *Nova Revija* published its fifty-seventh issue and caused a fierce debate in Slovenia's political life. The issue was devoted in full to the Slovenian national question, with the involvement of opposition intellectuals that expressed nonparty views. Significantly, unlike past occurrences when the authorities sanctioned, banned, and even imprisoned members of oppositional journals, this time the Central Committee of the League of Communists of Slovenia—backed by the presidency of the Socialist Alliance of the Working People—did not resort to administrative intervention and turned to democratic dialogue with the authors and editors. This opened the door for a more intense and articulated opposition in the following years.

Nonetheless, the next event that fueled existing public tensions even further was the JBTZ affair or trial (*afera JBTZ*). This refers to the arrest and prosecution of two *Mladina* journalists (Janez Jansa and David Tasic), the editor (Franci Zavrl), and a Slovenian sergeant of the Yugoslav People's Army (Ivan Borstner)—for alleged betrayal by publishing military secrets. These were in fact notes from meeting of the Central Committee regarding dissidents' arrests. The trial became a symbol, and a fight standing for the entire democratization of society, well beyond the release of four men. After the sentencing— which ignored public outrage—rallies and demonstrations intensified, with tens of thousands of participants calling for the protection of human rights. The intellectual reaction was not far behind, with Žižek and thirty-two other intellectuals publicly resigning from the Communist Party: "I was a member of the Communist party until 1988 when it became disgusting to remain in a party that defended militarism."[86] The resignation meant that a crucial link between the party and the left-wing part of civil society was broken.

In her positional account for the Ljubljana School's relation to the cultural arena, Renata Salecl pointed out that "the Lacanian movement in Slovenia was always on the side of the opposition. In the early 1980s when new social movements began to develop in Slovenia, it was really only Lacanians who gave theoretical support to these groups."[87] This theoretical support positioned Žižek's school with the general public aspiring for change, and particularly with the younger generation, which was exposed to and influenced by varied intellectual sources. Yet this positioning was not simply one-sided, against either the state or some conservatives. It was also a position from within the public, that of those seeking to extend and expand the change and not just accept it as a unitary shift from communism to capitalism. The school's position thus reacted to the cultural opposition's diverse intellectual origins: "The opposition movement in Slovenia has two quite distinct origins. On the one hand you have a nationalist intelligentsia, nationalist poets writing about national roots, etc. Their philosophical reference is Heidegger. On the other hand, you have the remnants of an old New Left connected to new social movements—peace, human rights movements, etc.—and, extremely important, a punk movement. (The band Laibach, for example.) It is precisely through punk that the pluralist opposition reached the masses. It was a kind of political mass education, and we supported it."[88] These seemingly contradictory elements of Slovenian culture are a direct effect of the turmoil in the political arena, as many social actors tried to be those who set the new cultural tone. To make this counterintuitive situation clearer, this is how Žižek bluntly puts it: "In Slovenia, civil society is equal to the right-wingers. In America, after the Oklahoma bombing, they suddenly discovered that madmen are everywhere."[89] As we saw earlier, once the Iron Curtain was lifted, what came out were not only good and progressive social forces but also the obscene underside of social antagonisms, that is, ethno-nationalism. This is why even the public sphere of civil society was not immediately critical, or consistently oppositional.

The school's intellectual tool kit was used by some cultural movements in their continuous effort to keep opposing and reinterpreting the limits of the situation. Interpretation that sometimes, in such paradoxical times—when the system was already self-critical—must also suspend itself in order to make the situation clearer rather than eclipsed by a debilitating multiplicity of meanings. Hence the personal and professional link between cinema and politics, corresponding to Žižek's desire of becoming a movie director turned philosopher. As he eloquently puts it, "Cinema is still the easiest way, like for Freud dreams were the royal way to the unconscious."[90] And because in modern societies culture is predominantly a segment of civil society, and not the state, public performativity is crucial for intellectual as well as artistic interventions.

It is therefore hard to overestimate the importance of the Slovenian NSMs during this time of transition. Some even compared them to Kant's French Revolution, since they are both considered *Signum rememorativum, demonstrativum, prognosticon*, that is, the historical sign for the progress of humanity toward the good, traced by the enthusiasm generated by these events. Yet it seems that without the strong support, intellectual and practical, of SIMs such as the Ljubljana School, both movements would have been less influential and effective. Following Močnik, this analysis has shown that Žižek, along with a specific Lacanian-Hegelian positioning, emerged from a distinct feature of the political-intellectual landscape in Slovenia, as it was accompanied by the unusual relationship between alternative culture and civil society, as well as the almost exceptional relationship between a generation of young intellectuals and alternative cultures, whether of punk, FV 112/15, or NSK. As Močnik recalls: "The intervention of Lacan was decisive; it enabled us to reformulate in a theoretically productive way the seeming dead-ends of the previous theories. Against dead-end formulas, I put first the Lacanian concepts that break the dead-end, and then the positive reformulation of the impasse."[91] The consideration of the very theoretical intervention as a political practice allowed the Ljubljana School to keep creating new links and positions—from formalism to structuralism and psychoanalysis—precisely as its very position.[92] The school's continuous intervention in the cultural arena, interpreting NSK's performances, maintained the position of the school as engaged intellectuals both theoretically with students and practically with the public. Gantar noted that the complex relation between civil society and alternative culture was to have an influence even beyond independence.[93] Dolar summarizes this incredibly formative period of his school:

> There was a very broad label under which we somehow congregated at the time, and this was "the alternative." I mean this in the eyes of the public, but this was also a self-designation. The alternative doesn't mean Lacanians, we are part of it, it would mean NSK, Laibach, punk, avant-garde movements in arts, avant-garde in theater, which was very important and very good at the time. This is a very different span, these things, and someone could squeeze this label of "the alternative," to the system, the party, the way the party was doing things. And there were alternative media; there was Radio Študent, which still exists, which was the alternative medium, and *Mladina* was an alternative medium. Reading *Mladina* what you could never read in the national newspaper. Reaching the public using all these alternative media communication channels was very successful. Slavoj was a great public presence, as a speaker, funny, . . . he's a showman, he's trying to be the showman, and when there were first elections for the presidency he ran for the presidency for post and came fifth. So he almost got it. So he had already public presence.[94]

To trace these performances and positionings, carried out by Žižek's upcoming intellectual interventions, it is useful to look at the School's own development, from its base of the troika, the recognizable front of the Ljubljana School. In addition to Dolar and Žižek, the third part is Alenka Zupančič. She was a student of both, and according to her, was "very efficiently corrupted" by Žižek's interventions, to the extent of deciding (in 1985) not to study natural sciences but philosophy instead. And so, in her worthy recollection of that formative period, she brings to light the most important feature of Žižek's performance, namely, the difference between his effective wit and the common intellectual's futile cynicism:

> One thing that was also extremely interesting for me, when this whole thing started in the eighties, was to see the difference between public intellectuals of that time, who were people perceiving themselves as these sage or wise men and women, giving wise advice and analysis of culture or whatever, and the way this other, my camp worked was very different. It was extremely witty; it was never from this point, if you just look at the

posture of people telling you on TV. Slavoj was on television, he even ran for the presidency, but it was never somebody telling you "OK, look at me, a very educated and clever person, I will tell you what to think." It was never this kind of posture of "I know better, I will tell you what to do."[95]

Negating the intellectual position that Baert has termed "the authoritative intellectual" and Lacan "the subject supposed-to-know," Zupančič goes on to explain Žižek's source of public attraction, stressing its difference from other philosophers of that time:

> Everybody was already playing with ironic distance all the time, so this was not subversive in any serious sense, but this was. And Slavoj was immediately able to see this, as opposed to the "then" public intellectuals who said, "Oh, but this is very strange, they don't have, they just repeat, they're fascists." People didn't know what to do with this. This was precisely what was so interesting about them. So in the way of how one speaks, and also for my part, when I'm given the chance or if I'm asked to do some kind of political interview, I hopefully, spontaneously try to keep faithful to this tradition of never trying to play the "OK, now I'm of a certain age, I've seen many things, so now I can tell you" game.[96]

Turning irony and cynicism into witticism and fidelity, Žižek reoriented the sociopolitical coordinates beyond their positive (the party's) or negative (the dissidents') opposition. He created a way to think outside this deadlock, in a way that superpositions the *yei* and the *nei* of the public: Critique? Yes. Irony? No. Not being cynical made him an odd (but honest) critic, positioned against the party but also against civil society. This superpositioning became all the more public with an increasing number and kind of interventions, amid the intensified political disintegration.

The position of artists such as Laibach and the NSK was complex, for, as Aleš Erjavec writes, "they deconstruct not only post-Socialist culture and history, but also the wish of the Western art system to see and identify the artist in such a culture as an asymmetrical and exotic *Other*."[97] Accordingly, Žižek positioned his intellectual interventions through a series of related concepts: (1) punk to *symptom*, (2) Laibach to *overidentification*, (3) and culture to *cynicism*. A description of each relation demonstrates Žižek's interventions and performativity more vividly.

First, as editors of *Punk Problemi*, Dolar and Žižek held a position that allowed them, again, to agree and disagree with common public discourse. They agreed with those who claimed that the punk movement was a symptom, yet they also disagreed on the meaning of this symptom, taking it seriously through theory rather than common sense. They argued in their interpretive interventions against the symptomatic reading offered by mainstream criticism. For example, in his 1981 editorial of the first *Punk Problemi* issue, Žižek provided a different diagnosis using the concept of symptom in a novel way, "marking the beginning of a completely new chapter of the relationship between socio-political reality, art scene and the critical journals."[98] According to Žižek's analysis "symptom returns our suppressed truth in a perverted form.... Punk literally enacts the suppressed aspect of 'normality' and thereby 'liberates,' it introduces a defamiliarizing distance."[99] This distance, however, is not cynical, keeping the symptom quiet instead of letting it speak. Attuned with the growing public interest in psychology, the self, and subjectivity, Žižek used this superpositioning to break with the objective "dogmatic Marxism" for prohibiting the subjective symptom (that Marx invented) to speak. He adopted an "orthodox Lacanian": "We need to read the Marxist symptom in the context of Freud and Lacan, and this is what I have done successively in my texts. We told the Althusserians we were with the Derrideans, and the Derrideans we were with the Althusserians, but we went with Lacan, alone as it were. Why? Because he allowed us the wife and the mistress, the both/and, not just the either/or."[100] After superpositioning the "orthodox" and "heterodox" positions from within the intellectual-philosophical arena, Žižek and Dolar showed how overidentification is more dangerous to the functioning of a self-critical, cynical regime (or subject) because it reveals its inner inconsistencies rather than just posing external objections from a different (usually moral) ground. Instead of maintaining a pseudo-critical distance using cynical wisdom, overidentifiers—those who take "things" (e.g., symbolic authority) too seriously—pose a greater risk to the sociosymbolic order since they practically demonstrate how the regime is not what it claims to be. More accurately, this is equivalent to a new society member insisting on deliberately violating the unwritten rules so to expose inconsistency of the written rules. As also noted by Parker, "in retrospect, it is now possible to see the phenomenon of NSK as 'a kind of theatricalization of a few Žižek theses,' but in the 1980s this was 'the language of the alternative society.'"[101] Activists from the NSK did attend Žižek's lectures but insisted that it was Laibach that first used the method of overidentification, and that Žižek then theorized what the group did. Thus, overidentification became one of the most recognizable oppositional methods of artistic and intellectual strategy for ideology critique.[102]

Third, Žižek relates cynicism and culture in his 1984 text (published in Slovenian) *Ideology, Cynicism, Punk*. It draws on the German philosopher Peter

Sloterdijk's *Critique of Cynical Reason* (1983) and blends it with his Lacanian conceptions of subjectivity.[103] Žižek begins with the accusations of fascism that targeted Laibach after their provocative TV performance in June 1983. Motoh claims that Žižek's text "explains the effect the Laibach performance had on the TV audiences and critics by their mimicking of the ideological ritual, without distancing themselves from it by irony or criticism. This act is exactly what is not permitted within the system. The ideology does not require the individual to *believe* in the rituals, but expects conformism in not ever admitting their disbelief."[104] In the text, Žižek introduced Sloterdijk's triad of cynical consciousness: naïve ideology—kynicism—cynicism. If the first position is a misguided belief in ideology, and the second is its enlightened denunciation, then the cynical contemporary subject denounces while acting as if it believes. As Žižek expressed it, the cynic knows full well that his ideology is false, yet he or she follows it nonetheless—or, in an early indication of what would become Hegelacanese, "reflection is already included in its position."[105]

Regarding Laibach's performances, Žižek linked the initial (pseudo-)critical reaction to it, as an ironic imitation of totalitarian rituals, with the underlying concern: What if they really mean it? This concern is there, supposedly, to evoke the conservative question, What if the public takes seriously what Laibach mockingly imitates? This reasoning is then contrasted with Žižek's interpretation of both Laibach and the public immediate response. He shows how Laibach "'frustrates' the system precisely insofar as it is not an ironic imitation but overidentification with it—by bringing to light the obscene superego underside of the system, over-identification suspends its efficiency."[106]

Laibach and NSK subverted the state's ideology because they did exactly what the cynical regime—keeping its "safe" distance—prevents its people from doing, that is, taking it seriously. Therefore, "overidentification here meant refusal of any distance, the taking of dominant symbolic forms at face value and, through repetition and reflexive considerations of their tactical impact, taking the response of the state to breaking point."[107] In his writings on such cultural and artistic performances, Žižek made overidentification "a way of breaking from the deadlock between apologists for the regime and the unwittingly loyal opposition, shattering the strategies of 'dissidence' that seemed simply to serve as another alibi for the regime. Through the 1980s the main focus was on state rituals, and in the 1990s the NSK set up its own embassies and consulates."[108] The punk movement, however, practiced another strategy. Attempting to expose the very cynical character of the regime, the movement first used a cynical tactic of sarcasm and irony to reveal the hypocritical ruling ritual. Yet Žižek's text also claims for another tactic in the movement's practice: the exposing of every quest for (lost) authenticity—

like that of the hippie movement or nationalistic right-wingers—as an empty gesture or funny pose. The punks' position, their pose, reflected the impossibility of this performative authenticity and the falsity of the escape, thereby "addressing the cynically spilt subject of the self-management system and enabling it to get rid of its habitual subjection to the system's automatism."[109]

Recently, in his preface to Monroe's extensive study of Laibach and the NSK, Žižek relates psychoanalytic theory, performance, and today's postmodern society: "Freud referred to 'acheronta movebo,' moving the underground, in the exergue to his *Interpretation of Dreams*, and this is what 'moving the underground' as a practice of the critique of ideology means: not directly changing the explicit text of the law, but, rather, intervening in its obscene virtual supplement. And this, precisely, was what Laibach were doing throughout the 1980s: instead of submitting the explicit ideology (of Yugoslav self-management Socialism) to rational critique or ironic subversion, their performances directly staged the underlying inconsistent mixture of ideological fantasies that sustained it—and this was what made them so unbearable."[110] Bringing this technique into the present, thus arguing for its relevance, he asks: "How to find a similar procedure today: is there, in our cynical 'postmodern' ideological universe, still a place for a Laibach-type intervention, or is such an intervention immediately 'co[-]opted,' neutralized?" Then he makes the surprising link to another (in)famous popular staging from our current global memory, namely the Abu Ghraib photos of American soldiers humiliating Iraqi prisoners. Against the ideological response of President Bush, denouncing the photos as deviance from American values, Žižek claims that this is not a deviation from a constituted value but a deviation constitutive of it. Hence "Bush was wrong: what we get when we see the photos ... is precisely a direct insight into 'American values,' into the very core of the obscene enjoyment that sustains the US way of life."[111] He concluded by arguing that "it is here that a Laibach-type intervention is needed: again, a direct staging of this obscene supplement, of the spectacle of barbarism that sustains our civilization.... Today, the lesson of Laibach is more pertinent than ever: only a direct confrontation with the fantasmatic core can actually liberate us from its grip."[112] This form of intellectual intervention, of arguing through everyday references to make a point about the subject and its—that is, readers'—relation to ideology, would become signatory of Žižek's performances.

Yugoslavia's Political Disintegration and Slovenia's Democratization

On May 4, 1980, at the moment of Tito's death, Yugoslavia's national debt was already $20 billion, and in the year after, the inflation rate was 45 percent.

Two other occurrences affected the disintegration of the Yugoslav Federation: the recession of the early 1980s in the West and the beginning of the political decomposition of the Soviet Union. Therefore, this period of the early 1980s was characterized by "the activity of Yugoslav cultural workers and intellectuals criticizing current policy, supporting political pluralism, opening taboo subjects, and increasingly emphasizing the national component of social life."[113] One major issue, and around which debates were held, was the rise of ethno-nationalism (and the figure of the Jew), with different parts of Yugoslavia claiming their self-determination. For example, on March 11, 1981, student demonstrations appeared in Kosovo's capital, Pristina, with demands for a "Kosovo-Republic."[114]

Together with this intellectual openness between the early and the late 1980s, Slovenia had experienced a process of political pluralization, with several mass demonstrations for (different kinds of) change. Against this background, first cracks appeared in the unity of the League of Communists of Yugoslavia, especially among Yugoslav writers and their associations. Thus a new tension supplemented the East-West division, as a rift broke between two opposing positions regarding the future of Yugoslavia: on the one hand was the "unitary" (Serbian and Montenegrin) position, and on the other, the "confederal" (Slovenian and Croatian). Slobodan Milošević, the charismatic Serbian politician, strongly denounced the confederative ideas at the eighteenth meeting of the Central Committee of the League of Communists of Serbia.

Another event that drew Žižek's political and intellectual attention was Milošević's visit to Kosovo in 1987, which became a turning point in the emergence of Serb nationalism as a specific retroactive formation of a chosen trauma. As Parker claims, Milošević "emerged from this experience a transformed person, wearing the armor of Serb nationalism," and then, "with the decision to bring the body of Lazar, the hero of the 1389 battle [against the Turks], on a tour of Serb villages and towns, the 'chosen trauma' that had been kept alive throughout the centuries was brought to life. This is how events in the 1980s served to reactivate 'affects' (intense bodily states that we experience as distinct emotions) connected with 'traumatized self-images.'"[115] The production of a past event to only then find it to be what caused the traumatic effect in the present is similar to Freud's analysis of the psychoanalytic symptom. Žižek would contextualize his and the Yugoslav situation through Lacan's interpretation of Freud, and would use it to demonstrate how this enjoyment—produced by a nostalgic yearning for a lost organic sense of community—is not just ideological but also, pathologically, the very condition to any ideological appeal.

The "Slovene Spring," between 1989 and 1991, saw the continuation of democratization and political pluralization. Most importantly, parties and coalitions (like the Slovenian Democratic Association, the Socialist Democratic Association of Slovenia, and the Greens of Slovenia) were formed through the challenging translation of civil opposition to political position. This was followed by multiparty elections and the plebiscite for the sovereignty of Slovenia.[116] Additional laws, regulations, and declarations were made to establish Slovenia's territorial, economic, and political sovereignty.

Despite being "semi-dissident" and unemployed, Žižek began his active political engagement in the second half of the 1980s. Before that, dissidents and critical intellectuals were Heideggerians, yet Žižek's team did not have good relations with any of them. Thus, Žižek aimed for a very limited goal in his political engagement: "It was simply to prevent Slovenia turning into another country like Croatia or Serbia, where one big nationalist movement hegemonized the entire thing. In that we succeeded, Slovenia is a country with a much more dispersed sense of place and the nationalist temptation is dissipated. So it wasn't a fundamental political engagement."[117] At the end of 1990, Žižek's Liberal Democratic Party lost the election to the broader Democratic Opposition of Slovenia (DEMOS) coalition. This was followed in 1991 by the formal disintegration of the Yugoslav state, with the anticipated international recognition of independent Slovenia and intensifying ethnic clashes in the region.

Žižek's interventions—which by then included newspaper and journal pieces, several books, and TV appearances—meant that he was positioned both intellectually and politically as an engaged local public intellectual. It seems that once his party was not elected to the four-member collective presidency, he made a decision: his intellectual interventions would be political interventions. As he put it, "I simply had to choose. Do I do serious theory or politics?"—and as for the elections he lost, he recalls that, "along with the old Communist Party, the Liberal [Democratic] Party is now part of the opposition bloc. But what defines the distinctive role of the Liberal [Democratic] Party is our opposition to the rise of this national-organic populism in Slovenia. Our aim is to promote pluralism, and an awareness of ecological issues, and to defend the rights of minorities. This is the kind of liberal tradition we represent. Not the purely capitalist values of the free market, not Friedrich von Hayek."[118] Žižek's attempt to intervene directly in politics and to put his theory to practice, involved not only personal positioning vis-à-vis other people or parties but also a conceptual positioning on the very meaning of concepts central to the changing public life. Thus, he insists, "we were engaged in a struggle for the rearticulation of this floating signifier, 'liberalism.' The term was associated, throughout Slovenia, with the idea of freeing ourselves from communist domination. It was extremely important who should succeed in occupying this ideological terrain, and in fact the right-wingers were furious."[119] According to Renata Salecl, the inability of the Liberal Democratic Party was connecting with the Green Party, which eventually became part of the center-right DEMOS coalition. Perhaps this inability resulted from the personal animosity between Žižek and the Green Party. She mentions that once DEMOS took power, it had "the same system as before," because, "until the fall of the regimes in East Germany and Romania toward the end of 1989, the aspiration of DEMOS was to be strong enough to be taken seriously as an opposition. It was only after these events that they themselves saw that there was a real possibility of winning power. Neither ourselves, nor the Communist Party, foresaw that this might happen—and now the real political problem is simply to stay alive."[120]

Unlike other Yugoslav republics, like Serbia and Montenegro, Slovenia was unique in that the left and liberal opposition were more organized, both politically and intellectually. This was due to Slovenia's access to and engagement with the West, and its being the richest, most ethnically homogenized nation, all the while having the smallest population in Yugoslavia. Building on more solid intellectual grounds, with dozens of vibrant journals and fewer ethnic cleavages, the Slovenian opposition was not based solely on small groups centered in universities. This organization prevented the opposition from consisting of far-right nationalists and steered public attention away from them. However, this opposition, of which Žižek was a part, did not manage to prevent the perverse situation whereby a capitalist ideology hegemonized the political arena, in the sense of allowing for multiple and even contradictory positions to emerge around a repressed social trauma. Using self-positioning to differentiate himself from that ideological hegemony, Žižek explains:

> Even for the Communist Party, the main economic points of reference are Thatcher, the Chicago school. Personally, I'm a pragmatist in this area. If it works, why not try a dose of it? But one should at least recognize that neo-liberal economics is not a neutral technical instrument—to use Lacan's terms, there are certain subject positions inscribed within it. We Liberals are the only political force opposed to this—the supposed "de-ideologizing" of the economy through the application of "neutral," technically efficient measures. The tragedy is that even the communists perceive this kind of Thatcherite or Friedmanesque economics as something ideologically neutral, as not involving any class- or subject positions.[121]

It is thus not surprising that Žižek's party did not resonate with the public, given that it was unable to create strong links and alliances with other parties and intellectual groups, which would go on to form the winning DEMOS coalition. The younger Žižek spoke faster, more theoretically, and less persuasively. This is why Žižek ended fifth and lost the 1990 elections, yet he "didn't take it too seriously." As he explains: "In terms of political posts, I was never interested in doing any cultural politics or whatever. The only thing that interested me—again the old story, but it's not a joke—was either being Minister of the Interior or Head of the Secret Service."[122] This was the end of his direct political engagement, yet this also cleared the path for future intellectual interventions, from books to films, through which Žižek's relation to politics was maintained publicly.

Žižek applied his synthetic intellectual approach to politics in a series of early international publications in English, analyzing contemporary ideological and aesthetic phenomenon.[123] In his *Eastern Europe's Republics of Gilead*, Žižek used the Lacanian notion of theft-of-enjoyment to address Yugoslavia's disintegration and the rise of ethno-nationalism.[124] The (emotional and physical) lack of the self is explained (away) by the other's excessive or surplus enjoyment. Taking Yugoslavia as a "case study" while generalizing its analysis beyond the "backwards Balkans" to US ideology of the 1980s and "late capitalism," Žižek showed how nationality has "built its own mythology narrating how other nations deprive it of the vital part of enjoyment the possession of which would allow it to live fully."[125] Thus, Žižek's analysis provided (the West) a description of how the national antagonism has already been structured and embroiled in the Yugoslav state apparatus and its forms of interpellation by justification and legitimization. Žižek made this political-intellectual (and even psychological) connection via already-established intellectuals such as Louis Althusser and Ernesto Laclau, known references in the field with some affiliation to Lacan, while he modified their position to accommodate his Hegelian framework. Althusser's concept of interpellation—given his existing yet ambivalent intellectual relation to Lacan, and the public relation to the self—is paramount in this positioning process: "Let us suppose that an Althusserian notion of interpellation gives us the main form of subjectification. Hysteria just means that the identification which should be produced through interpellation fails. . . . What Americans now call a 'borderline case' is not something radically new—it is just another form of the failure of identification, that is to say of hysteria."[126]

In the Yugoslav case, while the West enjoyed Eastern Europe's "reinvention of democracy," the same antagonistic form necessary to capitalist organization was actually reintroduced.[127] As a result, "when the lid of 'totalitarianism' was lifted, instead of the 'spontaneous' eruption of democratic desire that the West keenly looked for, what we saw were more ethnic conflicts, based on the constructions of different 'thieves of enjoyment:' as if, beneath the Communist surface, there glimmered a wealth of 'pathological' fantasies, waiting for their moment to arrive."[128] Žižek addressed these paradoxical conditions: "During the last ten to fifteen years, there has been a de-ideologization of power, and Marxists have usually been more dissident than non-Marxists. What was never reported in the West was that the people who benefited from this were the analytical philosophers in Belgrade, who were definitely not Marxists. You had a Communist regime openly supporting analytical philosophy of science. Their message to the power structure was clear: 'We are doing instrumental scientific research. We are no danger to you. You leave us alone and we will leave you alone.'"[129] Žižek suggested that in such paradoxical conditions, what is needed is more alienation, as a critical distance from the destructive fantasies of the new capitalist regime as an organic community. Thus, as Parker notes, Žižek resonated with an existing practice and theorized it: "The call for a 'distance' between the state and civil society repeats what Žižek had been calling for well before capitalism had been reintroduced. The strategies of resistance he had been advocating during the 1980s were already being used to contest the local bureaucracy and the grip of the Slovenian League of Communists."[130] The sensitivity to words and appearances, along political, intellectual, and cultural lines, has propagated "the idea that with this demystification of language self-management could be portrayed as a form of direct democracy."[131] This process would later be linked by Žižek to the Western culture of political correctness, as a symbolic euphemism of language that emerged at the expense of real social change. These convoluted relations to the West, intellectually drawing so much from it while remaining politically critical toward it, are also engraved in the formation of Žižek's Ljubljana School, with respect to its international recognition, as Dolar recalls:

> I think this was invented as a code. We first started being called the *Ljubljana (Lacanian) School*, a code, especially in America, as some sort of a handy way to tell people "there are some guys coming from Ljubljana and they will speak about Lacan." Obviously, this was the handiest brand, Ljubljana Lacanian School. It played to our hands. We had a completely open attitude; we didn't know how or why to insist on being labeled in a certain way. At some point, we were joking that people use this, and Slavoj loves this, as a joke, that somehow this caught on. It's a more imaginary (than real) designation.[132]

Slovenia between East and West   63

The political collapse of Yugoslavia was not a one-off event but a prolonged process of decay, and in fact, "long before the declaration of independence of Slovenia and Croatia in 1990, the state was already dead and existed only as an international legal entity."[133] This process caused a breakdown along cultural and intellectual lines, decomposing the meaning of contemporary public views regarding questions like "What collapsed?" and "What are we changing into?" By tapping into these fragmentary sentiments of public concerns, Žižek established a unique blended superposition and conveyed it to the local intellectual and political arenas. His interventional superpositioning was made through a specific "symptomatic reading" of the situation, as doubly critical—toward the old Communist Party and the new capitalist reformers. Influenced by the broader European context and spirit of May 1968, Žižek's early interventions (from 1972 to 1973), in newspapers, journals, and public events, resonated with the development of the emerging civil society and artistic scene while giving a voice to a "lost" generation. By ascribing new meaning to this "loss"—namely, the opportunity to reinvent Slovenia—Žižek also redefined the meaning of the social transition from communism to capitalism and associated what some perceived as catastrophic collective trauma with a notion of hope and a new, better future. This very move would be repeated, in form and content, in the global context too.

Only against this local background can Žižek's global intellectual emergence make sociological sense. He developed his superpositioning while reacting to a changing political situation that affected academics as well. His intellectual interventions—journals, articles, poems, and books—performed this superpositioning in a way that resonated with cultural sentiments and paved the way for direct political engagements. Yet because his superpositioning was directed at once for *and* against the state change, he was penalized from various positions, leading to his social and intellectual sacrifice:

> I did something for which I lost almost all my friends, what no good leftist ever does: I fully supported the ruling party in Slovenia. For this all my leftist friends hate me and of course the whole right wing. What the Liberal Democratic Party did was a miracle. Five years ago, we were the remainder of the new social movements, like feminist and ecological groups. At that time everybody thought that we would be vanishing mediators. We made some slyly corrupted, but good moves and now we are the strongest party. I think it was our party that saved Slovenia from the fate of the other former Yugoslav republics, where they have the one-party model. Either right wing like in Croatia or left wing like in Serbia, which hegemonized in the

name of the national interest. With us it's a really diverse, pluralist scene, open towards foreigners (of course there are some critical cases). But the changes of a genuine pluralist society are not yet lost.[134]

There are two primary conclusions to take away from this analysis of the political and cultural changes in Slovenia in the 1980s. First, Slovenia was in a unique position in the Yugoslav state, with regard to both the Western and Eastern powers. Yugoslavia's distance from Stalin(ism) paved the way for Western influence, yet still within the bounds of Marxist framework. Starting from the early Tito-Stalin split, Yugoslavia's independence had set it on a friction course with both Eastern and Western powers. Yugoslav intellectuals shifted the focus from the material base to the psychological-emotional affects with concepts like alienation. These developments allowed for every Yugoslav republic to establish its own nondogmatic Marxism. In Slovenia, the lack of a strong philosophical orientation was fertile ground for intellectual experimentation. Thus, led by young scholars such as Žižek and Dolar, structuralism was introduced to a terrain predominantly influenced by Marx, as the party's position, and by Heidegger as the opposition's.

Therefore, second, Slovenia's unique position facilitated the import of Western (specifically French and German) ideas and culture, expressed in interventional journals and networks. We saw how from the 1960s onward, a series of critical journals were launched, if only to be closed by party officials soon thereafter. Nonetheless, this founded a "journal culture," in which both intellectuals and the public found the journal to be a site for socio-intellectual debates, or political and cultural interventions—everything the authorities considered a threat. Although the party consistently tried to shut down such journals, culture solidified, transforming into NSMs and SIMs during Tito's decline. Crucial links were made in this period: inside Slovenia between artists (like NSK) and intellectuals (like Salecl and Dolar), but also outside Slovenia, like the links between Žižek, Močnik, Derrida, and Miller.

The intellectual blend that originated then, while mixing high theory and pop culture in a politically relevant way, is now the trademark of the Ljubljana School, the face and mouth of which is Žižek. Besides the importance of his early interventions in Slovenia, through which he held editing positions and created teams and collaborations, Žižek's entry to the global, English-speaking world was made possible by directing this new approach to the very political disintegration of Yugoslavia. Explaining to the West the opaque situation of the East, in the very theoretical terms and academic stages of the West, was a trigger for Western media and academia to learn the name "Žižek." As he explained the event of Yugoslavia's disintegration, he became recognized by the intellectual West and was positioned as a Lacanian thinker somehow related to the poststructuralist line of thought. As his name became synonymous with Lacan's, the global positioning was even clearer, although no less problematic given Lacan's own positioning. This positioning process that emerged in the specific context of Slovenia of the 1980s would continue along Žižek's growing succession and extension of his (also digital) performances, mainly in the United Kingdom and United States. That growth in the scope and breadth of his interventions is the focus of the next chapter.

2 If at First You Don't Succeed: The Emergence of Hegelacanese

Žižek's positioning as a local public intellectual in the context of Slovenia during the 1980s set the foundation for his intervention in other intellectual contexts during the 1990s. In this period, he reacted to a social—theoretical and practical—issues in a distinct performative way and via specific relations of team and networks, which together facilitated his positioning and determined its effectiveness. By this time, Žižek was an established local intellectual with a team of colleagues such as Dolar and Salecl, a global collaborative network with Jacques-Alain Miller (in France) and Ernesto Laclau (in the United Kingdom and South America), as well as a strong position in the local public sphere, as through the journals *Problemi* and *Analecta* (among others).

This shift from the local Slovenian context to the broader European context is the time when Žižek emerged as an international phenomenon, reacting to and resonating with, in form and content, the emerging new digital conditions of the "post-codex era."[1] This would be made clear toward the end of the 1990s, yet at their onset, lingering questions from the 1980s were still palpable. In a series of intellectual interventions, Žižek performed his superpositioning of the social and individual levels of analysis while dealing with the notion of the subject. Additionally, his superpositioning of high and low, which brings together high (intellectual) theory and low or pop (public) culture, has facilitated Žižek's intervention in the European intellectual arena. It also positioned Žižek as a sacrificial intellectual, performatively rejecting the position of the master, analyst, or "subject supposed-to-know"—all variations of the now outdated and declining "authoritative intellectual." This performative insistence on blending high theory and conceptions with pop culture and politics is emphasized explicitly in this 1991 interview of Žižek, where he was described by the British based *Radical Philosophy* journal through a political and intellectual contextualization:

One notable result of the recent political ferment in Central and Eastern Europe has been the emergence of new theoretical currents, often combining strands of thought which—to West European eyes—appear as starkly incompatible. Nowadays, one can meet young Soviet philosophers whose interest in the Frankfurt School, and in deconstruction, is matched by their keen advocacy of neo-liberal economics, and East European sociologists whose Foucauldian critique of Marxism and the one-party state is tempered by deep skepticism about the politics of privatization. One of the most complex and intriguing of these new syntheses is the "Lacanian-Hegelian-Marxism" which has been developed by Slavoj Žižek and his colleagues at the University of Ljubljana in Slovenia, the westernmost republic of Yugoslavia.[2]

Slovenia's own positioning as "westernmost" framed Žižek's positioning as part of a new intellectual syntheses that emerged from the changing political context of the 1980s and the globalizing context of the 1990s. Žižek's explanation of the East to the West, in Western theoretical terms and channels such as the *New Left Review*, started to position him as a prominent intellectual. To explain and demonstrate Žižek's unique blend as superpositioning, I turn to the European intellectual arena as the context of Žižek's intellectual expansion during the 1990s. The specific argument in this chapter is that Žižek became a prominent intellectual through a series of intellectual interventions in various intellectual fields, creating a superpositioned language that corresponds to several disciplinary jargons, making his thought applicable and attractive for diversified intellectual readerships and resonating with many of their interests and concerns. These various intellectual fields include psychology, psychoanalysis, Marxism, critical theory, sociology, film theory, literature, cultural studies, and political theology. By discussing issues that intersect these fields in a performative and rhetoric language, Žižek was relevant to different intellectual audiences through his weaving of different positions in these fields and creating his own.

Žižek entered the European scene armed with substantial relationships, which would later affect his rise as global intellectual. The most crucial of these were an international status of ambassador of science for the Republic of Slovenia (since 1991); his formation of the Ljubljana School; his teammates Dolar and Zupančič; his book series *Analecta* and several journals such as *Problemi*; and his network relations with Ernesto Laclau, J. A. Miller, and others.[3] But without an effective performance, maintained by and carried out with particular linguistic and rhetoric devices, relations do not last very long or far. Also, relations change over time and space. Intellectuals change their positions and their positioning with regard to others; or, others may change their positions, thus forcing a change onto the intellectual. Therefore, what is shown here is the maintenance of these relations *as* they change by means of positioning and repositioning. As a local public intellectual (between 1982 and 1989), Žižek published only locally in Slovenian. In general, performative terms, even when including the decade before 1982, that is, going back to 1972 (Žižek's first Slovenian book), Žižek had published twelve books in Slovenian and only one in English—*The Sublime Object of Ideology* in 1989. Yet *this* one created a shift in Žižek's intellectual interventions. As Dolar explains:

> There is a major shift in Slavoj's writing. His first book in Slovene is actually very difficult, *The Pain of the Difference*. This was '72. Slavoj tried very hard to have a book published in France, but eventually he had his fallout with [Jacques-Alain] Miller and he didn't publish it, and then [Slavoj] published it in *Éditions Lignes*. It didn't have any resonance, because it was a strange series for what he did. After '89, Slavoj's focus is entirely on English publications, in the sense of production. Whatever we published here of Slavoj, in these years, was written in English originally and we had Slavoj translate for us.[4]

There are many facets compounded in this passage, from the network relations and their real effects for intellectual production, to the reasons Žižek's book did not resonate in France. But for the moment, let us note that the shift to English is indicated by Žižek's overall production. Between 1990 and 2000 Žižek published fifteen books in English (four of which are coedited), but only eight (translated from English) in Slovenian. Intervening in both the intraintellectual and public intellectual arenas, 80 percent of the English books were published with Verso, and the other 20 percent with Routledge, Duke University Press, and MIT Press. With this remarkable level of prolificacy, which most intellectuals (perhaps) achieve in a lifetime, it is important to analyze the cause for this shift of performative position from Slovenian to English. Its effect was Žižek's emergence into the English-speaking world in parallel with English becoming the globalized language with the emergence of the internet. Put in terms of exportability, works written in English, as opposed to Slovenian, are better positioned to be translated and transmitted to others, given the dominance of English as a global language.[5] This is especially true for works that superposition French and German positions, resonating with the idea of the European Holy Trinity. This chapter exam-

If at First You Don't Succeed 69

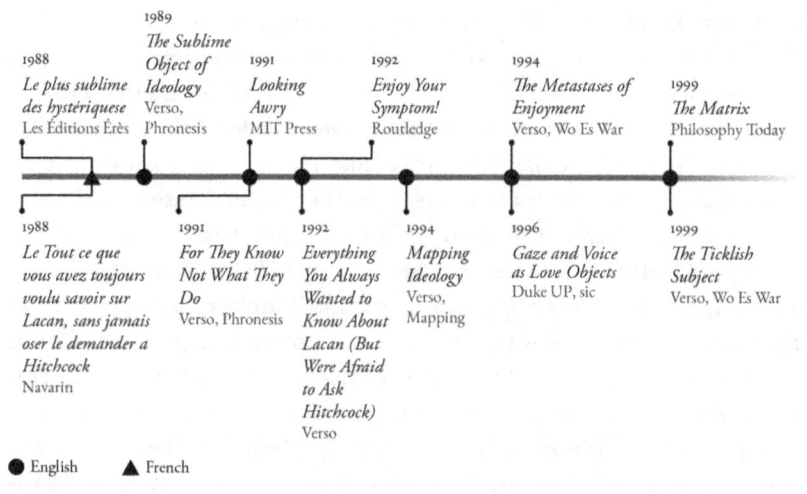

Figure 2.1: Žižek's formative intellectual interventions, 1988–2000.

Timeline (English, ●):
- 1989 — *The Sublime Object of Ideology* — Verso, Phronesis
- 1991 — *Looking Awry* — MIT Press
- 1992 — *Enjoy Your Symptom!* — Routledge
- 1994 — *The Metastases of Enjoyment* — Verso, Wo Es War
- 1999 — *The Matrix* — Philosophy Today
- 1991 — *For They Know Not What They Do* — Verso, Phronesis
- 1992 — *Everything You Always Wanted to Know About Lacan (But Were Afraid to Ask Hitchcock)* — Verso
- 1994 — *Mapping Ideology* — Verso, Mapping
- 1996 — *Gaze and Voice as Love Objects* — Duke UP, sic
- 1999 — *The Ticklish Subject* — Verso, Wo Es War

Timeline (French, ▲):
- 1988 — *Le plus sublime des hystériquese* — Les Éditions Érès
- 1988 — *Le Tout ce que vous avez toujours voulu savoir sur Lacan, sans jamais oser le demander a Hitchcock* — Navarin

ines how (and where) this process took place: the context, the relations, and the performance. I address first his French 1982 PhD, its publication in 1988, and its failed reception in French. Then I explain why the same manuscript was successfully published in English in 1989 as Žižek's inaugural English intervention. This formative intervention is analyzed in itself, followed by the consequent series of intellectual global interventions it sparked (fig. 2.1).

Why Žižek Failed in France

Žižek held a close relation to France, including to French theory, thinkers, and universities. Over the years, he maintained a dialogue with prominent French intellectuals such as Alain Badiou, Jacques Rancière, Claude Lefort, Étienne Balibar, and Jean-Claude Milner. This may lead one to conclude that if anything facilitated Žižek's emergence onto the global intellectual scene from that of the little country of Slovenia, it was (t)his French connection. However, Žižek received little attention in France, and his reception did not lead to any significant intellectual positioning. Indeed, "while Žižek currently enjoys remarkable visibility on the Anglo-American academic circuit, his presence on the French scene is relatively understated."[6] This rejection allowed Žižek to focus more on writing in English, penetrating the English global market, academy, and various publics. Given his unique performances and the processes of digital globalization, this turn to English positioned him as a prominent global intellectual. But first, let us revisit Žižek experience in France.

The spark of Žižek's French connection was the Slovenian sociologist and activist Rastko Močnik. After finishing his undergraduate studies in Ljubljana, he traveled to Paris for an MA and made a connection with Derrida, who was one of his teachers. In the early 1970s, Močnik introduced Žižek to Derrida. And just a few years prior to that, in 1969, Mladen Dolar also made his first trip to Paris, right to the aftermath of May 1968 events: "I saw Paris in '69 and the traces of '68 were there all the time. They haven't erased the slogans, the graffiti . . . just before I enrolled in the philosophy department, they took us to this dormitory, where we supposed to sleep in Saint Jean de Sey [in the Sixteenth], and there was a huge graffiti on that dormitory, *jouir sans entraves* [enjoy without borders]. It was a slogan from '68, original slogan, and this was there, in the building where I was going to sleep my first night in Paris. This was screaming at me, as an eighteen-year-old in Paris and you have this slogan in front of you. It was a time of an opening."[7] Dolar recalled that his formative year was 1980, when he got a chance to complete his studies in Paris after winning again, by "sheer coincidence," a French grant. The experimental university at Vincennes (Saint-Denis) hosted Dolar, as well as the most exciting Parisian intellectuals, including Lacan, Deleuze, and Badiou. According to Dolar, he was lucky enough to have personally experienced the lectures of the French structuralists, since 1980 was the last year when everything was in full swing. This stopped with the coincidental death of many of them, such as Barthes, Sartre, Lacan, and Foucault. As an example for the public influence of these lectures, Dolar explained that, "for Lacan, they hired the biggest lecture hall in Paris in Faculté de Droit, which is for around 1,100 people, but you had to be two hours early to get in. For Foucault, he had around 400 people and you only had to be an hour early. There was a kind of hierarchy. This intellectual stardom doesn't exist today."[8]

Žižek's unique personal and professional relations with J. A. Miller were already established as his PhD student and teaching assistant in the early 1980s at Université Paris 8. Moreover, Žižek later became a patient (analysand) of Miller. When comparing his French connection with other Slovenian intellectuals, Žižek explains:

> Others, if they went, they went elsewhere, to Germany, to the Anglo-Saxon world and so on. I don't think that many others went to France. No, no, no. It was our privileged link with Millerian Lacanianism, with *École de la Cause Freudienne*. But again, then, lately, already late '80s, we got into troubles. Because again, his orientation was too clinical for us. . . . But this is why we were even so attacked, because when then we established in the '80s, already late '70s, connections with French Lacanians, it didn't go too well because they didn't like our philosophical orientation. They were in-

terested in expanding their movement. They wanted us to return here and start practicing psychoanalysis, clinically. We didn't want to do this. We always remained philosophers.[9]

Here we can see why Žižek's interventions, and by extension his position as an intellectual, were rejected by academics in France. Specifically, we can discern two positions regarding Lacanian psychoanalysis. For Žižek, Lacan is a way of rehabilitating German idealism in general and Hegel in particular, "a way out" of the Marxist-Heideggerian deadlock; a form of situating today's culture with Plato's "idea." This move, according to the model of intellectual intervention (see fig. 0.2), initiates the first movement of intervention where the intervener moves from the intellectual to the public arena by using great figures of the past, and relating them to pressing matters of the present in order to produce a novel reading of the future. Žižek positioned Lacan as a source for philosophical thought, and in that he took Lacan outside of the clinic. For Miller, however, Lacan was first and foremost (a father-in-law, and) a theoretician of the clinical psychoanalytic practice. This oppositional positioning of practice (Miller and psychoanalysis) versus theory (Žižek and philosophy) led to a growing rift between the two, with material effects, beyond Žižek's first panic attack:[10] "Miller's refusal to publish the doctoral thesis that emerged from Žižek's period of study led to its eventual publication (in 1988) by *Les Éditions Érès*, an outlet for the human sciences with a strong commitment to psychoanalysis both theoretical and clinical. The book was entitled *Le plus sublime des hystériques—Hegel passe*, and published in the collection 'Point Hors Ligne.' It had little impact at the time and is currently out of print."[11] As Miller was a controversial figure with no prestigious academic position or status, and at odds with many other French intellectuals (Lacanian and others) who did not hold him in high esteem, having him as reluctant voucher was especially countereffective. Moreover, having Hegel as the main intellectual reference in the title did not resonate much in France, which lacked even a single "Hegelian" and was full of German-French rivalry.[12] In that period, following Foucault the intellectual trend in Paris was of "specific intellectuals," such as experts, and an anti-Hegel positioning against his panlogism. An earlier example is Althusser's influential essay from 1962, "Contradiction and Overdetermination," in which he launched a fierce critique of Hegel in an attempt to decouple his thought from that of Marx. As Žižek admitted, his "first French book (not counting the collected volume on Hitchcock),[13] *Le plus sublime des hystériques*, up to two-thirds of which I would say overlaps with *The Sublime Object*, while not a total fiasco, did not leave any serious impact. So you can see here how contingent these things are. For something which explodes here can practically disappear elsewhere."[14] Nonetheless, Žižek's French intervention did leave some mark in the intellectual arena, mostly within the lower ranks of academia. Here we can start seeing Žižek's sacrificial position (losing it in academia but gaining it in the public), which he frames as "working-class solidarity: the lower you got on the academic level, the more it was popular. All around I heard the same story: it was among graduate students that my stronghold existed, not among the top professors. I kind of like this."[15] Even today, some three decades after Žižek's first publication in France, Žižek's position in French is unclear. Only a small number of books are translated and inconsistently: each publisher has published just one or two books (these publishers include Fayard, Flammarion, PUF, Amsterdam, and Climats). According to Oltarzewska, "that the French publishing industry recognizes his importance but is unsure of where to put him is borne out by the fact that he has, to date, no fewer than eight publishers."[16] Therefore, a certain form of positioning, Žižek's superpositioning, can be useful and successful in one context but unsuccessful in another.

When comparing Žižek's interventions in the Slovenian, French, and English contexts, a few stark differences emerge, specifically involving space, time, style, and speed. Concerning space, the lack of an established psychoanalytic community in Slovenia allowed Žižek and his Ljubljana School to perform, publish, and teach more freely—without the critical attacks coming from other psychoanalytic rivals. His cultural and political interventions (in addition to his intellectual ones) resonated with the Slovenian public and granted him a significant position in society. But in France, there has been a long tradition of established philosophical and psychoanalytical communities, carrying some of the biggest names worldwide, from Lacan to Sartre and Althusser.[17] These established communities did not exist only intellectually, in academia, but also publicly, where a culture of philosophy and psychoanalysis developed with the emergence and export of French theory in the 1960s.[18] Together, both intellectual (i.e., philosophical and psychoanalytical) and public (i.e., cultural and political) spaces were more stratified, hierarchical, and codified in French than in Slovenian and, for other reasons, than in English.[19]

There was no room for Žižek in France, and even less so in Paris, with its intellectual pantheon. In addition, Žižek's superpositioning made it difficult to classify and categorize his work. This is why, without Miller's help, Žižek was able to publish his doctoral thesis as a book only with a relatively small and specialized publisher (Éditions Lignes). This publisher promotes intellectuals at the crossroads of literature, art, and philosophy (e.g., the uncategorizable Bataille). The series in which it was published, *Point Hors Ligne*, is a collection focused on psychoanalytic concepts for clinical practitioners and intellectuals from the humanities and social sciences. Surely not the most coherent body, with desperate aims, needs, and approaches, which makes it all the more difficult for the positioning, branding, and marketing of a new intellectual intervention.[20] Given the strong clinical psychoanalytic affiliation and the hierarchical philosophical space, "to this French public, Žižek's use of psychoanalysis must have seemed a touch unorthodox: whereas, in France, Lacan's theory has strong links to clinical practice, Žižek's Lacan is not only disconnected from the clinic but pressed into alliance with Marx and Hegel to yield a politicized reading of contemporary culture."[21] This different intellectual space construction (between Slovenia, France, and the United Kingdom and United States) is accompanied by the question of intellectual climate or timing.

As Laurent Jeanpierre indicated, following the events of May 1968, there was in France a growing dissatisfaction with Marx as a solution to the capitalist problem, a decline of master narratives, and distrust of "big" philosophical questions. At that time, associating a philosophized Lacan with a politicized Hegel was swimming against all currents. To these contextual determinations in space and time we should add Žižek's unique style that also contributed to his French rejection.[22] It seems Žižek's idiom and rhetorical language did not resonate well with French academic circles and publics, which may have been less open to textual experimentation and relied on its traditional way of academic writing: "As if this mixture of Lacanized Hegel and nonclinical Lacan were not disconcerting enough . . . , the context-specific logic of disciplinary boundaries, the expectation that a philosophical argument demonstrate qualities of orderliness and *sérieux*, a generalized disenchantment with politically engaged writing, a distrust of theoretical eclecticism did not augur well for Žižek's reception in France."[23] When it comes to style, Žižek's hybrid language, his heterodox (materialist) reading of Hegel, uncompromising use of Lacanian formulas and cultural references, and the ruthless "cut-and-paste" approach to composition—can all be wearing. Therefore, specifically in the French context, "there is a genuine risk that these uncontrolled surges of affect might hystericize the reader, not in the positive sense of inducing productive curiosity, more in the sense of triggering exasperated rejection."[24]

These language games—made of frequent neologisms and colloquialisms of words, capitalization and italicization of letters, as well as name-dropping, jokes, examples, and rhetorical questions—render the performative dimension palpable in and through the writing and create a hypertextual, hysterical quality of reading. Žižek's rate of interventions makes this performance even harder to follow, jumping from one discipline and jargon to another, visiting myriad cultural references and philosophical ideas. Even his stated ambition—to start with communism—could be intimidating and rejecting. Yet the lack of room and desire for his style in the French context facilitated his second global attempt in another, English context.

This different contextual framing, performed by a different publisher, title, preface, and so on, created a more applicable and attractive version of virtually the same intervention, which means, same content—different context. In the English context, *The Sublime Object of Ideology* was framed as part of Laclau and Mouffe's post-Marxist approach, which was still influential in academia since their own publication of *Hegemony and Socialist Strategy* a few years earlier in 1985. This does not mean that Žižek's project was understood as only post-Marxist; but it had a recognizable point of departure, which it lacked in French or France. As Homer puts it: "Žižek's work could not have been [rewritten in English] at a more opportune moment. In Eastern Europe, the historic collapse of 'actually existing socialism' and the break-up of Western Marxism seemed assured if not already complete. The intellectual currents of postmodernism and post-Marxism were at their most vitriolic and triumphalist."[25] This political and intellectual post-Marxist timing was to play a significant role in English reception and French rejection of *The Sublime Object of Ideology*.

Vouching as Positioning: Laclau Prefaces Žižek

During the late 1980s there was a pertinent question in intellectual circles of philosophers, critical theorists, and Marxist sociologists: Who is the subject? Particularly, who is the subject of the revolution and the driver of emancipation? After the failure of both Stalinist and Maoist attempts to realize a communist state and movement, respectively, the subjective referent to "the proletariat" was left unclear. This ambiguity intensified with the changing intellectual and political context: the world witnessed a great disintegration of the Soviet Union, and with it, of the communist alternative or threat to capitalism. Meanwhile, the rising form of capitalism was already distinguished from the classical, Fordist, centralized version. As "neoliberal," the new decentralized, techno-cultural, postindustrial capitalism also changed the public sphere and turned it into a digital space. With the decay of philosophy and philosophical systems, the rise of specialized expert as social scientists, and the emergence of the computerized, digital public sphere, the context and performance of intellectual interventions drastically changed during the 1990s.

Few interventional books that were published have materialized the intellectual and political problem of the missing (Marxist) subject: once workers were not so identifiable with the proletariat, the latter started losing its identity as the subject of political change. Badiou's *Théorie du sujet* (1982) is one of those books, and another is Laclau and Mouffe's *Hegemony and Socialist Strategy* (1985). Both tried to articulate the post-Marxist notion of the subject and a novel identity for the revolutionary subject after the failures of twentieth-century communism. *Hegemony and Socialist Strategy*, published in English, made the most effective global impact. Žižek enters into this theoretical problematic and practical deadlock in his first series of successful global interventions that positioned him as a global intellectual. The series includes several formative interventions such as books (some of which were later marketed as a set called *The Essential Žižek*), but also interviews, reviews, articles, talks, and films.[26] Through all of these, Žižek engaged in a complex positioning process that conditioned his future emergence as a global *public* intellectual.

With his inaugural English book in 1989, *The Sublime Object of Ideology*, Žižek linked his intellectual intervention to the problems of the time and entered the global intellectual scene, where English was the dominant form of intellectual globalization. We should also bear in mind that this book was not a product of a single stroke of genius or madness; rather, it was a result of a long and vast network of actions taken by Žižek and others. Importantly, Žižek had developed a language that created a signifying identity that could be associated with certain positions and ideas in a clustered fashion. Žižek achieved this by weaving Hegel and Lacan into what I refer to as "Hegelacanese." This language, as a form of speech-acting and performing, became the signifier for the Žižekian brand. It was the language that was rejected in its French form only to be embraced in English. This is Žižek's recollection of it:

> In [the] mid-'70s I met Ernesto Laclau, and he organized my first book, he organized *Sublime Object of Ideology*. Then I met also, at a big Lacanian congress, in the mid-'70s, Joan Copjec, who organized my next book, who [sic] was selling very well. It's still selling, *Looking Awry*. And with that, I was on. From that point I published whatever I want. I think it's simply applying Lacan to politics and to popular culture. This, and with a leftist twist, again, because you know, there were cultural studies [the field], analyzing popular culture and so on, but nobody connected this with Lacan and psychoanalysis, with subjectivity. This was the new thing, to give to it this

Lacanian twist. And it worked. It was incredible how quickly it worked. I was in demand—in one or two years everything changed. Because I remember that book, *Looking Awry*, it was immediately reprinted, translated.[27]

The superpositioning of other disciplines and positions, from psychoanalysis and philosophy to the social and individual, was crucial for the creation and circulation of Žižek's new language of Hegelacanese. In times of "the death of the subject,"[28] this connection of social issues to subjectivity signaled a new way of thinking about our times in an engaged way that allowed the reader or listener to bypass the common (noncritical) cynical position and to include him- or herself in the analysis as a participatory mechanism of identification—not unlike how football or music fans are attached to their performers.[29]

The Sublime Object was published during the transitional and eventful period of 1989, by London publishing house Verso Press. Founded in 1970 as the publishing house of the *New Left Review*, Verso established itself as a leftist, internationalist, and popular, market-savvy company, much unlike conventional university presses. Laclau already had a book series with Verso called *Phronesis*. Part of staging the intervention, the series' peritext declares its intentions and ambitions by way of positioning in time and space. Signaling its synchronicity with the present, the series description that opens the book states, "There is today a wide agreement that the left-wing project is in crisis." Next, it expands its relevance to the global world: "New antagonisms have emerged—not only in advanced capitalist societies but also in the Eastern bloc and in the Third world." And moving from the political to the intellectual, it mentions disagreements on the right theoretical strategy needed to deal with the crisis. Two positions are discerned: on the one hand, "there are those for whom the current critique of rationalism and universalism puts into jeopardy the very basis of the democratic project." On the other hand, that of *Phronesis*, "the critique of essentialism—a point of convergence of the most important trends in contemporary theory: post-structuralism, philosophy of language after the later Wittgenstein, post-Heideggerian hermeneutics—is the necessary condition for understanding the widening of the field of social struggles characteristic of the present stage of democratic politics."

Therefore, *The Sublime Object* is positioned within this framing, aligned with the series' objective of establishing "a dialogue between these theoretical developments and left-wing politics." This anti-essentialist position, labeled as the "sine qua non of a new vision for the Left," is used to resonate with the global political and intellectual situation of that time. As such, *The Sublime Object* became an intellectual intervention into the global, intellectual arena. Laclau himself was identified in several intellectual circles and held several positions among post-Marxists, French and South American Lacanian psychoanalysts, Argentine politicians, and European social scientists (in discourse theory). His wife, Chantal Mouffe, was also a recognized scholar who, after working at Columbia University in New York, became professor in London at the University of Westminster and in Paris at the Collège International de Philosophie. Given their mutual interest in Lacan, Laclau hosted Žižek in his *Ideology and Discourse Analysis* graduate program, at the Department of Government, University of Essex, where he worked as a reader of political theory.

Imperative to Žižek's emergence on the global scene was not only his inclusion in Laclau's book series with Verso, but also that Laclau prefaced *The Sublime Object*. This act was one of vouching as positioning, by which Laclau's already established and prestigious position (or sociocultural capital) as a global intellectual was bestowed onto Žižek. In the preface to the book, Laclau begins a peritextual positioning by situating *The Sublime Object*—and by extension Žižek—along an existing, recognizable narrative of reading the present through Hegel's dialectic and Lacan's subject. Žižek's name appears for the first time only after three long paragraphs, after Laclau positions Lacanian psychoanalysis. Labeling Lacanian psychoanalysis "a great intellectual tradition," Laclau positions (himself and) Žižek in favor of this tradition, as parts of it.

Another aspect of a great intellectual tradition is its ability to effectively influence differentiated intellectual currents. In his preface, Laclau positions Lacan both geographically and intellectually, arguing that in France and Latin America the Lacanian orientation was clinical and practical, whereas in Anglo-Saxon countries it was associated to the theoretical "literature-cinema-feminism triangle."[30] This association was made possible by an early reception of Lacan, especially in the United States, through the film journal *Screen* and partial translations in feminist studies (e.g., Jacqueline Rose's *Feminine Sexuality* from 1982). As Oltarzewska notes, "Žižek's specific contributions were his political credibility, his humor, light touch and pedagogical flair, his emphasis on the later (post 1960) Lacan, whose preoccupations (the drives, the act, *jouissance*, the Real) were less familiar to the Anglophone critic."[31]

For structural and historical reasons, in France "greater degrees of demarcation and confrontation have been maintained between intellectual currents,"[32] compared with the English Anglophone context, where Lacan was more closely related to the broad banner of "poststructuralism."[33] As Liu and Bailey recall, apropos of the invention of French theory in the Anglo-Saxon world, "Theory burst forth in the United States in 1966 with 'The Structuralist Controversy,' a conference at Johns Hopkins organized by Richard Macksey. Jacques Lacan, Jacques Derrida, and Roland Barthes took Baltimore by storm. Genuine excitement about new forms of French thought spread what Geoffrey Galt Harpham would retrospectively describe as an 'atmosphere of danger and charisma' at the peak of enrolments in the humanities, an apex of post-war growth and expansion in the fields it encompassed."[34] As was chronicled in the *Michigan Daily* of January 22, 1978, apropos of the English translation of Lacan's *Écrits*, "Only in England does Freud enjoy nearly the kind of stature he enjoys in America. In France, another man occupies the position of the grand figure of psychology. His name is Jacques Lacan."[35] Liu and Bailey link the rise of French theory in the United States to the context of disciplinary expansion, where the humanities were reacting to the growing public demand for higher education. With the inexpensive airline travel that became available during the 1970s and 1980s, French theory became "a methodology that bridged philosophy, literary criticism, linguistics, and anthropology," combining "meticulous close-reading with highly dramatic wordplay, both in written and oral rhetorical performances."[36] This expansion of the humanities and inclusion of Lacanian or French theory did not go without criticism, of what some considered a takeover.[37] Thus, positioning Žižek with relation to French theory also depends on the differentiated Lacanian position in these French and English contexts.

Particular to the latter was, as mentioned before, the *New Left Review*, which was instrumental in creating "intellectual vacancies" within the public intellectual arena in postwar Britain. These vacancies cried out for a nonnative speaker who was immersed in foreign theories. Furthering the work done by the *New Left Review* in creating a tangible venue for performing public intellectual interventions, the London Institute of Contemporary Arts held successful weekly talks and symposia, especially in the 1980s, which provided a popular English platform for foreign theorists to expound on their views. A testament to Žižek's successful English reception following his 1989 intervention was his first appearance at the institute in 1992.[38] The *London Review of Books*, established in 1979, also created a space for theoretical writing that operated in between academia and the culture industry. A review by the renowned British intellectual Terry Eagleton in November 1997 popularized Žižek further. Similarly, since its inception in 1982, *Channel 4* semiregularly screened interviews with intellectuals such as Derrida and showcased documentaries on literary theory. A possible result of Žižek's successful circulation of Hegelacanese in England was a series of late-night lectures by Lacan aired in 1993 to no fewer than 250,000 viewers.[39]

This intellectual context was hospitable for Laclau's preface of *The Sublime Object of Ideology*. He traced the Lacanian genealogy so to position Žižek within it and less with regard to the (controversial) banner of French theory.[40] The first generation of "old school" Lacanians (e.g., Octave and Maud Mannoni, Serge Leclaire) was introduced as focusing on the symbolic, a Lacanian concept that was instrumental in the middle period of his teaching. The second, younger generation (consisting of Michel Silvestre and J. A. Miller) focused on the real, the focus of his late teaching. In addition, Laclau mentioned two other orientations in Lacanian thought: German hermeneutic (led by Hermann Lang) and Marxist-structuralist (led by Althusser and Pêcheux). Only at this point did Laclau signal what individualizes Žižek and his book from previous positions of Lacanian psychoanalysis. He positions Žižek and his Ljubljana School using the Lacanian, post-Marxist, poststructuralist frame of *Phronesis*, and through the unique opposition to both Latin/French (clinical) and Anglo-Saxon (literary) positions. Without an explicit clinical or literal dimension, for "Slovenian theoreticians . . . Lacanian categories have been used in a reflection which is essentially *philosophical* and *political*."[41] Notwithstanding this seemingly essentialist position, what is important is Laclau's identification of "two main features [that] characterizes this school."[42]

The first distinctive feature is Žižek's insistent reference to classical philosophical texts and authors, and the second is the recurrent referencing to the ideological-political field. In fact, Laclau describes here the past-present movement of intellectual intervention (see fig. 0.2). He explains that Žižek links great figures of the past—such as "Plato, Descartes, Leibnitz, Kant, Marx, Heidegger, the Anglo-Saxon analytical tradition and, above all, Hegel"[43]—with present-day phenomena, from ideology and language to totalitarianism and democracy. This, I argue, is how Žižek enacts the intraintellectual intervention by positioning himself around a persistent deadlock in theory (of democracy, language, and so on). As Laclau himself admitted, "This does not mean that there has been complete agreement: in our view, the Slovenian school initially drew too drastic a line of separation between Lacanian theory and post-structuralism; we also have a number of reservations about their reading of Hegel."[44] Nonetheless, after creating some distance between Laclau and Mouffe's project and that of the Ljubljana School, Laclau acknowledges that the latter "represents one of the most innovative and promising theoretical projects on the European intellectual scene."[45] This intellectual vouching, coming from a renowned and connected academic such as Laclau, is (partly) why *The Sublime Object* became Žižek's inaugural and formative intervention.

Laclau then described the Slovenian Lacanian context in contrast to the French, Latin, and Anglo-Saxon contexts. From their considerable production, he notes a close link between the intellectual orientation of Slovenian Lacanians and their political engagement. Laclau mentions the weekly *Mladina* (described in chapter 1) as "the most important mouthpiece of this movement," with Žižek the main political columnist. Given this constant open channel between Lacanian intellectuals and the public, "Lacanian theory is the main philosophical orientation is Slovenia."[46]

Tellingly, Laclau provided some directions for the reader, or as he puts it, "a series of suggestions for the reading of this book."[47] The reason for this is straightforward and is related to the reason Žižek failed in France: "the reader could quite easily end up disoriented as to its literary genre."[48] Without a categorized genre, it is hard to position the author anywhere in the intraintellectual arena. Yet the right kind of framing and staging, the right directions, can indeed compensate for the troubling classification. Readers were told, almost as a warning, that what they hold "is certainly not a book in the classical sense."[49] Laclau's framing consists in mentioning that *The Sublime Object* does not argue systematically according to a plan, nor is it a collection of essays. It is, rather, "a series of theoretical interventions which shed mutual light on each other, not in terms of the *progression* of an argument, but . . . *reiteration* of the latter in different discursive contexts."[50] Laclau prepared the readers for the unusual style they were to encounter, what Barthes called a "writerly text," and framed it as an invitation for the reader to take part and "continue for him- or herself the discursive proliferation in which the author has been engaged."[51] And if that is not already inviting and exciting enough, the book's basic thesis relates itself personally to the potential reader as it is formulated around the notion of the subject.

According to Laclau's framing, "the basic thesis of the book—that the category of 'subject' cannot be reduced to the 'positions of subject' since before subjectivation the subject is the subject of lack—is formulated in the first chapter: each of the subsequent chapters which reiterate this thesis does so in a new discursive context."[52] In a clear case of superpositioning, Žižek's intervention is framed, both in terms of content (the subject) and of form (of iteration), as an innovative invitation: "This book also contains an implicit invitation to break the barrier separating theoretical languages from those of everyday life."[53] Again, what is emphasized by this framing (both as staging and incrimination) is the superpositioning of high and low, this time of theoretical languages—considered elitist and exclusive to experts—and of everyday languages used by the public. Providing these two seemingly opposing rhetorical reference points signals that a public intellectual intervention is in progress: intellectuals may find the formal language of theory useful and appealing, while the public may find the normal language more understandable. This is the movement of intervention that moves from the intraintellectual arena to the public intellectual arena. By situating this intervention vis-à-vis the theoretical deadlock of that time, namely the duality of structure and subject, Laclau suggested that such novel reading might provide a new way of dealing with the practical, political deadlock of democracy. Also, by referring to the linguistic problem that Žižek deals with in his book (e.g., descriptivism, naming, meaning), Laclau positions Žižek as a relevant intellectual to the growing discursive, performative, and linguistic tendencies in the humanistic and social scientific academia, all the while hinting that the actual language used in the book is inclusive and inviting.

In Laclau's preface Žižek was performatively positioned along specific intellectual and political axes. In fact, the readers are told, "for all those interested in the elaboration of a theoretical perspective that seeks to address the problems of constructing a democratic socialist political project in a post-Marxist age, it is an essential reading."[54] Of course, this superpositioning involves positioning others as well in a relational manner. Laclau emphasized Žižek's superpositioning in all levels (between high and low) of the rhetorical devices used to perform this intervention:

1. Level of referencing (classic and/or cutting-edge): referencing both classical philosophers and contemporary political and artistic figures means positioning Žižek as relevant for both the intellectual and the public arenas.
2. Level of claiming (general and/or specific): superpositioning is enacted in making a general claim about collective or social subjectivity yet in an individual way for a specific subject—namely, every reader of the book.
3. Level of tone (subjective and/or objective): Žižek's language is characterized as idiomatic, idiosyncratic, and unique. It is also an invitation to participate in the repetitively creative process of reiteration; his tone manages to be at once very subjective, and, in his abstractions, to capture the objective side of things.
4. Level of form (semantic and syntactic in/formal organization): Laclau noted that Žižek's book is not a typical intellectual intervention. Like his tone, the form of Žižek's intervention is mostly associative and informal but as a book it maintains some formality, an oscillation that will become Žižek's signature mark.
5. Level of metaphor (conceptual imagery of fact and/or fiction): given the ample cultural content ranging from the opera to cinema, Žižek super-

positions fact and fiction, opening up the space of their mutual articulation in a novel and unique position.

Therefore, to use Jacobs and Townsley's terms, Žižek started making frequent and interchangeable use of multiple rhetorical styles such as "making specific arguments," "making moral arguments," "asking questions," "reframing" and "providing information." He also relied on both direct (personally experienced) and indirect (objectively professional) claims to authority. This turned out to be highly effective in times when "the mass media itself, and the public communication it makes possible, are coming to serve as an independent basis of social authority."[55]

Laclau's positioning of Žižek, his book, and the Ljubljana School offered a way for the intellectual reader to read Žižek and situate him along some existing lines of thought and division. Without this vouching and transference of symbolic capital, the reader would have been less able to identify and position Žižek in the intraintellectual arena. Only after this link is established can Žižek start his own process of intellectual individualization in the actual text of the book. A close reading of *The Sublime Object of Ideology* is necessary to understand how this process began and how it led to Žižek's emergence as a global intellectual.

Per-formative Global Intervention

Žižek recalls: "The explosion was simply *Sublime Object of Ideology*, which is a miracle, even now. It was not so much because of Hegel, but because of this use of Lacanian concepts for the analysis of ideology. I was lucky to publish the right book at the right place at the right moment."[56] But what exactly was "right" in Žižek's book that made it his most cited work to date?[57] The answer is discernible in the following analysis of his introduction, as an exemplary case of Hegelacanese, which shows the weaving of Hegel and Lacan, or philosophy and psychoanalysis: (1) a lot of referencing, both classical and cutting edge; (2) claims that are both general and specific; (3) a mixed subjective and objective tone; (4) formal and informal organization; and (5) a metaphoric fusion of fact and fiction. Starting from his introduction, then, these Hegelacanese traits, indicated by his repetitive capitalized and italicized form, for example, are to be found practically in the entire Žižekian corpus.

In the very first paragraph of the introduction to *The Sublime Object of Ideology*, immediately after Laclau's vouching preface, Žižek opens with the following sentence: "In that book of Habermas' which specifically addresses the issue of so-called 'post-structuralism,' *Der philosophische Diskurs der Moderne*, there is a curious detail concerning Lacan's name."[58] By referencing another recognizable book and author, the very first sentence brings together the two intellectual traditions in contemporary Europe: German and French. Žižek thus starts his own endeavor, a forty-year expedition into the English world, by relating himself to the link between Habermas and poststructuralism. These two traditions will be superpositioned in creating his Hegelacanese position. And here, right at the beginning, Žižek uses a frequent rhetorical tactic to perform an invitation—he poses a question: why there is a refusal to deal directly with Lacan?

To begin addressing this question with the reader, Žižek referenced fourteen other intellectuals, all with a certain global recognition and position as Continental or European, in the following order: Habermas, Lacan, Hegel, Marx, Nietzsche, Heidegger, Bataille, Foucault, Lévi-Strauss, Freud, Jung, Laclau, Mouffe, and Derrida. After this intellectual material was already field-tested locally, it was woven into a single package, wrapped in a recognized and prominent intellectual such as Laclau (and not long after his own intellectual intervention together with Chantal Mouffe of *Hegemony and Socialist Strategy* in 1985).[59] The name-dropping is done, then, for a specific rhetorical reason. It already signals Žižek's mode of intellectual intervention, the repetition to be later characterized as self-plagiarism and mash-up. It also shows that positioning, or rather superpositioning, is taking place. As a rhetorical device, the names are mentioned as nodes in an intellectual map. This is a map in which every such name stands for a disciplinary position, from psychoanalysis to philosophy, literature, and anthropology, as well as for different political positions, between conservativism and radicalism. Each such name offers itself as bait to the reader, creating what appears to be a positioning trap—even if you recognize only one name of this list, you are immediately drawn to the entire Žižekian mapping. With this mapping, a narrative starts to emerge in a way that both constructs and demonstrates the argument.

However, presumably so the reader would not get lost, Žižek positioned all the references, and himself, around one book—Habermas's 1985 *Der philosophische Diskurs der Moderne*—that symbolized and embodied, for him, "the great debate occupying the foreground of today's intellectual scene."[60] Via a popular cultural reference to Sherlock Holmes, Žižek shifted the center of the debate, immediately taking the reader with him to this Other scene: "the Habermas-Foucault debate, is masking another opposition, another debate which is theoretically more far-reaching: the Althusser-Lacan debate."[61] Let us unpack this superpositioning performed in the first two paragraphs. First, Žižek performed this self-positioning in the intraintellectual arena specifically by identifying a theoretical deadlock, as the model of intellectual intervention prescribes. As in the context of Slovenia, this had been done by relating past figures (like Plato and Hegel) to present matters (of democracy and totalitarianism). Further, what do Habermas and Foucault stand for, and what is at stake in their debate, as the "foreground of today's intellectual scene"? And finally, why is this debate masking another debate, to the effect that the reader gets a debate between debates?

Jürgen Habermas, today "world-renowned as a social theorist, philosopher, and leading European public intellectual for more than five decades," was by 1989 already an established European intellectual known as a second-generation Frankfurt School.[62] A student of Adorno and Horkheimer, Habermas is known for departing from his teachers' pessimistic and overtly critical approach to society through adopting a more positive communicative approach. His position regarding language is what caught Žižek's attention. Cited almost thirty thousand times, Habermas's *Theory of Communicative Action* (volume 1, 1984) positioned him as a relevant intellectual to the growing linguistic emphasis in the social sciences. Departing from the Marxist materialist approach to sociopolitical issues, Habermas presented a more positive approach in situating language as a mediator between people. Building on language's rational discursivity, Habermas hoped to construct a more democratic society, in Germany and elsewhere. This is partly why he became so known in the West, for bringing the East—that is, communist Eastern Germany—closer to the Western democratic world. Habermas allowed democratic thinkers to harbor language's mediation and rationalism to project a better vision of and for humanity. But although this emphasis on language was in tune with the intellectual currents in the humanities and social sciences of the time, it also stood apart from the growing French critique of language and discourse as what separates people by inserting power relations into reality. The French negative or critical relation to language is shared by recognized currents such as deconstruction, poststructuralism, and postmodernism. For Žižek this results in the positioning of Habermas versus Foucault, whereby the entire political and intellectual arenas can be mapped with relation to the debate regarding language: Good or bad? Promoting rationalism, or enforcing coercion?

Before the reader can even take a position, the site of the debate is shifted, dislocated and displaced into another site, that of Althusser and Lacan. There is a superpositioned fourfold axis, which Žižek immediately links to the significant contribution of *The Sublime Object*: the subject. Žižek performed a Hegelian shift from *between* (German-French positions) to *within* (the French positions): "Why was the opposition Althusser-Lacan replaced by the opposition Habermas-Foucault? At stake here are four different ethical positions, and four different notions of the subject."[63] On Habermas's positive side there is "the Ideal of the universal, transparent intersubjective community [where] the notion of the subject is the old subject of transcendental reflection."[64] Against this positive vision, on Foucault's side there is "a turn against that universalist ethics which results in a kind of aestheticization of ethics: each subject must, without any support from universal rules, build his own mode of self-mastery."[65] Žižek presents his pathway to his own new superposition, aligned with the Other intellectual debate of Althusser and Lacan: "Habermas and Foucault are two sides of the same coin—the real break is represented by Althusser, by his insistence on the fact that a certain cleft, a certain fissure, misrecognition, characterizes the human condition as such: by the thesis that the idea of the possible end of ideology is an ideological idea *par excellence*."[66] With this statement, Žižek insists on the persistence of ideology despite the intellectual and political "end of ideology."[67]

By shifting the foregrounding intellectual debate from the Habermas-Foucault to the Althusser-Lacan axis, Žižek performed a shift from the conscious to the position of the unconscious. For both Habermas and Foucault, language becomes the way in which the subject recognizes itself as such, becoming conscious to and of itself, for better (with Habermas's self-rationality) or for worse (with Foucault's self-regulation). Yet with Althusser, and especially with Lacan, language also assumes the unconscious as the proper sociopolitical and ethical site. Also, Althusser is closer to Marx than Habermas is (let alone Foucault). Writing his master's thesis in 1947, "On Content in the Thought of G. W. F. Hegel," and publishing later influential books such as *For Marx* (1965), *Reading Capital* (1965), and *Ideological State Apparatuses* (1971), Althusser was firmly positioned as a neo-Marxist, trying to bridge Marxism and structuralism. In the latter work, which is considered a major breakthrough in twentieth-century Marxism, Althusser had already engaged with Lacan and the unconscious quite explicitly. He tried to explain the Marxist notion of false consciousness via Lacan's structural linguistic theory of the unconscious. For that he coined the influential concept of interpellation, with which he strived to explain the becoming-individual of the human subject, that is, the turning of subjects into capitalist individuals. Through these works, Žižek takes from Althusser something that eluded both Habermas and Foucault, namely, the imaginary process of identification prior to the symbolic construction of the self. In an era of growing focus on the psychological "I," this intellectual elaboration of its construction is of great public interest as it simply affects every self.

Žižek's superpositioning of the social and the individual is performed via the creation of the position of the subject (which is at once collective and unitary). This is done by bringing together high and low, theory and culture, with the intellectual division around language and the political division around representative democracy. A subjective effect of responsibility is created on the side of the reader, which is drawn into the debate, pushed to engage with it and take sides in it. Because of the Lacanian psychoanalytic pathway to the unconscious subject, social issues—of politics, culture, and ethics—are inscribed in the subject itself, thus allowing the reader to personally engage with these issues from a distanced self-position: "In this perspective, the subject as such is constituted through a certain misrecognition: the process of ideological interpellation through which the subject 'recognizes' itself as the addressee in the calling up of the ideological cause implies necessarily a certain short circuit, an illusion of the type 'I was already there' which, as Michel Pêcheux—who has given us the most elaborated version of the theory of interpellation—pointed out, is not without its comical effects: the short circuit of 'no wonder you were interpolated as proletarian, when you are a proletarian.'"[68] Žižek performed his own position in contrast to the Althusserian rendition of this identification as interpellation. He rearticulated the Marxist notion of ideology along the Lacanian lines of the unconscious. This allowed Žižek to be positioned inside the Marxist tradition and thus as an engaged, radical thinker with global consequences, despite his dealing with the subject and its feelings, which positioned him as a peculiar Marxist. Žižek becomes Marxist enough to resonate with the Marxists in and outside academia, while also being non-Marxist enough to attract other intellectual currents. According to Žižek, "Lacanian psychoanalysis goes a decisive step further than the usual "post-Marxist" anti-essentialism affirming the irreducible plurality of particular struggles—in other words, demonstrating how their articulation into a series of equivalences depends always on the radical contingency of the social-historical process: it enables us to grasp this plurality itself as a multitude of responses to the same impossible-real kernel."[69] In this claim Žižek resonates both with the leftist critical position of discursive formation (where the subject or the social is an effect of discourse) and with the critique of this leftist position—which may sound conservative—by which not everything is a language game. This is how Žižek is positioned between or beyond the left and the right in their common, already recognized positions, and is situated in the impossible quantum superposition of both and none. This is his insistence on the Lacanian notion of the Real, which will individualize his position with regard to other leftist critical thinkers who focus on the symbolic, such as Laclau, Butler, Habermas, and Foucault.

Nonetheless, Žižek paid tribute to Laclau for at least identifying this Real and utilizing it in social analysis: "It is the merit of Ernest Laclau and Chantal

Mouffe that they have, in *Hegemony and Socialist Strategy*, developed a theory of the social field founded on such a notion of antagonism—on an acknowledgement of an original 'trauma,' an impossible kernel which resists symbolization, totalization, symbolic integration."[70] This is how Žižek bridged the critical discursive-linguistic position, with the realist position usually adopted by rightists. By distancing themselves from Hegel and Marx, French thinkers such as Foucault and Derrida moved toward symbolic mechanisms that shape society. Against them and their symbolic position, the conservative reaction was defending the realist kernel that is beyond symbolic constructions. This is how no position was left for Marxists, and Marxism decayed and diluted, especially in the United States, where cultural Marxism became more dominant than the realist-scientific. Žižek performed a short circuit between these positions: he took some parts of symbolic constructivism, but he also maintained the Real nonconstructible kernel precisely as the critical point of his analyses. Thus he bypassed the entire intellectual arena and created a new position with immediate political and ethical consequences. More concretely, Žižek linked the Marxist notions of alienation, antagonism, fetishism, and revolution, with the Lacanian conceptions of separation, the Real, fantasy, and the act. This linkage amounts to a superposition which transgresses the intraintellectual arena. Žižek recognizes the global political (but also cultural and ecological) consequences of his intellectual intervention by relating Laclau and Mouffe's post-Marxist radicalization to the common or "traditional" Marxist position:

> Their term "radical democracy" is thus to be taken somehow paradoxically: it is precisely *not* "radical" in the sense of pure, true democracy; its radical character implies, on the contrary, that we can save democracy only by taking into account its own radical impossibility. Here we can see how we have reached the opposite extreme of the traditional Marxist standpoint: in traditional Marxism, the global solution-revolution is the condition of the effective solution of all particular problems, while here every provisional, temporarily successful solution of a particular problem entails an acknowledgement of the global radical deadlock, impossibility, the acknowledgement of a fundamental antagonism.[71]

It is only at this point, after the Lacanian and Marxist relation, that Hegel appears as Žižek's own contribution, literally creating his branded and generative language of Hegelacanese. Generative here means that Žižek's Hegelacanese turned his performances into a genre in and of itself, a generic repertoire that can be repeated, reiterated, and thus easily circulated. That generative language is asserted as the book's (and thus Žižek's) thesis: "That the most consistent model of such an acknowledgement of antagonism is offered by Hegelian dialectics."[72] Then, by way of a Polish military joke about a soldier shooting someone prematurely before curfew hour only because he knows that this person lives far away and will not make it home in time, Žižek positioned himself against a whole range of Hegel critics (from Althusser to Foucault and Habermas), who also shoot the Hegelian "absolute knowledge" prematurely before reaching it, as they "refute nothing with their criticism but their own prejudices about it."[73] This alignment of Hegel and Lacan is signaled in the threefold aim and structure of the book, which recalls Lacan's triadic structure of the psyche's Real-Symbolic-Imaginary, and echoes Hegel's triadic dialectics structure.[74] These aims are to introduce Lacanian psychoanalysis, to return to Hegel, and to contribute to the theory of ideology. The introduction thus concludes with a subjective tone of "belief" regarding the interconnectedness of these aims: "The only way to 'save Hegel' is through Lacan, and this Lacanian reading of Hegel and the Hegelian heritage opens up a new approach to ideology, allowing us to grasp contemporary ideological phenomena (cynicism, 'totalitarianism,' the fragile status of democracy) without falling prey to any kind of 'postmodernist' traps (such as the illusion that we live in a 'post-ideological' condition)."[75] Intellectually, then, Žižek is positioned with Lacan and Hegel, but against Foucault and Habermas, while staying ambivalent regarding Marx and Althusser. This positioning is then translated into the political, public arena: Žižek is positioned as a radical, critical, leftist intellectual, yet in a way that counters and challenges many leftist taboos. By promising to explain social phenomena in psychoanalytic terms, Žižek is actually offering to draw broader philosophical insights into the human condition, providing an engaged platform (rather than a product) that includes the reader as subject of the same world as the author, thus allowing the reader to contemplate his or her position in this shared world experience. This intervention as invitation to the invention of something new, textually and conceptually, individually and socially, became at once a political and intellectual thought experiment. His use of language, which includes many capitalizations and italicizations, preceded and anticipated the internet language of hypertextuality. It allows for emotions to be carried out in and through the text. Unlike the reserved, remote, and traditional academic writing, which tends to be as asubjective and disengaged with the text as possible, Žižek strives to insert and intensify, excite and incite the emotive element and hyperbolically amplify it by repeating himself (in form), by using the same jokes, examples, and rhetorical questions (in content), soon to be canonically recognized as his repertoire.

This is why his first book in English actually begins with a question. Structurally, of the three parts of the book—again hinting the dialectic—part 1 is entitled "The Symptom," and its first chapter is the question "How Did Marx Invent the Symptom?" This question is all about positioning.[76] First, it invites readers to a discovery expedition into the treacherous terrain of the psyche, thus including themselves in the picture. Second, it resonates with the growing psychological popular parlance. Third, it shifts the terrain unexpectedly to Marxism. In forming his investigation in this way, Žižek superpositions the individual discourse of pop psychology and the social discourse of revolutionary Marxism. Moreover, his superpositioning of leftist and rightist positions has created Žižek's own intellectual and political "third way."[77] He stood with the leftist Marxists, but from a post-Marxist perspective; thus, he was also with the critics of Marxism, but not for their rightist, conservative reasons. He also superpositioned the modernist and postmodernist positions, as he criticized both for their one-sidedness. Žižek's *The Sublime Object* became a tour de force of a new unique mode of thinking, in both form and content. He challenged conventional ways of writing and arguing, and presented a novel link between (past) intellectuals to (present) politics and ethics.

Yet Žižek's Hegelacanese had to be used more than once to establish itself as a formidable language. For that, Žižek continued to publish with Laclau's *Phronesis* series until, in 1994, he launched his own series with Verso, *Wo Es War*. This performative networking expanded from Europe to the United States with the 1996 launch of another book series, called *sic*, with Duke University Press, and the publication of a series of articles. Žižek then built on *The Sublime Object*'s success, and rehearsed his position in further publications, such as *Looking Awry: An Introduction to Jacques Lacan through Popular Culture* (1991) and *Enjoy Your Symptom! Jacques Lacan in Hollywood and Out* (1992 and reissued 2001). All these provided analyses of mainstream culture while bringing to life concepts such as jouissance (enjoyment), the symptom, and the Real. In these interventions (fig. 2.1), Žižek consolidated his idiosyncratic language of Hegelacanese and performed it in a narrative composed of series of engagements with intellectual, political, and cultural issues.

Narration as Intellectual Intervention

Importantly, Žižek positioned himself with relation to the predominant intellectual currents of his time, including deconstruction, poststructuralism, and postmodernism, but also analytic philosophy. All these intellectual currents consider language central to human existence, in various forms. For this reason, Žižek spent much space-time in his formative interventions dealing with the question of language, and specifically with speech-act theory, performativity, and descriptivism. In 1990, as the one with the last word, he contributed a final chapter, entitled "Beyond Discourse-Analysis," to Laclau's *New Reflections on the Revolutions of Our Time*. In it he reached beyond the common critical leftist position of discourse theory, which reduces reality to the symbolic, while not regressing to the precritical realism of the right.

Not surprisingly, Žižek's Archimedean point of reference is Laclau and Mouffe's own intervention from 1985, through which he performed his superpositioning. First, there is the common reading: *Hegemony and Socialist Strategy* is "usually read as an essay in 'poststructuralist' politics, an essay in translating into a political project the basic 'post-structuralist' ideas: there is no transcendental Signified; so-called 'reality' is a discursive construct; every given identity, including that of a subject, is an effect of contingent differential relations, etc."[78] After this spontaneous intellectual and political positioning, read through the common perspective, there is the usual criticism that this reading evokes: "language serves primarily as a medium of extra-linguistic power-relations; we cannot dissolve all reality into a language-game, etc."[79] The reader is immediately confronted with these oppositions, of the common reading and the common critique. Against this positioning Žižek argued that "such a reading misses the fundamental dimension of *Hegemony*, the dimension through which this book presents perhaps the most radical breakthrough in modern social theory."[80] Now, interest and anticipation are created, together with uniqueness of positioning.

In a world of constant focus on individuality and the self, no one wants to be identified as a commoner aligned with the common reading or critique. Hence the question Žižek provoked here is, What exactly is the "most radical breakthrough" in modern social theory? The answer Žižek provided highlights the Lacanian affinity between his project and Laclau's: "The real achievement of *Hegemony* is crystallized in the concept of 'social antagonism': far from reducing all reality to a kind of language-game, the socio-symbolic field is conceived as structured around a certain traumatic impossibility, around a certain fissure that *cannot* be symbolized. In short, Laclau and Mouffe have, so to speak, reinvented the Lacanian notion of the Real as impossible, they have made it useful as a tool for social and ideological analysis."[81] This is how Žižek relates himself to a major intellectual issue of his time, namely language, while he also pushed the common position beyond its existing (symbolic) limits. Rearticulating the Marxist (practice of) critique of ideology in the contemporary form of discursive analysis, again allowed Žižek to make his Hegelacanese a superpositioned heteroglossia, speaking in multiple tones, voices, and dialects at once. Soon after this intervention there appeared other books, a few more edited volumes, as well as films—all collaborative projects, which are material effects of Žižek's teamwork and network.[82]

In the second book published by Žižek in English, *For They Know Not What They Do* (1991), he updates the position he held in *The Sublime Object of Ideology*.[83] As Žižek recalls: "My second book was more substantial theoretically [than the first], but it is typically less popular with fewer obscene jokes and so on. So much depends on circumstances."[84] While the main title echoes Christ's remark from the Cross and Marx's definition of ideology, its subtitle already hints its developed superpositioning: *Enjoyment as a Political Factor*. This relation between the production of subjective enjoyment and the political, global situation is again the signature of Hegelacanese. And as that emotive language includes jokes, by way of its "destiny," Žižek performatively explained the development of his new position: "The background of the present book is best illustrated by the well-known Soviet joke about Rabinovitch, a Jew who wants to emigrate. The bureaucrat at the emigration office asks him why. Rabinovitch answers: 'There are two reasons why. The first is that I'm afraid that the Communists will lose power in the Soviet Union, and the new forces will blame us Jews for the Communist crimes'; 'But,' interrupts the bureaucrat, 'this is pure nonsense, the power of the Communists will last forever!' 'Well,' responds Rabinovitch calmly, 'that's my second reason.'"[85] Žižek's adaptation of his intellectual superposition to the current, post-1989 political and public situation is performed by the reversal of the two positions of the joke. Instead of Jews—as paradigmatic others—being afraid of communism's demise and then its prosperity, in the updated version they are afraid of communism's prosperity and then its demise. Before a linear reading would claim that nothing has changed in this reversal, in Žižek's speculative Hegelian reading, this (temporal) reversal changes everything. He explained that back while *The Sublime Object* was published, this joke was still effective. Yet: "The present book supplements the analyses of *The Sublime Object Ideology* by endeavoring to articulate the theoretical apparatus which enables us to grasp the historical shift indicated by the strange destiny of the Rabinovitch joke: the eruption of enjoyment in the form of the re-emergence of the aggressive nationalism and racism that accompany the disintegration of 'actually existing socialism' in Eastern Europe."[86] In contrast to the celebration of the demise of communism as the rise of democracy, Žižek identified in the very heart of democracy the roots for what soon thereafter would be called the Balkan War. While the right, as those (Yugoslav Marxists) in power faced defeat, and while the left celebrated the democratic freedom, Žižek performed an intellectual intervention by creating his superposition of criticizing both sides at once.

According to Žižek, when one (communist) evil was abolished, another one arrived (the national-democratic illusion of freedom). As its title indicates, this intervention also adds another aspect that allows Žižek to resonate with more publics than the expert, academic intellectual. By hinting at the public ignorance of the people proclaimed by Christ (and later by Marx), Žižek introduced theology to the intellectual and political arenas, two spaces that tended to be separate from religion. This positioning vis-à-vis religion, relevant for a wider public of priests and theologians, is related to both Hegel and Lacan. The former was known for his philotheology, to the point of wanting to replace God; the latter, a devout Catholic with affinity to Judaism, was clear about the relation between psychoanalysis and theology. Repeating Lacan's response to a student asking whether psychoanalytical treatment is tantamount to the religious confession, Žižek argued: "This is what the book's title aims at—psychoanalysis is much more severe than Christianity: ignorance is *not* a sufficient reason for forgiveness since it conveys a hidden dimension of *enjoyment*. Where one doesn't (want to) know, in the blanks of one's symbolic universe, one enjoys, and there is no Father to forgive, since these blanks escape the authority of the Name-of-the-Father."[87] In short, psychoanalysis, in- and outside the clinic, does not hold the subject, a person or a society, responsible only for what is said (or known), but also for what is not said (or unknown). Thus, even religious readers could find a clear yet "twisted" reference point in Žižek's work. In a reflective self-positioning, he admitted that in this book there are traces from its context of conception, so it is confused on purpose:

> What gives the book its "specific flavor," however, is not so much its content as its *place of enunciation*. It conveys the text of lectures delivered on six consecutive Mondays in the winter semester of 1989–90 in Ljubljana, Yugoslavia. The lectures served as an introductory course to Lacan, organized by the Slovene Society for Theoretical Psychoanalysis and aimed at the "benevolently neutral" public of intellectuals who were the moving force of the drive for democracy; in other words, far from assuming the position of a Master "supposed-to-know," the lecturer acted as the analysand addressing the analyst composed of his public. The lectures were delivered in the unique atmosphere of those months: a time of intense political ferment, with "free elections" only weeks ahead, when all options still seemed open, the time of a "short circuit" blending together political activism, the "highest" theory (Hegel, Lacan) and unrestrained enjoyment in the "lowest" popular culture—a unique Utopian moment which is now, after the electoral victory of the nationalist-populist coalition and the ad-

vent of a new "scoundrel time," not only over but even more and more *invisible*, erased from the memory like a "vanishing mediator." . . . Although the lectures are now "put in order," there is still in them more than a trace of the chaotic circumstances of their origins. These traces have been preserved deliberately, as a kind of monument to the unique moment of their enunciation.[88]

The content of the intervention thus reserves something in its form, and that is the political—but also intellectual—openness that Slovenia experienced during the transition period of the 1990s. Moreover, Žižek's self-positioning reveals his sacrificial intellectual position. Unlike the authoritative intellectual who identifies with the master and speaks from the position of the subject supposed-to-know, Žižek deliberately rejects this position, and in that he commits a public suicide of his social image (as a philosopher). In what resembles the dialogical, embedded intellectual, Žižek performed an act of subjective destitution, by which he rejects the position that is supposed to separate him from his audience or public. This raises the lingering question related to Žižek: how to take seriously someone who does not, in turn, take themselves seriously?

The next interventions in (t)his series involved more culture than politics, thus positioning Žižek as the "hippest" intellectual, up with the times and trends.[89] *Looking Awry: An Introduction to Lacan through Popular Culture* (1991) has a slightly different structure from the philosophical-political books previously published. More akin to a textbook, this intervention is meant to be a popular book for the intellectual reader. Similar to the triadic structure of *The Sublime Object of Ideology* and *For They Know Not What They Do*, this book is also structured in three big chunks or parts, mainly of already-published material now packaged together. However, each part is broken into bite-sized pieces that together compose something like a reader of Lacan and contemporary culture. Hence, this book is much less political and more intellectual, intended to be accessible for students and professional academics interested in the evolving object of culture.

In *Enjoy Your Symptom!* (1992) and *Everything You Always Wanted to Know about Lacan (But Were Afraid to Ask Hitchcock)* (1992), Žižek turned to classical cultural references in order to apply his Hegelacanese not only to politics but also to popular culture. The reason is that ideology, what we do without knowing, is immensely invested in culture. Films, novels, and other artifacts, even TV shows and commercials, provide Žižek with a vast pool of cultural material to be analyzed ideologically. These analyses resonated with an academic context whereby cultural studies was being forged as the new front of social sciences. Both books were published in non–university presses (in their academic series though), so as to be more accessible to various public while keeping a professional tone. In this turn to culture, Žižek became involved with additional intellectual disciplines beyond psychoanalysis and philosophy proper.[90] He engaged with film and cultural studies, attracting readers with backgrounds beyond philosophical and without stated political motivations. In these interventions Žižek utilized all his key rhetorical devices: questions, jokes, and examples. Particularly regarding the latter, being the matter of culture, he shows that examples—from TV commercials to Hollywood films—are valid philosophical demonstrative tools. Most philosophers and intellectuals underestimate the example, a tendency that goes back to Kant's description of it as the "go-cart of the judgment."[91] However, for Žižek, examples are prime devices for disseminating ideas. As McGowan argues, in Žižek's work the example has the status of a concept, as "it's the vehicle for the manifestation of speculative identity, the identity of identity and non-identity, which is Hegel's great philosophical discovery."[92] Instead of the common intellectual tendency of clinging to the argument and rejecting the example, in Žižek "an argument is just an example that doesn't realize it is an example."[93] The point of Žižek's frequent use of examples is that it "reveals the unconscious of an argument, and in the unconscious contradiction predominates."[94] As rhetorical devices, he does not hold that examples are beneath the philosopher's high-minded thoughts and abstractions.[95] Rather, examples from everyday life are the concretization of philosophy. In this way he performatively reverberates Plato's Idea of a postmodern examined life.

By using classical references such as Hollywood and Hitchcock, Žižek's exemplification is aimed at the heart of the mainstream—an aim that should not surprise us, given Žižek's insistence on psychoanalyzing the mainstream ideology embodied in everyday culture. More intellectually, these interventions provide a crucial contribution to the Marxist study of ideology as well as to the Lacanian study of culture. Now expanding these methods into new cases, Žižek's intellectual superpositioning was immediately grounded not only in psychoanalysis or philosophy but also in cultural and film studies. Through the Hitchcock edited volume, new intellectual connections were made between Žižek and American intellectuals, most noticeably Fredric Jameson, Eric Santner, and Joan Copjec, through which an alignment of positions took place.

Mapping Ideology was another edited volume with great impact on Žižek's positioning as an important intellectual with global reach.[96] This intervention positioned Žižek in the intellectual tradition of critical theory, Marxism, literature, and sociology. As an editor, Žižek played the curator of the newest exhibition of the concept of ideology, expanding its Marxist connotations to the psychoanalytic and sociological realms. The contributors were blended intellectuals from various times and disciplines, including Adorno, Seyla Benhabib, Lacan, Althusser, Michel Pêcheux, Terry Eagleton, Göran Therborn, Rorty, Bourdieu, Jameson, and, of course, Žižek himself. With this transdisciplinary international star list, Žižek not only related himself to them but also positioned the concept of ideology in a new, updated light. In the same year, 1994, Žižek had the opportunity to have his own book series with Verso. As he explains: "The Wo Es War series represents a certain reading of Lacan which is philosophical and which at the same time goes beyond the limitations of standard cultural studies in terms of its political orientation. My big ambition was to enable other people close to me, especially my Slovenian friends Alenka Zupančič and Mladen Dolar, to publish abroad. This was another reason why I wanted the series. But the basic orientation is the philosophical reading of Lacan plus this specific political twist. For this, I needed a series in order to develop a coherent project with a clear direction."[97] With a clear reference to Freud, this series provided Žižek with an intellectual site that allowed him to develop collaboratively and individually his new language of Hegelacanese into a continuous, coherent performance.[98] The series' opening statement declares its (and Žižek's) intellectual and political positioning: "*Wo es war, soll ich werden—where it was, I shall come into being*—is Freud's version of the Enlightenment goal of knowledge that is in itself an act of liberation. Is it still possible to pursue this goal today, in the conditions of late capitalism? If 'it' today is the twin rule of pragmatic-relativist New Sophists and New Age obscurantists, what 'shall come into being' in its place? The premise of the series is that the explosive combination of Lacanian psychoanalysis and Marxist tradition detonates a dynamic freedom that enables us to question the very presuppositions of the circuit of Capital."[99] Žižek is related here with Freud and the Enlightenment, yet is positioned against two dominant intellectual tendencies of the late capitalist context: pragmatism and New Age. Again, the past-present link is made clearly with a reference to Freud and associating him with the contemporary political situation. As the model on intellectual intervention suggests, Žižek identifies a deadlock in theory, namely how to instate the universal in a particular, relativistic setting, and then he opens up a path for a new singular way of dealing with that deadlock. The innovative combination of Lacan and Hegel is supposed to allow for a new reading of the future, since it includes the changes from capital's previous stage—where critical thought is still stuck and unable to mobilize the masses toward liberation.

Therefore, in his first *Wo Es War* book, *The Metastases of Enjoyment*, Žižek continues to develop his particular form of thought, applied now to woman and causality. Writing about femininity, sexuality, and "courtly love" amid the rise of feminist theories positioned Žižek as a relevant thinker engaged with timely issues. Noticeably, in an uncommon rhetorical self-positioning move, the book is appended with a self-interview entitled "Taking Sides." In it, Žižek is interviewing himself, posing questions to himself, and providing the reader with a "behind the scenes" thought process with which he answers his own questions. The self-interview began by explaining why subjective destitution is the necessary position of the analyst (who does not know) as opposed to the master (who does know). This former position is taken by Žižek; he becomes the analyst of global society and its symptoms.[100] The counterposition of the master as the subject supposed-to-know is an example of the authoritative intellectual speaking to his patients or publics from above, identifying with his assumed role and thus playing into the hands of the social order. The enjoyment of the master is gained by projecting a kind of fake sacrifice for the patient or public. However, Žižek's subjective destitution "is closely linked to another key Hegelian-Lacanian motif, that of the 'sacrifice of the sacrifice.'"[101] By adopting the position of the analyst Žižek is sacrificing the false sacrifice of the master that enjoys his image of a suffering individual working relentlessly for the greater (patient's and public's) good. That subjective enjoyment is concealed behind the rhetoric of sacrifice, the same one we get from contemporary leaders who claim to have given everything up for the nation, while gaining surplus profit and surplus enjoyment.

Once positioned against such pseudosacrifice, Žižek explained his turn to popular culture being the material "stuff" of ideological, fantasmatic investments. It is to where we project our symbolic relation to reality materially, and hence it is where we can discern our social symptoms. Then he engaged in a positioning process of prominent and recognized intellectuals such as Derrida, Heidegger, and Foucault, to emphasize the Lacanian position against all of them in a constructive, supplementary way that leaves an inclusive space for their followers. For instance, he described the persistence of latent violence in democratic societies, which includes sexism, racism, and nationalism. Žižek described this move from patriarchy to cynicism, when he identified a shift in the modality of power in late capitalism, a conceptual shift to which liberal feminist-postcolonial theories are blind. By moving from the master-father-leader figure of authority to the cynical one, power is not exerted in the old-fashioned coercive manner, but as a form of (knowledge-based) enjoyment. So the boss is also the friend, the father is also weak, and the leader is also a cynic. In this new modality of power, a critique that dwells in the cynical distance falls into the hands of those in power. Namely, if the leader does not take himself seriously, exposing him (and his crimes) as not serious is not a critical gesture. It is the same insight Žižek developed locally a decade before apropos of the Slovenian NSK art performances, which shifted the critical position from cynicism to overidentification. This insight is used by Žižek to construct his position as analyst of "postmodern subjectivity," where all are born cynics who do not take appearances for real but still act as if they did, relying on the linguistic performative power maintained by a cynical distance.[102] As Žižek exemplified, when

> asked about their attitude towards America, the Slovene post-punk group Laibach said: "Like Americans, we also believe in God, but unlike them we do not trust Him" (an allusion to the inscription on dollar banknotes, of course)! In so far as God is one of the names of the big Other, this paradoxical statement renders quite adequately the Lacanian attitude towards the big Other of language: a Lacanian is not a cynic who acknowledges only enjoyment; he counts on the efficiency of the big Other, yet he does not trust it, since he knows that he is dealing with an order of semblance.[103]

Importantly, this assertion of the Lacanian position is at once intellectual (siding with Lacan against common intellectual critics), and political (siding with a more radical form of critique). "Cynicism as reflected ideology" is further developed in Žižek's next publication in his own Verso series, *The Indivisible Remainder*, where he dwelled into German idealism and quantum physics, with constant reference to Lacan.[104] The intervention into science and especially physics opened a path for even more readers to engage with Žižek, although unfamiliar with the more philosophical content. Žižek's engagement with German idealism was not limited to Hegel, for it would be restricting for his overarching project. Thus he is engaged also with Kant and Schelling, which positioned him as more relevant intellectual to non-Hegelians.

A year later, Žižek performed another uncommon positioning move, establishing himself as an authority in German philosophy, with his publication of a coedited book with the late Schelling.[105] This time the book was not published with the European Verso, but with the American University of Michigan Press. At that time of expanding his output in the American market, Žižek also launched the collaborative book series with Duke University Press. The series, called *sic*, declared in its opening statement that it "stands for psychoanalytic interpretation at its most elementary: no discovery of deep, hidden meaning, just an act of drawing attention to the litterality [*sic*] of what precedes it."[106] It performed its contextuality and relationality as "different connections to the Freudian field," where "each volume provides a bundle of

98 CHAPTER TWO

Lacanian interventions into a specific domain of ongoing theoretical, cultural, and ideological-political battles."[107] Then Žižek performed his superpositioning first by characterizing his series as neither "pluralist" nor "socially sensitive," and second by asserting that "it disregards any form of correctness but the inherent correctness of theory itself."[108] So although analyzing the practice of everyday life in a concrete and critical fashion, Žižek places theory as the ultimate stake, criticizing both the left and the right for their lack of theory (as thinking).

This superpositioning became quite explicitly intellectual in his next 1997 *Wo Es War* intervention, *The Plague of Fantasies*, which Žižek opened with a popular cultural reference and linked it with Lacan's unconscious: "The Unconscious is outside, not hidden in any unfathomable depths—or, to quote the X Files motto: 'The truth is out there.'"[109] Then he opposed two intellectual positions to create his own, by recalling Lacan's distinction between two types of the contemporary intellectual—the fool and the knave:

> In short, the right-wing intellectual is a knave, a conformist who refers to the mere existence of the given order as an argument for it, and mocks the Left on account of its Utopian plans, which necessarily lead to catastrophe; while the left-wing intellectual is a fool, a court jester who publicly displays the lie of the existing order, but in a way which suspends the performative efficiency of his speech. Today, after the fall of Socialism, the knave is a neoconservative advocate of the free market who cruelly rejects all forms of social solidarity as counterproductive sentimentalism, while the fool is a deconstructionist cultural critic who, by means of his ludic procedures destined to "subvert" the existing order, actually serves as its supplement.[110]

Žižek's superpositioning is declared in the usual method of identifying an opposition, a dualism, or a dichotomy, and then showing how its two sides are actually of the same coin, an understanding with a practical subjective effect of traversing the fantasy: "What psychoanalysis can do to help us to break this vicious cycle of fool-knave is to lay bare its underlying libidinal economy—the libidinal profit, the surplus-enjoyment, which sustains each of the two positions."[111] In rejecting both of these positions, and what they stand for intellectually and politically, Žižek is using Hegelacanese to create his new position. Žižek's next intervention in his *Wo Es War* series is *The Ticklish Subject* (1999). Prior to another Hegelian triadic structure, the introduction continues the intellectual-political positioning. In a clear Marxist reference, Žižek declared: "A specter is haunting Western academia . . . the specter of the Cartesian subject. All academic powers have entered into a holy alliance to exorcize this specter . . . : the New Age obscurantist . . . and the postmodern deconstructionist . . . ; the Habermasian theorist of communication . . . and the Heideggerian proponent of the thought of Being . . . ; the cognitive scientist . . . and the Deep Ecologist . . . ; the critical (post-) Marxist . . . and the feminist."[112] Using a common, classical intellectual reference, Žižek drew a map of these positions which he found problematic for neglecting the Cartesian subject. The Lacanian twist added to the Marxist reference and Cartesian tradition is that this subject, the (in)famous *cogito*, is essentially the subject of the unconscious, not of consciousness. However, while performing an intellectual-political self-positioning, the introduction noted, "While this book is philosophical in its basic tenor, it is first and foremost an engaged political intervention, addressing the burning question of how are we to formulate a leftist anti-capitalist political project in our era of global capitalism and its ideological supplement, liberal-democratic multiculturalism."[113] This self-positioning, as an engaged intellectual against the common intellectual currents, is transformed into a superpositioning of both the rightist-capitalist position and the leftist-liberal position of multiculturalism. After pivoting the present intellectual arena around the great past reference of Descartes, Žižek's position actually incorporated all the others positions, while his incorporation also rejects their exclusive reasoning. And by linking this past reference to the present global political context, he reacted to its global issues and created a novel reading of the future. Superpositionally, Žižek was not against multiculturalism or human rights, rather, he posited that these cannot be a basis for a global leftist anticapitalist project.[114]

This position was not performed using only the book form of intellectual intervention. Žižek's academic articles were published since the late 1980s and during the 1990s, but they drew little attention given their marginal, localized outlets. By putting much effort into conveying lectures into books and bypassing the academic journal article form, Žižek signaled his positioning regarding the academic establishment as a whole. While most academics move from lectures to articles to books, Žižek performed a short circuit between the first and last stages. His preference for the book form goes to the heart of knowledge production in the digital era, where books are in fact easier to come by. He also reflects an image of a serious or classical, general and global intellectual, in opposition to the expert intellectual that focuses on topic-based journal articles derived from his predefined expertise. Here we see again Žižek's sacrificial position. Limiting his article output while its value is increasing in academia hindered his "seriousness" in these academic terms and in the eyes of other academics. Yet if Žižek aimed to reach the global public, as an generic and diversified collective that is not restricted to particularly academic or nationalistic interests, then the book form was a much more effective disseminator than journal articles. This is especially true when combined with newspaper articles, films, and internet presence. So before using other forms of intellectual interventions, Žižek started mixing all these and experimenting with them. Thus, significant articles in their public reach and effect dealt with popular issues such as culture and politics rather than with theory and philosophy. One such example is his frequent use of the interview as a channel to explain his thoughts and contextualize them more informally. Žižek's participation in *A Critical Sense: Interviews with Intellectuals*, edited by Peter Osborne and published in 1996 with Routledge, positioned him (on the back cover) as one of "today's most important thinkers." Another illustrative example is the journal *Lacanian Ink*, renamed as the website Lacan.com, which, since its collaborative establishment by the Argentine Josefina Ayerza in 1990 and 1997, respectively, operated as an early international and digital hub for spreading "Jacques Lacan in the US." It featured articles from Miller, Žižek, and other Lacanian intellectuals. In this way, Žižek started to gain online presence, with the maintenance help of others.

By commenting on public issues, both political and cultural, his interventions resonated further and with even more publics. This was evident in his commentary of the popular motion picture *The Matrix*.[115] Released on March 31, 1999, the movie hit a particular cultural timing. On the break of the new millennia and the rise of smart digital technology, *The Matrix* touched upon numerous philosophical and religious ideas, from Plato's Allegory of the Cave to Lewis Carroll's *Alice's Adventures in Wonderland*. By commentating on it, Žižek positioned himself as a savvy intellectual, up with the times, able to relate to the global publics' interests and concerns. Žižek's first intervention, in the form of a public lecture on *The Matrix*, was delivered first to the International Symposium at the Center for Art and Media in Karlsruhe, Germany, on October 28, 1999. As part of the repetitive performative repertoire, it was then turned into an article and published by the journal *Philosophy Today*, before it was compiled in collected essays on *The Matrix and Philosophy* and translated into Italian, Spanish, Hebrew, Turkish, Korean, and other languages. Remarkably, Žižek's diverse intervention did not start with the film itself but with the viewer's position, thus bringing the reader into the conversation while superpositioning the intellectual and the idiot: "When I saw *The Matrix* at a local theatre in Slovenia, I had the unique opportunity of sitting close to the ideal spectator of the film—namely, to an idiot. A man in the late [twenties] at my right was so immersed in the film that he all the time disturbed other spectators with loud exclamations, like 'My God, wow, so there is no reality!'

I definitely prefer such naive immersion to the pseudo-sophisticated intellectualist readings which project into the film the refined philosophical or psychoanalytic conceptual distinctions."[116] By distancing himself from the spontaneous intellectualization of the film, Žižek identified with most viewers or readers, who are not intellectuals, while stimulating their intellect. This move of not identifying with the intellectual amounts to a critique of that intellectual position. As Samuels noted: "The rhetorical strategy of this first stage of Žižek's argument here is to paraphrase the various common (mis)readings that academics make concerning this particular issue, which in this case concerns the question of the ultimate meaning of this film. This opening move allows Žižek the chance to gather together many of his different readers and to show them how they are all wrong."[117] In this way he opened up an intellectual space but from another nonintellectual vantage point: "It is nonetheless easy to understand this intellectual attraction of *The Matrix*: is it not that *The Matrix* is one of the films which function as a kind of Rorschach test, setting in motion the universalized process of recognition, like the proverbial painting of God which seems always to stare directly at you, from wherever you look at it—practically every orientation seems to recognize itself in it?"[118] Žižek's use of the device of the rhetorical question, again, is meant to bring the reader into the picture. Then, his relation of psychology and subjectivity to the context of virtual reality greatly resonated with the public sentiments that made *The Matrix* into an era-defining blockbuster. Žižek used this public interest as an opportunity to introduce more widely and simplistically his Hegelacanese: "What, then, is the Matrix? Simply the Lacanian 'big Other,' the virtual symbolic order, the network that structures reality for us."[119] From this point onwards, the reader is actually learning about the functioning of the Lacanian concept of the big (unidentifiable) Other via a series of critical exemplifications from *The Matrix* (and its sequels) but also from other movies, novels, and plays.[120]

By the time Žižek had written about *The Matrix* in 1999, he had already intensified his personal engagement with cinema. He made two appearances in documentaries on the Slovenian collective art movement NSK and its subgroups Laibach and Irwin. Although made as fringe films not intended for the wider public, *Laibach: A Film from Slovenia* and *Predictions of Fire* allowed Žižek to experiment with this medium of digital and performative intellectual intervention, bringing his showmanship to the fore.[121] The latter, directed by the American Michael Benson, exposed Žižek to a North American audience after winning Best Documentary Award at the Vancouver International Film Festival of 1996. The effect of such showmanship is captured in a third documentary from the same period, only this time about Žižek himself, making him the object of inquiry and interest. In *Liebe Dein Symptom wie Dich selbst!* (*Enjoy the Symptom as Yourself!*) Žižek admitted his awkward emergent position in the Western Anglo-Saxon academia: "When we published the book on Hitchcock, when they invited me to Berkeley, California, they told me that they invited me—friends of me [sic]—because they wanted to prove to people that I really exist. The legend in Berkeley was that this is a practical joke played by some French intellectuals who invented Slovenia, and that we do not exist at all. So people were really shocked there that we really exist."[122] It seems that Žižek's reception in North America was one of doubt, in that a marginal Slovenian intellection could have produced such a sophisticated book on Lacan and Hitchcock. This translates into Žižek's hysteric position of speech which would accompany his performance for years to come. Yet effectively it pushed him to "prove" his existence, using all possible channels of communication. As a German documentary intended for a rather small audience of academic inner circles, it nonetheless helped popularize Žižek's ideas, as they were carried out by his significantly distinct showmanship of vulgar language, jokes, examples, and rhetorical questions.

This film allowed him to bring his ideas, style, and method to the live digital public sphere. Standing in front of the camera and playing the intellectual, Žižek simultaneously performed an anti-intellectual move and arguing that he "hates professors who believe that they really are professors."[123] Žižek became known for his nonacademic suicidal, sacrificial performance, not only for his ideas but also for his show, which appears funny, grotesque, and provocative at once. In other words, Žižek tapped into the contemporary mode of enjoyment not because of what he means but for what he does. His subjective doubt is exactly what annuls the position of the master authoritative or expert intellectual, and even suspends the possibility for a true dialogue as the dialogical intellectual would have wanted.[124] Instead, Žižek's subjective doubt is used as a sacrificial rhetorical device to resonate with the reader's or viewer's own self-doubt (are we really what we appear to be?), thus inviting the individual to cast doubt on his or her own way and life. As noted before, Žižek's intellectual interventions are not conventional philosophical treatises. They continuously oscillate as if split between a philosophical analysis of contemporary psychoculture, and a psychocultural analysis of contemporary philosophy. This oscillation will cast doubt on Žižek's positioning as a philosopher, a doubt that Žižek would deal with openly for decades. Yet this doubt proves critical in maintaining multiple and varied interpretations of the Žižekian position.

3 Going Global: Narrating the (Traumatic) Present

The 1990s were, for Žižek, years of theoretical innovation and publication, network extension, and intellectual establishment. This chapter provides a close examination of the following decade, between 2001 (in the context of the 9/11 event) and 2011 (the Arab Spring event). Žižek's interventions at the start of the twenty-first century shed necessary light on his superpositioning process, as he moves (according to the model of intellectual intervention, see fig. 0.2) from the intraintellectual (academic) arena to the extraintellectual (public) arena, and from past references to present affairs and to future consequences. This is done by rearticulating a practical deadlock, namely the critique of capitalism. Echoing Jameson's "narrative as a socially symbolic act," Žižek's narration of the present offered general publics a consistent yet varied platform for an alternative critical understanding of the current condition, ultimately positioning Žižek as an engaged global *public* intellectual.[1]

Žižek's Hegelacanese, once applied to contested global public events such as 9/11, the 2008 global financial crisis, and the Arab Spring, was performed in a unique digital dissemination and resonated with a global public. Importantly, Žižek provided a provocative meaning to the cultural global trauma of 9/11, and became a pivotal public figure with public reach. Žižek continued this narration of global events that appealed to the general, global public. However, by repeating his repertoire in various public—political and cultural—arenas, Žižek was also exposed to diverse intellectual positioning; by exposing himself to such positioning, achieved by reviews and critical evaluations of his work, Žižek also engaged in a public debates that rendered him the go-to philosopher at the start of internet age. Therefore, this chapter analyzes Žižek's interventions in their multiple forms, starting with these reactions from various intellectual and general publics.

Reacting to Žižek: Reproduction between Reception and Rejection

Between 2001 and 2011, Žižek published eighteen manuscripts in English and twelve coedited books. During this time, he published only six books in Slovenian, indicating his turn toward a global (and English-speaking) public. Moreover, we can see that Žižek resonated with the intellectual community by the number of books dealing with Žižek's thought, which during this period rose to twenty-seven, in addition to over fifty articles written about him.[2] Such attention suggests that Žižek's positioning as a global intellectual was effective, as no other intellectual had, in that time, received such a high number of book-length reactions.[3] Žižek also expanded his publishing connections, working in this period with around ten main publishers worldwide, including university (Duke, MIT, Chicago, Columbia) and nonuniversity (e.g., Verso, Continuum, Routledge, Polity) presses. This expansion was predicated on Žižek's earlier performative interventions that exposed him to diversified receptions, which would later condition his 9/11 intervention. But it is worth taking a short detour to understand why Žižek was so attractive to so many readers and publishers.

In his authoritative studies of the changing publishing industry over the past thirty years, John Thompson reports three main findings: first about the increasingly direct relation between publishers and readers, second about the decoupling of content and medium caused by the digital revolution, and third about the "hidden revolution" that affected more the process of publishing than the book as its product. When the digital revolution started in the 1980s, many predicted the death of the book. Conversely, Thompson has found that if anything, the digital revolution immortalized the book, as it gave it a new digital format—the e-book. As he put it: "With the rise of the internet in the 1990s, the weaving together of information and communication technologies and the growing availability of personal computers and mobile devices with high-speed internet connections, it became possible not just to transform supply chains, back-office systems and production processes, but also to revolutionize the ways in which consumers, i.e., readers, acquire books, the form in which they acquire them and, indeed, the ways in which the readers of books relate to those who write them."[4]

As the publishing theorist Bhaskar noted as well, publishing cannot be divorced from content.[5] But as the digital revolution took off in the early 2000s with the inventions of new e-readers, content producers faced another problem than the one they were used to. Instead of content scarcity, they try to avoid attention deficits at all costs. Interestingly, in this competition over readers' attention span, academic publishers are leading the adaptation race.

Familiar with early versions of digitalization, academic publishers produce more specialized works in fewer quantities but at higher prices than commercial presses, which made their products better suited for digital printing. Moreover, as the digital revolution in publishing intensified, it lowered the field's entry barriers, thus allowing for many new actors to enter in the form of self-publishing or crowdfunding. So while the traditional publishing model was based on a unilinear model of communication, now publishers have to rely on dialogical forms of information and communication flow, and be in closer, more direct contact with readers. Only this way will they be able to "bring books into existence and to connect writers and readers who wish to communicate through and around the form of the book."[6] Or, in the words of a chief executive officer of one of the large trade houses: "The essence of the digital transformation is that we have to become much more reader-centric. We have to become much more consumer focused as publishers."[7]

Thompson suggests that some of what explains the stubborn persistence of the book—for example, the fact that print books continue to constitute roughly 85 percent of the US book market—is that it is different from a screen-based digital culture. Specifically, the book still allows for a different user experience, one that facilities two great desirables of our time: the desire to disconnect, and the ability to have control over time. In addition, he reminds us that "we should not underestimate the importance of books in helping to cultivate the kind of critical and informed culture that is essential to what we could call a vibrant public sphere."[8] As a thinker whose content is extremely digitizable, with its fast production rate, the copy-and-paste textual quality, and the growing media buzz around his quirky yet catchy name, Žižek would become a digital, not analog, intellectual par excellence.[9] His work also combines both genres and circles that have become quite distinct over the years, mainly in the United States: the scholarly-scientific and the literary-intellectual.[10] Even when looked at through the academic publishing prism, Žižek's texts have a double sense of both the (progressively shrinking) scholarly monographs and the (still flourishing) textbook publications. Surely he writes monographs, yet his rate of publication allows for publishers to repetitively treat his work as if in progress, continuously adding updated versions, as for textbooks. This production is an important cultural and intellectual endeavor since books are "a readily accessible medium in which individuals can provide sustained, in-depth analyses . . . which can inform and stimulate debate in other media" interventions.[11]

An intervention, in the more popular sense of the term, designates an external abruption or sudden cut interfering with the normal routine of the intervened. So when close friends of someone wish to change what they consider to be a destructive behavior of that person, they arrange an intervention. This analogy between practical and intellectual interventions shows that an intervention can be understood as an event, something that happens rather than is, and the effects of which can range between maximum and minimum. A maximum effect of an intervention would be the complete change of the intervened, whereas a minimal intervention would leave no change or trace. In line with positioning theory's vocabulary of effects, it is to these effects of Žižek's performative and generative intellectual interventions that one has to pay attention in order to evaluate his emergence as a global public intellectual. Referring to *The Sublime Object*, Dolar recalls the network relations that facilitated Žižek's global expansion:

> His success in '89 very happily coincided with the downfall of socialism. He was the man who could first talk back, privately, and also gave an explanation to the story, about the Eastern bloc, and Stalinism, and the way it worked, and the powers, etc., as someone who knew the whole thing from the inside. Because for most Western sociologists, social scientists it was a kind of exotic tribe. Because Slavoj's book made it big also in America, immediately, in the early '90s, he had his first invitations to places America in the early '90s, immediately. Ernesto [Laclau] at that time had a standing and his preface (to Žižek) was effective.[12]

In the previous chapter we saw how Žižek utilized his connections in France, the United Kingdom, and the United States to create a network of Lacanian and Hegelian intellectuals with a strong leftist political tendency. Although he gained a global intellectual position due to his series of interventions, his repetitive and signatory performance, and his style of writing and speaking, Žižek continuously positioned himself as an anti-intellectual: he made several remarks against pseudointellectualism and rejected the positions of the "authoritative," "expert," and "dialogical" intellectuals. Moreover, his performances were not entirely within the academic tradition: his style was a hybrid of sophisticated concepts and the simplest everyday language and examples. His preferred form of intellectual intervention, the book, distanced himself from the paywalled and hierarchical journal-based culture of contemporary academia. In creating this distance from the common intellectual as the subject supposed-to-know, Žižek had already begun to occupy the sacrificial intellectual position. Akin to Socrates's sacrifice of his life for corrupting the youth of Athens, Žižek's sacrifice is performed digitally, in the form of academic shaming. A media-academia trade-off results whereby an intellectual who intervenes in the public arena while still active in the intraintellectual arena will lose professional credibility. For Žižek, academia rejected him for not being a serious enough of academic. As Zupančič reflects:

> Academia is like any other [field] . . . , there are all these kinds of internal, not only jealousies but also power struggles, and I guess there are people who are much more comfortable relying on and allying with all these institutional "proofs of excellence," or whatever you call it, which are classical academic references—the way you behave yourself, the journals in which you publish, the language you use, all this stuff—and who very often are jealous of success of certain other styles of writing. Of course, particularly by then, these types of writings get dismissed as simply philosophically nonrelevant. The more they have followers and the more powerful, they say, "This is simply populist writing, it has nothing to do with serious work."[13]

By preferring to not participate in the academic game by its own rules and to not accept the common academic publishing hierarchies, Žižek was not performing the common intellectual performance. To put it bluntly, while telling sexual and vulgar jokes, Žižek appears less of an intellectual while appealing to the public as "one of us." Evidence for the lack of academic engagement with Žižek's thought, notwithstanding his intellectual global stardom, is found in the Open Syllabus Project. "Opening the curricular black box," this project provides open access to 1.1 million (English-language) syllabi.[14] For example, as of 2019, Bourdieu's total count is 14,910 appearances, and his most cited work, *Distinction*, has a count of 2,918 and a score of 91. Comparatively, Žižek's numerous books have total appearances of 1,206, and his *Sublime Object* has only 377 appearances and a score of 13. Interestingly, he appears much more in English literature than in philosophy departments. This academic marginalization is also reflected in the survey undertaken with Žižek followers: few were first introduced to Žižek "in class" (18 percent), and the more common ways were "through a friend/family member" (25 percent) or "in a book/article/talk" (37 percent).

It is noteworthy that *New Theories of Discourse: Laclau, Mouffe, and Žižek* (with over two thousand citations) is one of the first two books to engage with Žižek as an object of study and thus position him as a global intellectual. With the growing intellectual and public interest in the concept of discourse, Torfing's positioning of Žižek as a representative of a *new* theory of discourse was effective in linking Žižek to diverse theoretical issues of the present. The second book that engaged with Žižek was *The Žižek Reader* (also published in 1999). Few intellectuals attain a status (or corpus) that warrants a reader for their work. This form of a book is addressed to the public; a selection of texts provides a shortcut into the intellectual's thought, especially when contextualized in practical and less theoretical terms. The reader is then able to position the intellectual as a central figure in the intraintellectual arena. Importantly, *The Žižek Reader* brought a minority intellectual to the public, responding to growing demands at the time to diversify the extraintellectual arena. This benefited not only Žižek but also the publisher's own relevance. *The Žižek Reader* was edited by Elizabeth Wright and Edmond Wright (from Cambridge University) and published by the prestigious Blackwell Publishers. The back cover engaged in intellectual positioning by declaring that "the *Reader* not only provides careful explications of the individual extracts within each section but also connects these extracts in a general introduction, mapping the shifts in Žižek's thought within the Lacanian framework."[15] Then, the editors acknowledge Žižek's superpositioning on the topic of feminism: "The essays on woman after feminism offer feminism ammunition from unexpected sources, within a reading of Lacan that goes counter to his ambiguous reception by feminists."[16] In this sense, Žižek both agrees and identifies with feminism, yet from a position that most feminists do not currently take. Indeed, in his own reflective preface to the *Reader*, Žižek articulates his common mode of superpositioning, negating both positions of left and right, as well as those of the intellectual and the public, and creating his unique sacrificial superposition called "burning the bridges." Let us see how this works.

Žižek begins with a cultural common reference, the motion picture *Titanic* (1997). He draws our attention to the ending scene in which, after the clash, Rose says to her lower-class lover Jack, "Nothing can take us apart! I'll never let you go!," while actually letting him go into the deep, freezing water. This scene then becomes a "perfect" exemplification of Lacan's assertion that having the status of a symbolic authority "has to be paid for by death, even by murder, of its empirical bearer."[17] Žižek confesses: "When my dear friends . . . approached me with the proposal to put together a Žižek Reader, my first reaction to it was: isn't the price for this elevation to the status of an author who deserves a Reader that one is treated as a kind of living dead, no longer acknowledged as a living and developing entity? Isn't it that, at some level, at least, an important aspect of me has to disappear into the dark abyss of the past?"[18] Once Žižek assumes this sacrificial position, the acquiescence to be fossilized alive, he also realizes this as an opportunity to clarify his relations through taking intellectual stands: "[the editors] forced me to confront the unpleasant, but unavoidable, question: where do I stand with regard to the present theoretical imbroglio in which deconstruction and the cognitive sciences, the tradition of the Frankfurt School and that of Heideggerian phenomenology, New Age obscurantism and new historicism, fight for hegemony?"[19] Žižek answers this question with a reaction to his general public reception as postmodern: "In contrast to the cliché of the academic writer beneath whose impassive style the reader can catch an occasional glimpse of the so-called lively personality, I always perceived of myself as the author of books whose excessively and compulsively 'witty' texture serves as the envelope of a fundamental *coldness*, of a 'machinic' deployment of the line of thought which follows its path with utter *indifference* towards the pathology of so-called human considerations. In this respect, I always felt a deep sympathy for Monty Python, whose excessive humor also signals an underlying stance of profound disgust of life."[20] Žižek's disgust of the academic, common intellectual life cannot become clearer than when he proclaims, "So if the present Reader succeeds in burning the last bridges that may appear to connect me to the hegemonic trends in today's academia and force its readers to perceive my work the way it stands alone, I am well ready to pay the price of assuming the status of a living dead."[21] In this move, Žižek both assumes and rejects the position of an authoritative intellectual, enjoying its universal and general status while denying its elitism and exclusivity.

Beyond *New Theories of Discourse: Laclau, Mouffe, and Žižek* and *The Žižek Reader*, the global reception of Žižek in the late 1990s related to the active role of publics and audiences, particularly the mediation of other intellectuals who positioned Žižek in certain intellectual and political positions. As an intellectual audience, these mediators—editors and publishers, interviewers, and critics—facilitated the public image of Žižek. Hence, by the beginning of the twenty-first century Žižek was positioned as a global intellectual that resonates both with the theoretical deadlock of discourse (analysis) as critique, and the practical—political and public—deadlock of constructing a new, futuristic vision of society.

Acknowledging the active role of publics and audiences, Stuart Hall's reception theory discerns three positions that an audience can take: the "dominant-hegemonic," the "negotiated," and the "oppositional." The dominant positioning of Žižek was achieved by interventions such as *The Žižek Reader*, where there was little misunderstanding or miscommunication in the decoding of Žižek's messages. Hall explains that this position "will allow the transmission of ideas to be understood the best, despite certain frictions that may occur due to issues of class structure and power."[22] However, Žižek's reception is not only an either-or, yes-no question. For a long-lasting positioning, a diversified reception is better than a unified one. In Žižek's case, the dominant position received and deciphered his messages according to his terms, but there were also other positions that were "negotiated" and "oppositional."[23] These latter positions took some parts of Žižek's messages and deciphered them in a partial or unintended way, positioning him differentially in both the intraintellectual and the public arenas. Žižek's messages were then reproduced in various ways and to varying degrees.

The "negotiated" position typically arose with regard to Žižek's unidentifiable position. Given his superpositioning, the inability to identify a clear position on the one hand made it harder for the public to develop a readership reminiscent of the Romantic cult of genius, but on the other hand it allowed for a multiple and evolutionary progression of Žižek's arguments and performances.[24] A second feature that further developed the negotiated position of Žižek in the eyes of the public was the repetitive form of his interventions. For example, in his review of three of Žižek's 1997 interventions in the London Review of Books, Terry Eagleton found Žižek's superpositioning—always opting for both and none—as both an advantage and a disadvantage:

> Žižek himself is both dauntingly prolific and dazzlingly versatile, able to leap in a paragraph from Hegel to *Jurassic Park*, Kafka to the Ku Klux Klan; but just as Lacan's fantasy-ridden world of everyday reality conceals an immutable kernel of the Real, so Žižek's flamboyant parade of topics recycles, in book after book, to this very same subject. The almost comic versatility of his interests masks a compulsive repetition of the same. His books, as in Freud's notion of the uncanny, are both familiar and unfamiliar, breathtakingly innovative yet *déjà lu*, crammed with original insights yet perpetual recyclings of one another.[25]

Another review of Žižek's "sublime repetition" also evoked this *déjà lu* not only as a guiding trope but also a result of Žižek's work. Elam argued that "it would be fair to go so far as to say that the most repetitious moments in *The Sublime Object of Ideology* are also the best."[26] Yet she also pointed out a difficulty in enunciating the Žižekian position: "If Žižek's attempt to restrain the sublime to the level of the ideological finally fails, it is because the attempt itself comes to seem more ideologically motivated than sublime, a strange sentiment that itself testifies to an unthinkable breach between the two terms."[27] Like her, Gigante positioned Žižek in the Lacanian tradition, and specifically related Žižek's ambiguous position to what he sacrificially calls "critical self-creation":

> Like others, such as his mentor Jacques Lacan, he assumes a theoretical stance which sets out to transgress boundaries between philosophy, psychology, literature, politics, film, and popular culture. But where Žižek is

unique, and where he makes his radical break with other literary theorists who take up a position, any position at all that pretends to some notional content or critical truth, is in the fact that he fundamentally has no position. His recent outpouring of critical texts ... describes a hybridized critical identity that is almost impossible to pin down. Rather than importing interdisciplinary texts and events to his own theoretical perspective, he functions as a "vanishing mediator," mediating between various theoretical points of view.[28]

Identifying Žižek's superposition, a position composed of others, as "having no position" is an indication for the price that such positioning process entails. The negotiated position of Žižek is thus developed around his ambiguity, a reception also found in Edward O'Neill's "Last Analysis of Slavoj Žižek":

In the *absence* of any detectable method, a dizzying array of wildly entertaining and often quite maddening rhetorical strategies are deployed in order to beguile, browbeat, dumbfound, dazzle, confuse, mislead, overwhelm, and generally subdue the reader into acceptance. Example after example is supplied, but the principle that makes them examples is *not itself given*. . . . One concept is defined in terms of another, which is then defined in the same way, ad infinitum. What's being explained is *mixed* in with what's doing the explaining in a *circular* fashion so striking that it may well count as both a novelty and a technical innovation in the practice of interpretation. Concepts are "applied" *without any boundaries* on either the concepts or the scope of their application. Arguments and interpretations are *hastily summarized* rather than being patiently outlined. Finally, sheer rhetorical force substitutes for argument.[29]

Notwithstanding these issues with Žižek's work or rather style, O'Neill still positions Žižek within his team and networks through which his interventions are produced: "He has co-authored a volume with Judith Butler and Ernesto Laclau and has written forewords, introductions, afterwords and whatnot to three other books. He has edited or co-edited four more volumes, and he has another on the way. And, somewhat inexplicably, there is even *The Žižek Reader*—in case people find it hard to lay their hands on Žižek's work. Indeed, it seems that not only might readers be aware of Žižek, it would be quite hard not to be."[30] Like O'Neill, by reviewing Žižek's most cited works, *The Sublime Object of Ideology* and *Looking Awry*, Lechte maintains a negotiated position despite proclaiming "Žižek should be read."[31] Although Lechte acknowledges Žižek's effective use of Lacan's psychoanalytic theory, he critiques his position apropos of language: "Finally, the following question is indicative of a crucial line of inquiry that remains absent from Žižek claims about metalanguage. If indeed Lacan showed that metalanguage (objectifying) is both impossible and unavoidable... from what position can we truly know this?"[32]

Unlike the negotiated position, which reproduced parts of the Žižekian position, the oppositional position rejected the preferred reading and favored its own. In Žižek's context, it usually touched upon the position of theory in general and French theory particularly. Regarding the reception of theory in the United States, Shumway critically described a star system operative in the humanities with the same features of classic Hollywood.[33] In a recent article in the *Los Angeles Review of Books*, Liu and Bailey explain, "The signature feature of star systems is the dyadic star-fan relation that orients the operations of the broader institutional nexus, from staging publicity events and interviews, print and televised, to film production itself. The Hollywood star exceeded the frame of the cinematic image, projecting the possibility of intimacy with a continuous star personality."[34] This is described as a shift from institutional to personality-invested authority, where in the context of mass media and the growing influence of celebrity culture, "the dyadic logic of stardom entered the Ivory Tower itself."[35] Once conferences were televised and circulated digitally, they provided a new public stage for virtuosic performances of intellectual interventions, where, for example, Derrida's "deconstruction of action" became "personality is construction." Criticizing theory became a way of criticizing a theorist; this was how the oppositional position to Žižek developed.

Although this position is emphasized in the next chapter (and decade), by the start of the twenty-first century, Žižek had already identified the problematic role of (Lacanian) theory in relation to public and intellectual contexts. As he superpositioned Lacan in *Between Cultural Studies and Cognitivism*, he argued, "We are witnessing today the struggle for intellectual hegemony—for who will occupy the universal place of the 'public intellectual'—between the postmodern-deconstructionist cultural studies and the cognitivist popularizers of 'hard' sciences, that is, the proponents of the so-called 'Third Culture.'"[36] This struggle, which first caught the attention of the general public through the so-called de Man affair (in which opponents endeavored to prove the protofascist irrationalist tendencies of deconstruction), reached its peak in the Sokal affair.[37] In cultural studies, "theory" usually refers to literary or cinema criticism, mass culture, ideology, queer studies, and so forth. Žižek resonated with the (danger in the) growing use of scientific ("university") discourse to ideologically abolish the position of the subject and with it any critical positioning: "Although, of course, the regression into authoritarian prophetic discourse is one of the dangers that threatens cultural studies, its inherent temptation, one should nonetheless focus on how the cognitivist stance succeeds in unproblematically presenting the framework of the institutional academic university discourse as the very locus of intellectual freedom."[38] And it was not only the position of theory that was opposed, but also Žižek's specific use of it.

According to the American philosopher Noah Horwitz's oppositional—"contra the Slovenians"—position, "even if Žižek's understanding of Hegel were correct, (a seemingly Lacanian) Hegel and the Hegelianized Lacan Žižek articulates do not match up with Lacan's actual position. The attempt to make the Lacanian subject into the Hegelian self-consciousness is precisely symptomatic of the risk of foreclosing the specificity of the psychoanalytic intervention in thought and culture."[39] Distinguishing Lacan's and Hegel's positions, Horwitz claims that for Lacan the split of the subject is between consciousness and the unconscious, whereas for Hegel it is between universal and particular. By positing that the very link between Hegel and Lacan is untenable, Horwitz opposes Žižek's main superposition. He even cites Lacan's own words in his defense, and warns of the risk of making Lacan into the ultimate German idealist, Hegel. Thus he negates Žižek's reading of Hegel as a materialist and relies instead on the canonical positioning of Hegel as an idealist. Horwitz's opposition is brought to the fore the most when he claims that the unconscious in Hegel is not, as it is in Lacan, "structured like a language." This differentiation prevents, supposedly, the Žižekian move of superpositioning Hegel and Lacan, as he practically overlooks what these thinkers actually wrote and forces his own theory on them.

This form of opposition is more broadly linked to Žižek's positioning vis-à-vis theory and his relation to the long controversy between the German-Franco and the Anglo-Saxon intellectual traditions. While the Anglo-Saxon tradition is considered more pragmatic and less obscure, its epistemology is refracted in the performative style of its adherents. In 2001, Hanlon suggested an inevitable clash between Žižek and Chomsky: "The best counterpoint to suspicions such as Chomsky's may well be found in the work of Slavoj Žižek, whose frenetic endorsements of Lacanian theory achieve a dense complexity even as they provide moments of startling (and typically humorous) clarity."[40] Žižek's superposition of these two positions will be defended in a series of digital correspondence between them, explained later. Yet for Žižek's position to further solidify in the public, an interpretation that became a narration of present-day events positioned Žižek as a global public intellectual, one who is relevant to more publics than one and resonates with more concerns than one.

By the early 2000s, Žižek had been positioned through the dominant, negotiated, and oppositional positions, which facilitated his general movement of intervention. This diversified positioning gave him a robust standing in the intraintellectual as well as a gateway to the extraintellectual arena. Thus, by the time 9/11 occurred Žižek was well placed to provide a global rendering of the event while also being received by diverse groups.

The Meaning of Global Trauma: 9/11 and the War on Terror

More than any other event, the attack on New York City's World Trade Center on September 11, 2001, marks the dawn of the twenty-first century. It sparked a wave of legal, political, social, and economic consequences with global reach. Following this event, a global "war on terror" was launched by several Western countries, led by the United States. As such, this event also drew intellectual attention performed in various publications from leading global intellectuals, including Chomsky, Baudrillard, Virilio, and Žižek.[41] Taken as a global cultural trauma, 9/11 was also used by Žižek and others to position themselves intellectually-theoretically and politically-publicly.[42]

According to Alexander's cultural trauma theory, trauma is a social process carried out by carrier groups that attribute moral significance to violent and controversial events.[43] These groups provide a narrative for such events, touching upon the social group's identity and memory. The theory's focus is on the social conditions as well as the public performances that position some events, values, and collective agents with regard to a certain cultural trauma by charging it with symbolic meaning. Alexander explains, "The cultural construction of collective trauma is fueled by individual experiences of pain and suffering, but it is the threat to collective rather than individual identity that defines the suffering at stake."[44] Similarly, in his interventions on 9/11, Žižek performed as a speaker of a carrier group (of intellectuals) in front of the global public audience that was reacting to the painful event. Alexander adds that a successful construction of cultural trauma rests on the cultural dichotomous classifications (good-bad, saviors-destroyers) leading to the creation of a new master narrative: "In one sense, this is simply telling a new story. Yet this storytelling is, at the same time, a complex and multivalent symbolic process that is contingent, contested, and sometimes highly polarizing. For the wider audience to become persuaded that they, too, have *become* traumatized by an experience or an event, the carrier group needs to engage in successful meaning making work."[45] A successful intellectual intervention in the context of a cultural trauma must then deal with four aspects:

the pain resulting from the event, the victims that suffered it, the related audience, and the responsibility of the perpetrator.

Žižek performed his 9/11 intervention in a series of texts and appearances, first published for the American leftist, independent, and nonprofit online magazine *In These Times*, then in the respected journal *South Atlantic Quarterly*, and then as a five-essay book for Verso, entitled *Welcome to the Desert of the Real*.[46] In fact, here we can see the association between the growing online culture and this particular turning point in Žižek's trajectory, as an early version of this text was circulating somewhat informally from September 14, 2001, through email lists (Listservs), particularly *Nettime*. In the latter intervention, Žižek articulated his superposition regarding the traumatic event by referencing *The Matrix* (and his recent analysis of it). The title recalls Morpheus, the resistance leader, welcoming Neo the hero into the real reality—as the desert of the real—to which Neo awakened after realizing that reality is not real but symbolic (constructed by the Matrix). Then, in his style of the rhetorical question, Žižek used the repetitive "what if" device to ask, "Was it not something of a similar order that took place in New York on September 11?"[47] The answer, according to Žižek, stresses the importance of theory in catastrophic times, so as to understand how we provide meaning to such traumatic events. By enacting a subjective, inclusive tone, Žižek again invited readers to think reflectively about their own positions. He also related 9/11 to the context of digital globalization and its new political economy, by using both cutting-edge (*The Matrix*) and classic (Lacanian) references. Žižek created his position through a cultural narrative drawing from the metaphor of Hollywood cinema and drawing on a logical persuasion: "As we were introduced to the 'desert of the real,' the landscape and the shots we saw of the collapsing towers could only remind us of the most breathtaking scenes from innumerable Hollywood disaster movies. The unthinkable had been the object of fantasy. In a way, America got what it fantasized about, and this was the greatest surprise."[48] Against the common positions on the event, which are the "good: we deserve it" and the "bad: we didn't deserve it," Žižek articulates a superpositioning by introducing the unconscious as an unintended consequence of a certain ideology. By suggesting that Americans unknowingly wanted this trauma, Žižek made a claim for a provocative position, at once shocking and attractive. As he explained his meaning construction: "The towers symbolized, ultimately, the stark separation between the digitized First World and the Third World's desert of the real.' . . . Whenever we encounter such a purely evil Outside, we should gather the courage to remember the Hegelian lesson: In this evil Outside, we should recognize the distilled version of our own essence."[49] In this way of translating the event to Hegelacanese, the victim-perpetrator division is blurred, and the responsibility is shared. Linking past figures such as Hegel and Lacan with present current political and ethical affairs, Žižek was performing an intellectual intervention into the public arena. He then linked the present—analyzed in his counterideological manner—to the possible future of victims and perpetrators alike, creating a shared space for both: "We don't yet know what consequences in economy, ideology, politics and war this event will have, but one thing is sure: The United States, which, until now, perceived itself as an island exempted from this kind of violence, witnessing these kind of things only from the safe distance of a TV screen, is now directly involved. So the question is: Will Americans decide to further fortify their sphere, or risk stepping out of it?"[50] Traversing the fantasy of an island detached from the problems of the Other world, the trauma was exactly this realization of self-vulnerability, that Americans are as vulnerable as everybody else. Following this traumatic encounter with the Real (as the impossibility point of the symbolic fantasy):

> America has two choices. It can persist in or even amplify its deeply immoral attitude of "Why should this happen to us? Things like this don't happen here," leading to even more aggression toward the Outside—just like a paranoiac acting out. Or America can finally risk stepping through the fantasmatic screen separating it from the Outside world, accepting its arrival into the desert of the real—and thus make the long-overdue move from "A thing like this should not happen here" to "A thing like this should not happen anywhere!" For [George W.] Bush, as for all Americans today, "Love thy neighbor" means "Love the Muslims." Or it means nothing at all.[51]

By repeating this argument several times in different forms and mediums, Žižek made his performance last and his position the common reference point for intellectualizing the meaning of such a collective cultural global trauma. In his book version, Žižek framed this line of argumentation as the hidden truth of the situation using an iconic part of his repertoire, the missing-ink joke, according to which in America, or the West, "we 'feel free' because we lack the very language to articulate our unfreedom."[52] This canonical and political joke—whereby a worker from East Germany is sent to Siberia and reports back that the only thing missing there is red ink, as the means to write critically—is an intellectual pathway to understand how ideology controls and censors the means that critique it. This insight echoes Žižek's analysis of the Slovenian situation, where after the disintegration of communism, critique was fully immersed in the capitalist system (of economy, politics, and education) and thus disintegrated as well. Now applying this insight to the global, digital, and traumatized context, Žižek's book intervention, *Welcome to the Desert of the Real*, was published in Verso's 9/11 series, which declares: "Probing beneath the level of TV commentary, political and cultural orthodoxies, and 'rent-a-quote' punditry, Baudrillard, Virilio, and Žižek offer three highly original and readable accounts that serve as fascinating introductions to the direction of their respective projects, and as insightful critiques of the unfolding events. This series seeks to comprehend the philosophical meaning of September 11 and will leave untouched none of the prevailing views currently propagated."[53] The reviews of Žižek's intervention, which further the positioning process, touch upon its performative rhetorical elements. Sloan relates Žižek's style and stage by describing it as a "free-associative geopolitical tour" that includes "concerns about the *mauvaise foi* of the contemporary left and ruminates on revolutionary ethics, Balkan politics, the Israel-Palestine conflict and the potential of Europe as a counterweight to US imperialism."[54] Highlighting Žižek's positioning as global intellectual with a wide public relevance, Sloan also reproduces his position on 9/11 with relation to its popular reactions: "Some have commented that the US collective fantasy of invulnerability was shattered by the intrusion of reality on September 11. For Žižek, it is almost the reverse. Prior to September 11, Americans lived in a 'reality' in which terrorist attacks and Third World poverty existed as fictional film and TV news images (regardless of being experienced by real people elsewhere). The attacks brought these *fantasies*, not those realities, crashing into the collective 'reality'—hence the sense of déjà vu (which was only heightened by the repeated TV showings of the crumbling World Trade Center towers)."[55] By repeating Žižek's psychoanalytical interpretation of the event and the popular public reactions to it, Sloan plays as a mediator between his position and the public's, while resonating with the latter's common turn to psychology to explain traumas. He echoes Žižek's analysis according to which "the American experience of September 11 was made more complex by the fact that those who live in an artificially constructed virtual universe feel an urge to 'return to the Real' although it is traumatic—even if they cannot be said to *want* it, they are nevertheless *fascinated* by it."[56] In Žižek's interpretation of the trauma, the pain exceeds those who physically suffered from the attacks as symptoms and includes all who suffer from its present conditions, that is, global capitalism. Further, the victims are thus not only Americans, but all those who inhabit the virtual reality culture of the digital public space. Through this claim, Žižek relates the actual victims of the trauma to the wider audience of the global Western world, which had considered itself the wider victim of the "clash of civilizations."[57] Importantly, Žižek's interpretation of the event has broadened the notion of responsibility to include not only the direct perpetrators but also those who contributed to and participated in their shared fantasy (of a harmonious digital safe haven) and its popularization. Žižek pushes this broadened notion of responsibility to his analysis of the authentic act, as the practical way the reader as subject can assume that responsibility and act accordingly. This aspect of the act is where positional negotiation begins, because it involves a position on violence, with relation to the practical (and public) role of theory. As noted by Sloan: "If theory can be effective in relation to world history, it is in this sort of serious grappling with questions about our responsibility. The point is not necessarily to agree with Žižek—indeed, some would say he borders on encouraging extremist and irresponsible action—but to bring such debates, and a more profound understanding of ideological effects in general, into the forefront of our work."[58] Also, Glass's comprehensive review of the series of intellectual interventions regarding the meaning of 9/11, published for the journal *Historical Materialism*, indicates:

> Only Žižek, whose study, if far more lengthy and nuanced than the other two, maintains a certain cautiously optimistic investment in the possibility of "an authentic *ethical act*" in response to contemporary developments. Celebrating the Israeli reservists who refuse to serve in the Palestinian territories, Žižek offers the gesture of "refusal" as a model for ethical action, concluding that "our duty today is to keep track of such acts, of such ethical moments." Furthermore, Žižek goes so far as to suggest a larger political program, a sort of geopolitical act of refusal: "The Left should unashamedly appropriate the slogan of a unified Europe as a counterweight to Americanized globalism."[59]

Favoring (Melville's) "Bartleby politics" as an active ethical refusal that interrupts the normal repetitive routine, Žižek's superpositioning of thinking and acting suggests a form of taking responsibility that includes all those subjected to Americanized globalism, which is basically everyone.[60] In allowing resistant or critical individuals to imagine a shared front, Žižek performed an invitation to responsibility taking as a way of thinking and acting differently. So although "Žižek views the US as morally confused about such ambivalence and confusion after 9/11,"[61] he "doesn't so much deal with the reality of 9/11 but rather the conception of it." He says: "The only way to conceive of what happened on September 11 is to locate it in the context of the antagonisms

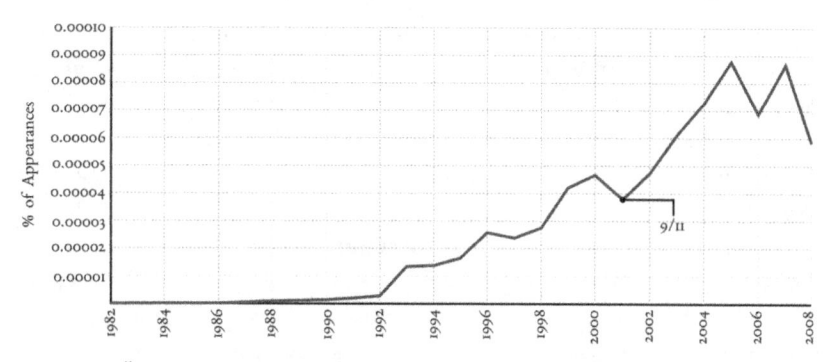

Figure 3.1: Žižek's mentions in English-language books, 1982–2008, indicating an increase after 9/11. Source: Google Ngram Viewer, August 19, 2018.

of global capitalism."[62] In identifying a conceptual culprit rather than a human one, Žižek traversed the divisive friend-enemy language used by President Bush and his opponents, as noted by Lecouras: "The President had the responsibility to explain any confusion in the minds of America's people by couching the event in stark moral terms. Baudrillard, Žižek, and Virilio are doing something quite different from the President; they point to the collective responsibility of this country in this terrible event."[63] The collective responsibility is derived from the collective (and yet effectively subjective) "passion for the Real," which "leads to its opposite—the theatrical spectacle."[64]

This line of interpretation that links virtual reality and digital media with the traumatic event of 9/11 apparently resonated with many because it was both unexpected and productive. Google Ngram provides one way of tracing the effects of Žižek's interventions and his diverse reception. As the data from Google Ngram shows (fig. 3.1), between 1989 and 2001 Žižek gained a recognized position with noticeable presence in the English-language books corpus. However, after 2001 there is a noticeable surge in Žižek's presence. I argue that Žižek's interpretation of the global trauma of 9/11 resonated with the general public in the search for the meaning of this event, leading to an intensified intellectual and public engagement with Žižek.

With the growing public interest in the internet, the latter was a recognizable point of reference for relating everyday individuals to the collective trauma. Glass notes Žižek's style of provocation: "One of Žižek's many rhetorical questions asks, 'are not international terrorist organizations the obscene double of the big multinational organizations?'"[65] Žižek linked the popular and practical support in big corporations with its unintended (and hence Real) consequence in the form of destructive terrorist groups, thus revealing the complicity of ordinary consumers in producing their worst nightmares. It seems that without Žižek's interventions the concept of the Real would have remained publicly unknown, as Žižek "almost single-handedly popularized [it] for his English-speaking audiences [and] provided the theoretical arsenal with which scholars of cultural studies engage the contemporary world."[66]

Yet not everybody liked Žižek's use of trauma as part of his theoretical arsenal. For instance, a senior Cambridge philosopher, when asked about Žižek, provided another use or rather misuse of intellectual responsibility: "Žižek is totally irresponsible, he has gained an enormous following, especially among young children, and he is irresponsible with his influence, with all his preoccupation with subversion and trauma."[67] More specifically, in his review of intellectual interventions regarding 9/11, Wolin follows the canonical mapping of the intellectual field, noting the division between the constructive (positive) Habermas and the deconstructive (negative) Derrida. Wolin also positions Derrida as a follower of Heidegger in his critique of Western reason. Then, reacting to the twentieth-century context he claims, "As a result [of professional specialization], the realm of public philosophy has been abandoned to the so-called left Heideggerians—the likes of Jean Baudrillard, Slavoj Žižek, and Paul Virilio—who have succeeded in filling the vacuum with a vengeance."[68] In his critique of this negative, destructive (given its Nazi connotative) reading of 9/11, Wolin turns the subjective tone and engaged rhetoric into a source of aversion toward the West: "What makes the interventions by the so-called left Heideggerians so odious is that their rhetoric rarely rises above the level of *Schadenfreude*. . . . In keeping with this perspective [of seeing the US as a technological Moloch], the pamphlets of Žižek and Baudrillard exude a barely concealed glee about Osama bin Laden's 'divine surprise' in September 2001."[69] Nonetheless, Žižek's intellectualization of the 9/11 trauma via cultural means positioned him as a global *public* intellectual, relevant in the making of meaning for readers across the globalized world. Tellingly, it even provoked some to revisit the concept of cultural trauma along Žižekian lines: "In our own current era in which millions of people are economically poor while most of the affluences and prosperities are concentrated in the hands of the few, shifting Alexander's original definition of cultural trauma leads me to coin the term 'capitalist trauma' which can be juxtaposed with Fanon's violence and Žižek's 'systemic violence.'"[70] Such connections and juxtapositions facilitated Žižek's popularization as a source for an intellectual (superpositioned) understanding of global politics and subjectivity, as well as popular culture and philosophy.

Popularizing Žižek: The Media-Academia Trade-off

After 2002, interest in Žižek grew considerably in the global public arena. With an established intellectual, albeit complicated, position, Žižek utilized his Hegelacanese in both the form and the content of his interventions. These forms include books—by him, on him, and in collaboration with him—newspaper articles, cultural pieces, filmed interviews, and movies. The effects of such interventions were the popularization of Žižek, which led to his establishment in the extraintellectual arena as well as a growing critical reaction from academia.

Prior to 2001 there were only two books about Žižek (by the same publisher); since then, there is an average of two books per year, with more than ten publishers involved. These books about Žižek have positioned him along intellectual and political lines. Intellectually, this positioning is both in terms of his own positions—for Lacan and Hegel, against Foucault and Habermas—as well as in terms of the disciplines he fits in, from cultural studies to literature, theology, media, and philosophy.[71] Politically, this means engaging with his political positions, theories, and programs.[72]

These texts concerned with Žižek took on several forms, including interviews, introductions, and applications to various fields. Together they popularized Žižek as a global public intellectual relevant for many audiences and disciplines.[73] Significantly, Žižek was featured as one of the objects of study in the *Key Contemporary Thinkers* series for Polity Press in 2003, alongside notable intellectuals, from Wittgenstein to Keynes. The back cover of the book described the reception of Žižek: "hailed as the most significant interdisciplinary thinker of modern times." In the preface to her 2003 book, *Žižek: A Critical Introduction*, Sarah Kay anticipates the "field-in-waiting" of Žižek studies. She also notes, apropos of his style, that "Žižek's writing is a distinctively hectic *omnium gatherum*, but this makes it difficult for readers to pursue particular themes."[74] She organizes the book as a form of thematization of Žižek's work, creating a sort of Žižekian canon of thought. Providing the reader with a glossary of Žižekian terms also codifies his language of Hegelacanese, rendering it legible for comprehension and dissemination. After surveying the themes of culture, philosophy, psychoanalysis, and ethics, Kay explains his politics with an emphasis on the notion of responsibility that he had been developing since 9/11. She later quotes from an interview he gave soon after the event, emphasizing the present-future link of his intellectual intervention into the public arena: "We face a challenge to rethink our coordinates and I hope that this will be a good result of this tragic event. That we will not just use it to do more of the same but to think about what is really changing in our world."[75] Kay continues: "His recent works may not be a form of symbolic *activity* that would make the world a better place. But if they expose us to the real, provoking us to rethink our entire situation, then they are a form of political *act*."[76] Polity published another introductory book on Žižek only one year after being featured as a key contemporary thinker, this time in its *Conversations* series. *Conversations with Žižek* is a compilation of five interviews which form a "behind the scenes" perspective on Žižek, signaling his position as an intellectual worth knowing. This book exposed a private, informal side of Žižek, facilitating a closer identification with his work, motivations, and desires.

As narrator of the present with interventional commentaries of current political affairs, theoretical issues, cultural artifacts, and scientific innovations, Žižek bridged the intellectual and the public in his first publication for the *Guardian* appeared on July 23, 2002, concerning the Leninist legacy of the left.[77] The intervention was a book review of a German biography of Lenin, which Žižek tied to the present global political deadlocks. This positioning as an expert of the East to the West granted him access to numerous public outlets. Beyond newspapers interventions which continued with his *London Review of Books* piece on biogenetics, he has been responsible for a globetrotting Lacanian intellectual school, as well as for a vibrant political Lacanian left.[78] Interventions such as *How to Read Lacan?* have positioned him as an authority on this novel perspective on the world and the human subject, as they resonate with the dominant psychological discourse and the global digital context. Interventions such as *Iraq: The Broken Kettle* resonated with the changing global political context. Collaborative performances—such as *The Neighbor*, coauthored with Eric Santner and Kenneth Reinhard, and *Hegel and the Infinite*, coauthored with Clayton Crockett and Creston Davis—positioned Žižek in the intersection of various academic disciplines and materialized his network connections worldwide.[79]

His own intellectual individualization was achieved through Žižek's self-identified magnum opus. To generate attraction, *The Parallax View* is described on its back cover as "Žižek's most substantial theoretical work to appear in many years."[80] Published under his *Short Circuit* series by MIT Press, and enjoying the public credibility of the latter's staging and framing, *The Parallax View* initiates Žižek's attempt to go beyond readings of Hegel and Lacan and highlight key concepts that package and contain his entire thought. "Parallax" is Žižek's term for his superpositioning, a creative process of repetition and modification of other positions.[81] Such reflective branding of his performative mode helps popularizing Žižek's shifting positioning and provides several publics with single point of reference to Žižek's whole intellectual corpus.

The reviews of the books were diverse and related Žižek to his several intellectual and political contexts, such as the "Hegelian Reformation" or Lacanian tradition. Mostly, though, they focused on the most popularizing element of Žižek, his style, transmitted even in his texts. In his review for *Political Theology*, Ted Smith doubted the very meaning of a magnum opus from an incessant writer.[82] For Fredric Jameson in the *London Review of Books*, "the parallax position is an anti-philosophical one, for it not only eludes philosophical systemization, but takes as its central thesis the latter's impossibility."[83] Terry Eagleton, in his review for the *Free Library*, claimed that "Žižek is that rare breed of writer—one who is both lucid and esoteric. If he is sometimes hard to understand, it is because of the intricacy of his ideas, not because of a self-preening style. In fact, his style briskly deflates the pompous self-importance of the superstar theorist."[84] Adrian Johnston, while reviewing for *Diacritics*, argued that the style employed by Žižek as a method of both analysis and writing is strongly shaped by Lacan and his theory: "Lacan's strange style, the difficulty of the ways in which he conveys his teachings in both spoken and written formats, is part of his pedagogical technique in the training of aspiring future psychoanalysts ... to engage in analysis even while learning about analysis."[85] While taking Lacan outside of the clinic and to the public, beyond its intended practical clinical framework, Žižek provided an attractive way for analysis to be performed in and through his interventions. Žižek thus extended the Hegelian and Lacanian pedagogical insight to the whole globe, the general global public, accessed digitally and textually.

Using his American connections, Žižek established his third English-language book series, *Short Circuits*, with MIT Press in 2003. This collaborative series positions itself and its editors in its series description using the rhetorical question and the metaphoric conceptual imagery: "A short circuit occurs when there is a wrong connection in the network—wrong, of course, from the standpoint of the smooth functioning of the network. Is therefore the shock of short circuiting not one of the best metaphors for a critical reading? ... The starting premise of this series is that Lacanian psychoanalysis is a privileged instrument of such an approach. This, then, is not a new series of books on psychoanalysis, but a series of 'connections of the Freudian field'—of short Lacanian interventions into art, philosophy, theology, and ideology."[86] The description highlights Žižek's signature style of superpositioning other texts, authors, and positions. It also positions itself as a series of Lacanian intellectual interventions reaching beyond the intraintellectual arena and into fields of great public concern, such as religion and culture.

124 CHAPTER THREE

Based on the high public value and recognition of MIT as a scientific authority, Žižek's first intervention in this series, *The Puppet and Dwarf: The Perverse Core of Christianity*, superpositioned the two most attractive social discourses: religion and psychology.[87] The back cover of the book recognizes Žižek's position as "an academic rock star," "the wild man of theory," and "one of our most daring intellectuals"; the praises identify him with Socrates, possible only after a ten-year psychoanalysis with Lacan. In the introduction, "The Puppet Called Theology," Žižek again uses classical past references, from Marx to Benjamin, to relate to present-day affairs such as modernity and religion. Before defining modernity as the social order that reduces religion to a particular cultural sphere, he reverses Benjamin's positioning of idea and matter, or idealism and materialism: "Today, when the historical materialist analysis is receding, practiced as it were under cover, rarely called by its proper name, while the theological dimension is given a new lease on life in the guise of the 'postsecular' Messianic turn of deconstruction, the time has come to reverse Walter Benjamin's first thesis on the philosophy of history: The puppet called 'theology' is to win all the time. It can easily be a match for anyone if it enlists the service of historical materialism, which today, as we know, is wizened and has to keep out of sight."[88] Through this unique, performative articulation, Žižek superpositions Marx and his antitheological position, arguing against a vulgar materialist position that diminishes the efficacy of the symbolic. Thus, in the particular context of increasing religious fundamentalism and the war on terror in Iraq and Afghanistan, Žižek confronts Christianity, both because of the (renewed) global public interest in religion and as a way to get out of the deadlock in belief and knowledge.

In parallel, Žižek expanded his work in new avenues and mediums. He entered pop culture proper through his intervention with American retailer Abercrombie & Fitch in 2003, which exposed him to a wider, younger public as a global public intellectual. This is how the website Critical-Theory describes this intervention, a decade afterward: "Slovenian critical theorist Slavoj Žižek isn't always spending his spare time marrying Argentine models or psychoanalyzing toilets. Back in the day, the philosopher also found time to write ads in Abercrombie & Fitch's 'Back to School' catalogue. At one point, Abercrombie & Fitch was trying to appeal to 14-year-old douchebags by publishing soft core porn under the auspices of product catalogues. At another point, Abercrombie & Fitch decided to try a permutation of softcore porn and Slavoj Žižek's rambling. The results are amazing."[89] Between 1997 and 2003 Abercrombie & Fitch printed *A&F Quarterly* as a cultural manifesto—"at once a magazine and a catalogue."[90] The 2003 "back to school" issue, featuring Žižek, opens with the correspondence between him and the former editor in chief Savas Abadsidis. In this exchange the editor positions Žižek as a philosopher with an "act" of superpositioning. As he wrote: "Dear Slavoj, ... we've never had a philosopher write the text for our images before, so write what you like. We're looking for that 'Karl Marx meets Groucho Marx' thing you do so well!"[91] To which Žižek replied: "Dear Savas, Friend! This is all I was able to do in these crazy circumstances! Feel free to use ... or not use, and you can also use just parts of my comments!"[92]

Žižek's response highlights his spontaneous and definitive character, unlike common philosophers or academics who are so restricted—legally and emotionally—with their writings. Page 4 of the issue describes Žižek in the following way, after already hinting at his superpositioning as Marx meets Marx:[93] "Slavoj Žižek is a man who will tell you something about anything. A Slovenian national, all heavy eastern European accent and nervous energy, he'll expound on Lacanian-Marxist theory or get caught up with why he thinks Linda Fiorentino is so sexy. Sometimes both at the same time. He's widely considered the most important philosopher working today, but here at A&F we like to think of him as our own academic-at-large. So what better time to consult him than at Back to School?!"[94] Although the beginning of the text might remind us of the authoritative intellectual who speaks about everything, the rest of it immediately denounces this position, emphasizing Žižek's origin, physique, demeanor, scope, and essentially, his eccentricity. Considered an academic-at-large, this issue popularized Žižek in exposing his name and thought to a younger, nonacademic public. However, writing on the rise and fall of the catalog, Riley-Adams recalls, "After six years, the magazine was put down due to a combination of overzealous sexuality, offensiveness, and high costs."[95] She opens her analysis with Žižek's own words from that issue: "'Sometimes in the news you don't even know what is publicity and what is news ... What do I see? A truly modern synthesis. Shit, why not have a cake and eat it too? You can have critical theory and nudity and enjoy it!' Spun the right way, his optimistic perspective sounds like every content marketer's dream—you can have your journalism and your marketing working together. But the statement is also indicative of the pages in which it's printed."[96] This kind of superpositioning, namely of journalism and marketing, allows Žižek's intervention in *A&F* to bring together his repertoire (of rhetorical questions, jokes, and examples) with key theoretical concepts such as object-cause of desire, act, and sex, presenting them as hot public topics served as invitations to (his) thought:

> The naked couple without a spectacled teacher would be reduced to two clumsy ignorant unable to perform the act.

> The object of desire is hidden behind the thigh but the true cause of desire is the tattooed cross on the arm. Is it not clear that we really make love with signs, not with bodies? This is why we have to go to school to learn sex.
>
> No way to escape sex—even in pure mathematics, it will haunt you: how much energy is released when two bodies hit each other? Or is it that pure mathematics is much sexier than sex?[97]

When Žižek was asked by the *Boston Globe* about this awkward choice of intervention, which effectively made him "an internationally renowned intellectual writing copy for a clothing catalogue," his response was: "You've got me there. I spent literally ten minutes on this assignment, just free-associating. I was in theoretical despair! If I were asked to choose between doing things like this to earn money and becoming fully employed as an American academic, kissing ass to get a tenured post, I would with pleasure choose writing for such journals!"[98] Elsewhere he remarked: "I didn't even know if I'd be paid, but I did it in five or ten minutes, gave some Lacanian comments and so on, and then he told me 'Okay, you get $10,000, is that okay?' And of course it was okay, because I didn't count on anything."[99] Such interventions might have positioned Žižek as a publicly relevant and timely intellectual, but they also positioned him as a sacrificial intellectual, looked down upon as clownish, more populist than popular.

Žižek's 2003 interventions were effective enough, though, to resonate with the public concern about the changing moral world. Particularly, his interventions had a feverish pace to them, mirroring the profound global shifts of the time. His preoccupation with films and cinema paved the way for his "aired" cinematic interventions, which started with public TV appearances and continued as YouTube clips. One noteworthy appearance was in 2004 on the American program *Nitebeat*, directed and hosted by Barry Nolan and aired on (NBC's) CN8 television channel, which was available to Americans living in the northeastern United States.[100] The purpose of the appearance was to discuss the recent publication of *The Puppet and Dwarf*. Here we see again that media are central not only because they "are purveyors of objective information to individual citizens poised to vote or debate but also because they provide a common cultural repertoire that makes deliberation possible (and even desirable) in the first place."[101] Nolan introduced and positioned Žižek (with noticeable hesitation about the pronunciation of his name, interpreting this as a sign for the difficulty of reading Žižek) as Lacanian: "Jacques Lacan was a French psychoanalyst. He makes Freud sound like a simple Valley Girl. Lacan's theory of how the self works is so complicated it makes my teeth hurt to think about it.... [Žižek's book] takes a look at modern Christianity from the viewpoint of Lacanian psychoanalysis. Or at least that's what I think it's about."[102] On his part, Žižek reacts to the uncertain pronunciation of his name and introduction of him in a way that performs on camera his sacrificial positioning: "I prefer it [my name] the wrong way. It makes me paranoiac to hear it the right way." In this self-distanciation from his proper name, Žižek denounces the self-valorization of the authoritative intellectual commemorated by the name. By not taking his name and self in the seriousness usually projected onto them from the public (in this case the host), Žižek disrupts the imaginary identification with his persona of an intellectual, thereby shattering the (public) illusion of himself as a subject supposed-to-know.

In the show, Žižek projected himself as one of the public, an accessible, approachable thinker whose experiences and observations can be shared globally without the elitist education of the authoritative or the specific expertise of the expert intellectual. Thus, when the host argued "This is the most complicated book I've ever tried to read," Žižek responds with a broad generalization of his book: "Strange, because the goal of the book is, on the contrary, to make Lacan back into someone whom even your grandma could understand." Then the viewer gets a shift, typical of Žižek, which dislocates the particular intervention and situates it in the context of his meta-argument of narrating the present and its global symptoms: "The thrust of the book is not so much Christianity, the basic idea is the following one: today there is a certain common agreement that certain things are going on: we need more tolerance, people no longer believe, ideology is over, too much consumption, lack of true authority. I try to undermine these things, not in the sense of defending authority, but in the sense of proving how it is the exact opposite which is going on."[103] In his Hegelacanese, Žižek superpositions the popular secular and religious positions by emphasizing the fundamentality of belief prior to its social institutionalization (by the market or the church).[104] He locates God in speech, as the necessary gap between speaker and listener, which means that from the moment we are in language we share a presupposed divine dimension and practice it. Žižek's superpositioning created and developed his position that attracts both religious and nonreligious audiences. This fascination with Žižek was further encouraged through provocative titles and use of the rhetorical question, such as implied in "Why Only an Atheist Can Believe."[105] Linking this theological question of God to the political question of community Žižek interprets the Christian notion of Holy Trinity as the social grip that brings people together as a community. This link allows Žižek to create his unique political theology, to intervene in the politics of neighbor trouble, and to shift its aim toward communism as the material base of collective belief (*in* the collective).[106]

In these interventions, Žižek's superpositioning is performed in his typical way later turned into a famous meme: "what if the opposite is true?" In the earlier mentioned interview with Nolan, he first asserts that among the public there are some repetitive complaints, such as lack of authority. The negation of that claim would be that there is no lack of authority. But Žižek is superpositioning these positions, showing that the lack of authority is itself a form of a more sinister authority. He exemplifies this position in a way that relates to contemporary familial experience. He differentiates the "good old-fashioned father" from the "tolerant postmodern father": on a Sunday afternoon upon visiting grandma, the old-fashioned father commands his child to go and behave; the tolerant father appeals to the child's feeling and says, "You know how much your grandmother loves you, but nonetheless you should only visit her if you really want to." Taking the side of the child, Žižek analyzes in this way the postideological form of authority: "This apparent free choice secretly contains a much stronger order: not only you have to visit grandma, but you have to like it!" As noted by Smith in his review of Žižek, this is how he superpositions common accounts of late modern life and constructs from them his own repertoire position: "Both biopolitics and narcissism have promised to offer comprehensive accounts of late modern life. But the two appear to be contradictory. How can there be too much discipline *and* too much narcissism? How can Michel Foucault and Christopher Lasch both be right? Žižek does not split the difference between these views, but arranges them as a parallax shift. They are, he writes, 'two sides of the same coin.'"[107] The *Nitebeat* interview in 2004 became Žižek's introduction to the broader popular American public. The interview's trajectory exemplifies Žižek's public exposure, from television to social media and film. It was uploaded on YouTube and circulated via the internet as well as being inserted as one scene of *Žižek!*, the documentary film. From 2004, Žižek's cinematic interventions expanded, popularizing him even more as a reaction to the digital global context of new social networks and media—to go viral, one must go digital, and that means going visual.[108] Appealing to common public intellectual discourses of biopolitics, narcissism, and cyberspace, while also going beyond them, Žižek generated more interest in his form of thought.[109] His long professional and personal infatuation with cinema opened up a path for Žižek to star in his own films.

After the German fringe documentary on Žižek from 1996, the next movies he performed in were *The Reality of the Virtual*, *Žižek!*, and *The Pervert's Guide to Cinema*.[110] Of these three, the latter was the most successful, showing Žižek's development in front of the camera, which moved from a "talking heads" performance (fig. 3.2) to a documentary and, finally, to an actual discussion of public issues, namely films. These movies created (by repetition) Žižek's canonical repertoire that would follow him for years to come. In them, the viewer sees his kitchen organization, his toilet-as-ideology analysis (fig. 3.3), his performance of Judith Butler asking (performatively) "What is a bottle?," the missing-ink joke routine, his (cult) relation to Lacan, the *Nitebeat* interview, the "What is philosophy?" question asked from his bed (fig. 3.4), the analysis of Coca-Cola as object-cause of desire, the meaning of Stalinism, and so on.

With an 88 percent approval rating on *Rotten Tomatoes*, *The Pervert's Guide to Cinema* (directed by Sophie Fiennes), which echoes Douglas Adams's popular *Hitchhiker's Guide to the Galaxy*, is perhaps Žižek's most successful cinematic intervention. The site's "critics consensus" proclaims that "Slovenian philosopher Slavoj Žižek forgoes the textbook stuff for a fun, probing look at cinema and the human emotional response to it."[111] This is reflected in the style of the film itself, whereby Žižek is inserted into famous films from the 1930s to the 2000s (ranging from Hitchcock to David Lynch), making him part of the films while he analyzes the cultural and political motifs in the real scenes of the movies via a repetitive use of his Hegelacanese.

In his review of the film for the *New York Times*, Holden recognizes Žižek's position of Hollywood as a dream factory, and Freud as the teacher of how to decipher them and find their real meaning. Holden claims that "after watching *The Pervert's Guide to Cinema*, you may never see these directors' movies the same way again. It is almost as if those filmmakers received instructions from Freud himself on how to visualize his ideas."[112] Žižek thus resonated with the digital context in which visualization is the most effective way to disseminate ideas, especially when the content of that visualized thought is pop culture. Also, recognizing Žižek's unique superpositioning, Holden notes: "Mr. Žižek is a little bit like the Wizard. If he is a compelling speaker (despite his thick Eastern European accent), he is also an academic magician and master of intellectual sleight of hand. Many of his statements, especially those rooted in contradiction and paradox, have the ring of brainy hocus-pocus. The teachers we remember most fondly are often the ones who entertained as they enlightened, through hyperbole seasoned with grains of salt. Mr. Žižek belongs in that company."[113] The subjective effect of Žižek's performance, namely the "brainy hocus-pocus," is a result of Žižek's constant oscillation be-

Figure 3.2: Žižek in *The Reality of the Virtual*, directed by Ben Wright (2004), 01:47.

Figure 3.3: Žižek in *The Pervert's Guide to Cinema*, directed by Sophie Fiennes (2006), embedded in *The Conversation* by Francis Ford Coppola (1974), 43:46.

Figure 3.4: Žižek in *Zizek!*, directed by Astra Taylor (2005), 31:57.

tween existing positions. Žižek's attraction is akin to that of the elusive magician combined with the charisma of the pop star and the accessibility of the teacher. The entertaining and enjoyable effect of Žižek's written and spoken performance is also captured in Bradshaw's review of *The Pervert's Guide* in the *Guardian*: "Unruly thinker and critic Slavoj Žižek gives us a highly entertaining and often brilliant tour of modern cinema."[114] In producing this enjoying effect of his engaged (and subjectivized) style, Žižek uses his movies to performatively denounce the intellectual (objectivized) posturing, thus rejecting his assumed subject supposed-to-know position. This act of intellectual individualization creates a distance between himself and some French intellectuals who had already participated in films about themselves. As Andrews claims, Žižek "speaks with concern about the tendency for documentaries on intellectuals to humanize them by showing routine foibles we all share. One cannot help but think of the recent *Derrida*, which showed the Father of Deconstruction unable to locate his car keys."[115] However, such an experimental cinematic performance, comes at a positioning cost, as indicated by Lee in reviewing the film for the *New York Times*: "Academic circles may debate whether Mr. Žižek is a legitimate philosopher or merely an especially learned and witty synthesizer. For the general audiences who flock to his lectures, it's enough to witness the ontology of difference explained vis-à-vis Woody Allen's 'Love and Death,' and to grapple with the notion of chocolate laxative as an 'almost Hegelian direct coincidence of the opposites.' You'll never look at 'The Sound of Music' (if not the reality of the virtual) the same way again."[116] Beyond this sacrifice of "legitimacy" of intellectual position (given the media-academia trade-off), the film positioned Žižek with the digital times, as more approachable and accessible for the general public. For example, in *Žižek!*, Žižek also shows how he writes, in a performance that relates to his particular form of writing, as if providing explanation to his incomparable rate of publishing: "I have a very complicated ritual about writing. It's psychologically impossible for me to sit down, so I have to trick myself. I elaborate a very simple strategy which at least with me it works: I put down ideas, but I put them down usually already in a relatively elaborate way.... Then, at a certain point, I tell myself 'everything is already there, now I just have to edit it.'"[117] By relating to himself in psychological terms, Žižek already signals his commonality with the popular turn to psychology to understand ourselves. He admits to his associative writing, and explains his way of making "writing disappear." This strategic position on writing behooves the internet era of endless repetitions, where a readership can develop with no reading being done.[118] As a result, this attitude deprives Žižek of his academic prestige, as he explains toward the end of the film, when asked by a student about his success especially in the United States—a place that he critiques so frequently:

> Let's be quite frank. At a certain superficial level I am relatively popular, but me and my friends, I don't think you can even imagine how non-influential we are within the academia. Why is there this necessity to portray me as somebody who can only thrive through jokes and so on? And even my publishers buy it; they always, at Verso, gave hints at me, "You're just making jokes," then I told them "Ok, now you will have a book, Lenin texts, which will not have [jokes]," their reproach was "Wait a minute, where are all the jokes, nobody would buy the book." I'm almost tempted to say that making me popular is a resistance against taking me seriously. And I think it's my duty for this reason to do a kind of a public suicide of myself as a popular comedian or whatever.[119]

The media-academia trade-off, as Žižek notes, made him popular at the cost of creating a ridiculous image of him. Assuming the "subjective destitution" of rejecting the authoritative intellectual position is termed by Žižek as a "public suicide," sacrificing his public image at the altar of Theory.[120] Lemieux also notes Žižek's own sacrificial position as a public intellectual in the media-academia trade-off: "[He] tries to remove himself from the public image that one gave him: Slavoj Žižek became a media character who lives through conferences and, now, cinema. In fact the media entertains Žižek's popularity, not its academic fame nor the depth of his thought. It is because one talks more of his celebrity than of his philosophy that Žižek has had this reputation."[121] Žižek's mediatic success as visibility and recognizability came at a price to his academic prestige; the popularity in the extraintellectual arena undermined his relevance in the intraintellectual arena. In the post-codex, digital era of the internet, with the growing importance of the visual over the written, Žižek's repetitive performance is the form that undermines his academic position as a serious scholar, yet it injects his thought into the public sphere with such efficacy to be circulated and exchanged as a cultural trope. Théron highlights the "unclassifiable" stylistic matter that makes Žižek's performance so appealing in the digital context: "His process of writing with copy-and-paste, back and forth, constant re-using of material already present in preceding works, books, interventions, altogether with a writing of the recovery. The sense of déjà vu, sometimes felt with the reading if this work in spiral is not due to the carelessness of the publisher, but to the movement of the writing which aims, each time, to reconfigure by the assemblage of its enunciation the situation of its own reception: retroactive performativity of the communication or of the Hegelian dialectic."[122] This is not to say that Žižek was completely removed from the intraintellectual arena entirely. Since the establishment in 2004 of the Birkbeck Institute for the Humanities (BIH) in London, Žižek has been its international director. The institute aims to stimulate interdisciplinary research and public debates. Focusing on promoting new ideas, BIH has a renowned two-week course, the London Critical Theory Summer School, which brings together many global intellectuals. Importantly, it also has a strong online presence with an updated podcast channel, offering many lectures to the global public.[123] In addition, since 2006, Žižek has been a professor at the European Graduate School (EGS). The EGS, founded in Switzerland in 1994, strives "to be a university that would function beyond the many constraints of traditional disciplinary structure while stimulating work leading to respected and well-recognized academic degrees. The EGS seeks to intervene in a global context where education is increasingly structured by instrumental ends that favor the development of technical expertise and frustrate fundamental questioning."[124] Being a somewhat experimental global university, the EGS shatters the common academic teaching-research divide, and promotes a teaching that is in itself an active form of research.[125] With a list of renowned intellectuals—such as Agamben, Butler, Negri—who are featured in an intense series of televised lectures, the EGS provides a public platform for intellectuals to disseminate their ideas to the public as well as attract potential students. From 2006, as a result of the inauguration of YouTube, EGS and BIH videos have been circulating endlessly on the internet, reaching over one hundred thousand views for philosophy

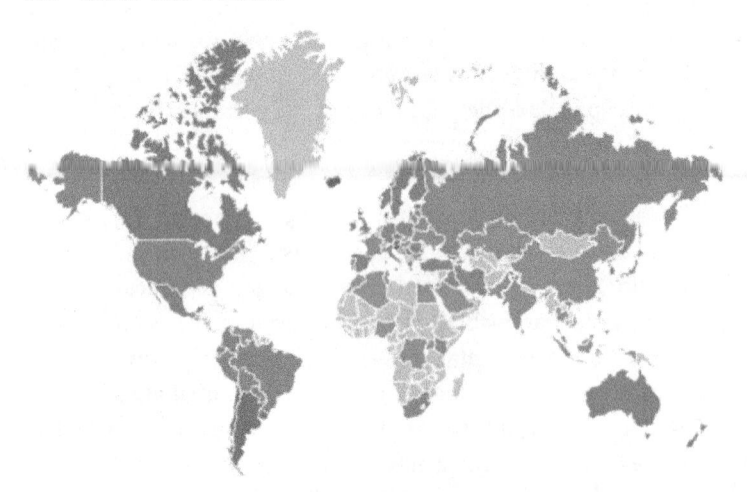

Figure 3.5: Digital interest in Žižek over region, 2004–2019. Source: Google Trends Search, January 3, 2019.

lessons (!), and expanding Žižek's exposure worldwide (fig. 3.5). Such oral performances are much more attractive in a context of visual and auditory rather than written, knowledge transmission. This is demonstrated by my survey, whereby a quarter (26 percent) of respondents admit they do not own any of Žižek's books, while more than two-thirds (69 percent) report they have watched "over 10" of his online videos. They create Žižek's readership not so much by reading his books but by watching his lectures, consuming his ideas through the digital page, namely the screen.

If such interventions solidified Žižek's position as a global public intellectual, the establishment of the *International Journal of Žižek Studies* (IJŽS), founded in 2007, solidified his intellectual position as an academic object of study. Reacting to Žižek's varied public image, recognized and undermined at once, the *IJŽS*'s description repositions him by asserting: "Despite such predictably caricatured media portrayals as 'the Elvis of cultural theory' and 'the Marx brother,' Žižek has attracted enormous international interest through his application of otherwise esoteric scholarship to contemporary mass culture and politics.... With a desire to avoid [. . .] mere hagiography, IJŽS's Editorial Board and the Journal will be devoted to engaging with the substantive and provocative implications Žižek's work has for a range of academic disciplines."[126] The journal positions Žižek not only as thinker but also as a source for the thought of others, peoples and disciplines. The journal made "Žižek" into a brand and a position in and of itself, though containing and composing (of) many others. It turned his defiance of easy categorization into an advantage and a vantage point through which Žižek can be hybridized further by other intellectuals in various academic fields in the intraintellectual arena. For example, in an interview with a journalist interested in packaging Žižek for mass consumption, Tony Brown of the journal's editorial board notes:

> Žižek is alive, which allows him to answer back. Derrida once claimed that people treated him as though he were dead before he actually died, since they were too ready to sum up the import of his work. Žižek always resists such encapsulations of his work and forces us to carry on thinking. He readily challenges people trying to sum him up. Hence his presence on the Board of the journal is unsettling rather than anything else - unsettling in a positive way. Anyone who tried to pin him down would be beating him up, intellectually speaking. Since Žižek is very alive he is able to kick back, interrupt encapsulations, celebrations, as well as criticisms.[127]

Through a variety of intellectual interventions from books to films, including a reader and a journal devoted to his thought, Žižek's unique Hegelacanese made it to the public's ear in the first decade of the twenty-first century. This performative language made itself transmittable and relevant for understanding political events as well as cultural artifacts, all in the continuous search for meaning in the meaningless postmodern digital revolution. Žižek resonated with common public concerns about the global situation, providing a master narrative as his argumentation for understanding the present. Also, he projected a notion of responsibility that includes readers as active participants in the same present. Žižek's movement of intervention from the intraintellectual to the extraintellectual arena, and from past-present (deadlock in democratic theory) to present-future (deadlock in critical practice), established his global position as public intellectual as a popular narrator of the (traumatic) present, notwithstanding his sacrifice as a professional academic. Hence, when the financial crisis hit in 2008, Žižek was primed to analyze (willingly or not) this global subject (as society and one of its issues).

The Present between Risk and Opportunity:
The Financial Crisis and the Arab Spring

In addition to the collective cultural trauma of 9/11, the financial crisis of 2008 and the Arab Spring of 2011 are so far considered as the global opening shots of the twenty-first century. Both have had lingering political effects such as the migration crisis, Obama and Trump, Grexit and Brexit, and consequently, lots of intellectual interventions.

The 2008 financial crisis hit at around the time of Žižek's *Violence*, in which he examined the mechanisms of the systemic, objective violence that people today are globally subjected to.[128] As a response to the crisis, he published two influential books, *First as Tragedy, Then as Farce* and *Living in the End Times*; he also published a series of newspaper articles, such as for the *London Review of Books* and the *Financial Times*, dealing with the meaning of the crisis.[129] From these contributions, Žižek also provided a text that was animated into a popular short clip for the series *RSA Animate*.[130] Through all those interventions, Žižek performed his ascription of meaning to the shocking events and positioned himself as the narrator of the (traumatic) present. In his rhetoric style, using his repertoire of questions, examples, and jokes, he maintained the consistency of his performative and repetitive act of intellectual and political interventions. In his interventions Žižek superpositions the public's common reactions to the event, attempting to construct a new third way. In the *London Review of Books* he argued for the primacy of thought in the era of activism and positioned himself beyond the dichotomous "to do or not to do" practical deadlock: "Faced with a disaster over which we have no real influence, people will often say, stupidly, 'Don't just talk, do something!' Perhaps, lately, we have been *doing* too much. Maybe it is time to step back, think and *say* the right thing. True, we often talk about doing something instead of actually doing it—but sometimes we do things in order to avoid talking and thinking about them. Like quickly throwing $700 billion at a problem instead of reflecting on how it came about."[131] By positioning thought as the true form of acting, Žižek narrates a possible future derived from his intervention: "What all this indicates is that the market is never neutral: its operations are always regulated by political decisions. The real dilemma is not 'state intervention or not?' but 'what kind of state intervention?' And this is true politics: the struggle to define the conditions that govern our lives."[132] Žižek's style reflects the public audience of these outlets he uses. Writing for the general public in a clear and direct form, he refrains from using of classical references. Although, to maintain his intellectual standing and to distance himself from journalists with no theory, he still utilizes metaphor with an intellectual undertone:

> 9/11 and the current financial meltdown, an instance of history repeating itself, the first time as tragedy, the second as comedy. President Bush's addresses to the American people after 9/11 and the financial meltdown sound like two versions of the same speech. Both times, he evoked the threat to the American way of life and the need for fast and decisive action. Both times, he called for the partial suspension of American values

(guarantees to individual freedom, market capitalism) to save those very values. Where does this similarity come from? . . . The financial meltdown has made it impossible to ignore the blatant irrationality of global capitalism.[133]

By linking 9/11 and the financial crisis and positing them as the global initiation of the twenty-first century, Žižek provides a narrative of the present that is derived from his intellectual and political positioning. He evokes a meta-argument that provides meaning to the rapid changes of global society. Yet he also maintains his rejection of the authoritative intellectual, by consistently shying away from being a thought engineer and provide ready-made solutions to preexisting problems. This is demonstrated in a 2009 interview with the *Financial Times*:

> Does the crisis herald revolution? "No, no, no. I am an extremely modest Marxist," he replies, rather disappointingly. "I am not a catastrophic person. I am not saying that revolution is round the corner. I am fully aware that any old-style communist solution is out." However, he insists, the financial crisis has killed off the liberal utopianism that flourished after the collapse of the Soviet Union in 1991 and all the grand talk about the "end of history." The terrorist attacks of September 2001 and the financial meltdown have exploded the myth that the market economy and liberal democracy have all the answers to all the questions.[134]

Žižek's meta-argument links his own experiences and analyses of the Soviet disintegration to the present predicament of the financial crisis, as part of his opposition Francis Fukuyama's claim of the end of history. His performances on public TV channels such as BBC's *HARDtalk* in November 2008, and the Dutch *Tegenlicht* in March 2010, have popularized Žižek's narration of the present and exposed his controversial thought publicly and digitally.[135] In an exceptional way, facilitated by his frequent visits to London, Žižek made himself available for studios that invited him not only for a brief news analysis, but also to feature as the main guest in an hour-long popular shows, where he reiterated his written interventions.

By using this classical Marxist trope as a launch pad to his analysis, in *First as Tragedy, Then as Farce*, Žižek employs his superpositioning on the financial crisis by first rejecting both sides of a popular dichotomy: either financial speculation (as the hazard) or real economy (as the remedy). Pointing out their mutual complicity, he claims that we cannot have the one without the other: "The paradox of capitalism is that you cannot throw out the dirty water of financial speculation while keeping the healthy baby of real economy."[136] This is also done by positioning himself in opposition to other prominent intellectuals: "There should thus be no surprise that the financial meltdown of 2008 also propelled Jacques-Alain Miller to intervene in such a "constructive" way, to prevent panic. . . . [']he message of his weird text is clear: let us wait patiently for the new 'subject supposed-to-know' to emerge. Miller's position here is one of pure liberal cynicism: we all know that the 'subject supposed-to-know' is a transferential illusion—but we know this 'in private'; as psychoanalysts. In public, we should promote the rise of the new 'subject supposed-to-know' in order to control panic reactions."[137] Arguing against such cynical wisdom and its defeatist liberal position, Žižek also provides the contours of the present by mapping existing positions and superpositioning them into creating his own: "We can thus construct a matrix consisting of four positions (or attitudes toward ideology): (1) liberal, (2) cynical fetishist, (3) fundamentalist fetishist; (4) ideologico-critical. Unsurprisingly, they form a Greimasian semiotic square in which the four positions are distributed along two axes: symptom versus fetish; identification versus distance."[138] Mapping is an efficient superpositioning technique, for it casts a net of positions, allowing many diverse readers to position themselves in it, if not transgressing it altogether as Žižek attempts to do in his interventions. After such mapping, Žižek's effective performance condenses the many (positions) into the one (question): "The only *true* question today is: do we endorse the predominant naturalization of capitalism, or does today's global capitalism contain antagonisms which are sufficiently strong to prevent its indefinite reproduction? There are four such antagonisms: the looming threat of an *ecological* catastrophe; the inappropriateness of the notion of *private property* in relation to so-called 'intellectual property'; the socio-ethical implications of *new techno-scientific developments* (especially in biogenetics); and, last but not least, the creation of *new forms of apartheid*, new Walls and slums."[139] That mapping of positions and antagonisms provided the public with a succinct way of capturing Žižek's own position and thought. It also related Žižek to the political, cultural, and scientific contexts of the globalized world. In addition to his textual interventions, Žižek joined the Occupy Wall Street protests in New York City on October 9, 2011. In the aftermath of the financial crisis, he used the (Zuccotti) park as stage and performed a global public intellectual intervention with an inciting speech in front of the crowd. The staging was classical: standing on an improvised podium, and surrounded by an engaged mass of protesters—and recorders—of the event. It was transcribed and circulated online first by the movement's own website and then as it was covered by the *Guardian*, the *Washington Post*, the *Observer*, and other outlets. In his speech, which included a Q&A session with the crowd, Žižek engaged in a pathos of struggle and positioned himself with the crowed, calling them all "winners." He repeated his joke of the missing-ink and pushed for a more active thinking about "the morning after" the protest, so not to end up with an ineffective "decaffeinated protest." Žižek also positioned the crowd along the communist lineage, though from an updated, novel reading of it: denying the common meaning of that "system which collapsed in 1990" and framing communism's significance around the care for the commons.[140]

As a performance, Žižek's interventions were effective in narrating the present between its risks and opportunities. One such exemplification of the effects of Žižek's narration of the present is the retroactive positioning of it by others. Transmitted in a cartoon form, Gelgud portrayed Žižek in 2018 as the one that had predicted the wave of populism following the 2008 financial crisis. His idea is that Žižek's *First as Tragedy, Then as Farce* "frames the first decade of the twenty-first century as having begun on September 11th, 2001 and ended with the financial meltdown," and "foresees the rise of white nationalism that many have been so surprised about" (fig. 3.6).

After participating in a few more cinematic interventions together with other popular intellectuals, such as Judith Butler and Antonio Negri, Žižek was in a prime—global public intellectual—position to narrate the Arab Spring event of 2011, which draw much intellectual and public attention.[141] As a popular movement that preceded and facilitated Occupy Wall Street, the Arab Spring was a global political event that also created some intellectual dividing lines. In a series of written and televised interventions, Žižek narrated the Arab Spring, siding with the protesters while relating it to his meta-argument in his particular performative style using his repetitive repertoire. In a piece published for the *Guardian* in the midst of the event, on February 10, 2011, Žižek opens his intellectual intervention with a positioning that links past references to the present event: "One cannot but note the 'miraculous' nature of the events in Egypt: something has happened that few predicted, violating the experts opinions, as if the uprising was not simply the result of social causes but the intervention of a mysterious agency that we can call, in a Platonic way, the eternal idea of freedom, justice and dignity."[142] By framing the event as an instantiation of a Platonic Idea, Žižek already invites an intellectualization. Yet by positioning himself against the side of experts and on the side of the general (Western) public gazing the eventful spectacle from a (geographical and conceptual) distance, Žižek insists on a universal position claiming that "The uprising was universal: it was immediately possible for all of us around the world to identify with it, to recognize what it was about, without any need for cultural analysis of the features of Egyptian society."[143]

140   CHAPTER THREE

Figure 3.6: Comic of Žižek and the 2008 financial crisis. Source: Nathan Gelgud, "Here's How Slavoj Žižek Predicted the Future Post-2008 Financial Crisis," 2018, https://www.instagram.com/gelgud/p/Bgo2n3bB88J/?hl=bg.

Such a reading of a global event with traumatic political consequences allowed one to transcend the Egyptian particularity and understand the event through one's own political experience. In appealing to the subjective feelings of protesters, precisely by adopting their singular position in society—going against their "normal" routine particularization—Žižek allows for this universal positioning to emerge.

While most intellectual reactions to the event, such as Filiu's or Alexan-

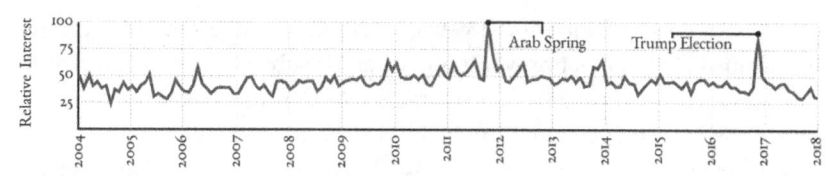

Figure 3.7: Digital interest in Žižek over time, 2004–2019, indicating increased searches during the Arab Spring and Trump election. Source: Google Trends Search, January 3, 2019.

der's analyses, focused on the particular aspects of the Arab Spring, Žižek extracted, packaged, and circulated a universal position.[144] In his analysis, Žižek performs a link between the meaning of the present and the future by tackling a practical deadlock: "It makes sense that so many people on the streets of Cairo claim that they now feel alive for the first time in their lives. Whatever happens next, what is crucial is that this sense of 'feeling alive' is not buried by cynical realpolitik."[145] The rejection of that cynical position is related to Žižek's old critical analysis of the postmodern cynical subject. Again, he positioned himself in opposition to the major popular opinion coming from a US president: "When President Obama welcomed the uprising as a legitimate expression of opinion that needs to be acknowledged by the government, the confusion was total: the crowds in Cairo and Alexandria did not want their demands to be acknowledged by the government, they denied the very legitimacy of the government."[146] Žižek denies both the anti–Arab Spring position, which was popular among the global right, and the pro–Arab Spring position, which welcomed the event insofar as it lacks revolutionary potential. By attempting to keep the revolution alive as the spirit of the people, Žižek is positioned with the public and against it simultaneously; with it—contra its political and intellectual rulers but against it—denouncing its habit to normalize (as repress) traumatic events. Žižek is, on the contrary, inviting the global reader to encounter the Real which resists and subsists beyond any symbolization. The effects of such invitation can be seen in his increased web-search interest (fig. 3.7). Similar to *First as Tragedy, Then as Farce*, Žižek's book intervention on the Arab Spring—*The Year of Dreaming Dangerously* is short and concise.[147] Contrary to his recent and longer *In Defense of Lost Causes* and *Living in the End Times* that are around five hundred pages long interventions into the ideologico-political global situation, the Arab Spring intervention was published in a small and short form, appealing to the general public in terms of reading requirements such as time and background.[148]

When writing on the Arab Spring Žižek's position is already recognized as communist and is read as such.[149] In accordance to his universal position, on the back cover of the short 135-page analysis of the event, after praises such as his being "a great provocateur," Žižek already narrates the present in a global form that links East and West, namely, the Arab Spring and the Occupy Wall Street movement: "Call it the year of dreaming dangerously: 2011 caught the world off guard with a series of shattering events. While protesters in New York, Cairo, London, and Athens took to the streets in pursuit of emancipation, obscure fantasies inspired the world's racist populists in places as far as Hungary and Arizona, achieving a horrific consummation in the actions of mass murderer Andres Breivik. . . . [T]he events of 2011 augur a new political reality."[150] In a more detailed form than his *Guardian* piece, Žižek's *Year of Dreaming Dangerously* begins with a reference to Marx's concept of domination and to Freud's dream-work, thus linking the problem of ethnicity as a thing in the context that is commonly called postideological. While other intellectuals such as Alexander and Filiu remained confined to a nonsubjective style of writing, Žižek's style takes the position of the protesters, while projecting future possibilities of the Arab Spring and the Occupy Wall Street. He did so through a common cultural reference of the TV series *The Wire*. Emphasized here is again the past (Marx)—present (the events, *The Wire*)—and ("signs from the") future movement of intellectual intervention. Such short, concise, and global performances positioned Žižek as an engaged global public intellectual. Consequently, he was invited to explain his position in the midst of the global political upheaval in several TV appearances. Thus, in 2008 Žižek appeared in a televised interview about his views on "the Iraq War, the Bush Presidency, the War on Terror & More" for *Democracy Now!*, a central leftist digital global news outlet.[151] In addition to continuous public interventions such as personal interviews about his tastes and political analyses of 9/11, Žižek also appeared in the Australian Broadcasting Corporation's program *Q&A*, in the episode entitled "A Very Dangerous Q&A."[152] This dialogical episode, in which the public asks questions answered by experts, was a part of the Festival of Dangerous Ideas (founded in Sydney in 2009), in which Žižek was the only academic panelist among four other journalists. In that episode Žižek responded in his remarkable—direct, vulgar, informal, common—performative way to questions about sexuality, psychopaths, economics, the Arab Spring, and WikiLeaks. When asked directly about his views on the happenings in the Middle East, Žižek responded with his common rhetorical tool kit of the culturally referenced joke (taken from François Truffaut's 1973 movie *Day for Night*); he positions the West as a man trying to sleep with a woman (the East) and, after a long time, when she agrees, the man is literally caught with his pants down, unable to perform.

Metaphorically, Žižek aims to debunk the Western liberal cynical hypocrisy by which Westerners support the (Middle) Eastern democratic, secular revolutions—insofar as they turn out to be Western themselves and nothing else or beyond. As he puts it, "Now that we got it [the desired object—an Eastern popular mobilization free from religious and totalitarian control], we are afraid!"[153] Žižek also links the social-political situation with the individual-sexual situation by emphasizing the dual (Christian and communist) concepts of love and revolution. He adds to his repertoire phrases such as "sex is masturbation with an object." In these types of provocation, Žižek performs a superpositioning between the critical and conservative positions: if the conservative position is for tradition and against (pure) love and revolution, and if the critical position is articulated as multiple partners and political reforms, then the critique becomes itself conservative. Thus, in the context of emerging (so-called) transgressive sexual and political forms, Žižek repeats and advocates the position of love being the real fear of today's subjects who repress that there is no love without the fall (in love), and no revolution without the fear (of loss). The attempt to go beyond calls for "continuity and stability" and to transgress the Eastern "passion for the West" (of becoming secular and liberal like the West), is tantamount to Žižek's attempt of creating a new global collective self.

Žižek's position on the Arab Spring was not only received in the desired, intended, dominant way. Being a communist, some critics found his narration of the event as part of his communist agenda, understood as repeating mistakes from the past and not reinventing a new future. For example, the Tunisian philosopher Mehdi Belhaj Kacem related Žižek's analysis of the event to the fact that the Stalinist and Maoist regimes have failed and should not be repeated, as even Marx, prior to the Leninist deviation, based communism on democracy. Rejecting communism and opting for democracy—as if the two were mutually exclusive—Kacem concluded that the "radical chic" was not only late to react to the event but was also clueless about it: "What I've read from Badiou and Žižek on the Tunisian revolution is absolutely useless. Tunisian philosophers have told me they regret that a Deleuze, a Foucault, a Derrida isn't still around. They would have found the right, resonant words to take the measure of the event."[154] As is clear from this remark, Žižek's intellectual positioning is an ongoing process based on his interventions, their performative form and rhetorical content and style, his relation to other intellectuals, and concepts in their specific context of articulation. This ongoing process would take an unexpected turn from general reception to widespread rejection.

Žižek's superpositioning along different contexts discussed in this chapter showcased how he performed the sacrificial position of the intellectual narrator. Specifically, by commentating on global events, interpreting them and ascribing novel meaning to them, Žižek linked the notion of trauma both to theory and practice. As such, in his apogee he performatively utilized his (a) Hegelacanese, enacted through various mediums and reaching numerous publics; (b) repetitive repertoire of rhetorical questions, jokes, and examples; (c) effect of enjoyment derived from the superpositional intervention; and (d) resonance with the public interest in subjectivity (sex and love), theology (God and belief), and violence (law and war). As they are performed in the extraintellectual public arena, Žižek's interventions have effects beyond the academy or any closed network of intellectuals. They penetrate the global public through his digital, printed, and oral performances, repeatedly undermining Žižek's (authoritative) intellectual position.

4 *The End of Žižek: Performing the Sacrificial Intellectual*

In the first decade of the twenty-first century, Žižek simultaneously expanded his reach to the global public arena while also opening himself to growing critique through the media-academic trade-off. As a consequence, his positioning became increasingly complex. Materialized in specific debates with various prominent intellectuals, and carried out in the digital public sphere, the critique against Žižek challenged his position as a philosopher, a leftist, and an intellectual. Soon near the publication of his second magnum opus, this critique came both from other academic intellectuals, who positioned Žižek as a jokester, a charlatan, and Eurocentric, and from public figures and activists, who positioned him as a rather conservative, privileged, and chauvinistic figure.

Žižek's various critics focused on his style, particularly his views on race, sex, and politics. However, as shown in this chapter, Žižek's reaction to this multiform critique, specifically by superpositioning philosophy and antiphilosophy, demonstrates the end of his intellectual interventions as both goal (as purpose) and terminus (as final development). He made the critique of the traditional philosophical style a philosophical practice, and on the way scarified his position as a philosopher. Recasting a digital light on the Socratic sacrifice for corrupting the youth, Žižek's continuous and lasting effect, namely his offering—as real consequences in the world in the form of social groups, concepts, and followers—is evidence to his successful sacrificial intellectual positioning.

Žižek outside the Academy: Jokes, Jokester, and Pedagogy

Concerning the question of style of the philosopher and the writer, Lambert asks, "Can we today any longer imagine a philosopher who doesn't entertain an essential relationship to the question of style? Can we imagine a philosopher who didn't write?"[1] His answer is that today's philosopher must reflect on the formal and material conditions of his or her philosophical project as a project of writing. The question of style and of writing more generally involves thus the question of power, the power to write and to resist through writing. As Derrida remarked in an interview, academic writing is one form by which institutional power and authority are excreted, when intellectuals are supposed, expected, or pressured to write in a certain acceptable way.[2] Therefore, intellectuals that protect "themselves against these questions [of power] and the transformations that these questions call for and suppose, they are also protecting the institution against philosophy."[3] This relation between the practice of writing and the theory of (doing) philosophy is all the more emphasized in the contemporary digital context, which erodes conventional notions about the value of philosophers, the role of universities, the production of knowledge, and, as shown, the position of the intellectual. Simply put, when an intellectual performs in the conventional manner, she or he is positioned as an academic intellectual rather than a public one.

Conventional in this (codex) context means, for example, teaching in a university and publishing a few books written with asubjective tone, lacking any jokes or common, popular examples. This performance limits the intellectual intervention mostly to the intraintellectual arena. It perpetuates and reproduces what Michel de Certeau called the "myth of education" and "the ideology of informing through books" that allow economic inequality to persist.[4] What we encounter today across the Western (capitalist) world is what Davis terms "the psychotic academy." As he puts it, "America seems only concerned with questions that already have answers and thus puts philosophy and thinking into the tame existence, safely labeling it a 'department' in a [corporative] university or college."[5] More broadly, his claim is that in today's neoliberal context, thinking becomes more and more dangerous and is therefore suppressed, paradoxically, even by the very agents supposed to support it. A precise political style of thinking, writing and acting, is at stake here.[6]

The conventional, "psychotic" style of thought actually restricts it to preexisting questions, thus reducing it to a problem-solving automaton. Davis contrasts this style with that of Žižek, which he calls the "180" pedagogy. According to him, "the point of this style of thinking is first to: (a) avoid freezing the act of thinking by releasing thought's desire to flow through its unfolding, but, and this is the second point: (b) without letting the process either dissolve into a nothingness or returning on itself and collapsing into a self-reifying monistic structure."[7] While opening the question of a work's unity to seemingly endless appropriations, what some cultural sociologists have termed "maximal" and "minimal" interpretations, Lambert reminds

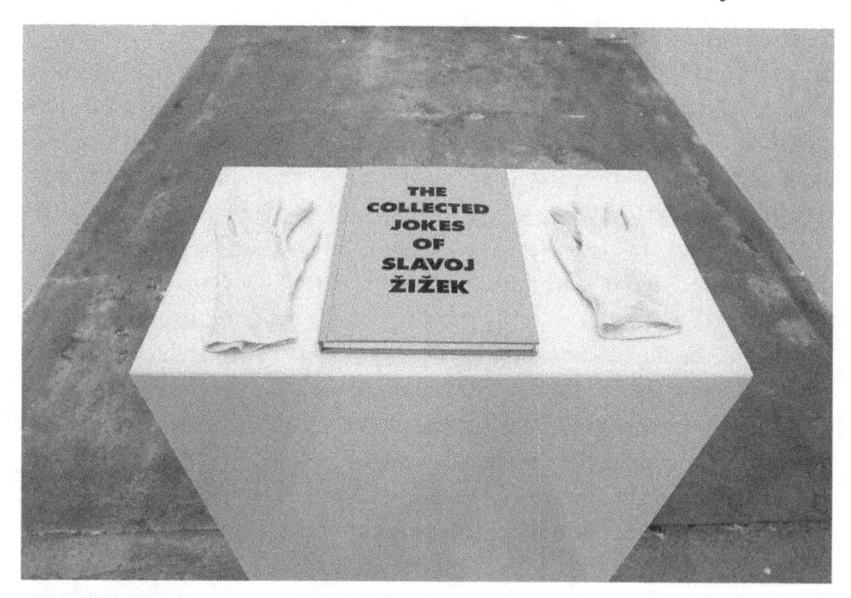

Figure 4.1: *The Collected Jokes of Slavoj Žižek* (2011), by the Norwegian artist and author Audun Mortensen, www.audunmortensen.com.

that any "'style' functions like a foreign language within language, and as a second-level order of signification, or new convention by which the work is determined, even if this determination is only 'contingently' fixed and can undergo further translation or repetition."[8] From this perspective, by being positioned by many (even contradictory) interpretations of his style of interventions, Žižek maintained a unique performative superpositioning, rendered in his Hegelacanese and his repetitive repertoire of the rhetorical questions, jokes, and examples. In this sense, "it seems that we have located the essence of [his] style in this event of appropriation of a singular and unique idiom, from the moment that this idiom is already handed over to the powers of repetition and imitation, revealing instead a discourse that is strangely divided from itself at its very origin."[9]

One such example for Žižek's use of repetition as a style of performing is Žižek's book of jokes. A joke is a rhetorical tool that achieves several goals: it emotionally incites the listener; it creates a consistent performance when repeated; it becomes an indicator of the performer; and it is an effective practical tool for "hitting" a theoretical point. Žižek's frequent use of jokes as an integral part of his rhetorical repertoire became so ubiquitous, that it was the subject of a single-copy coffee-table book by the Norwegian conceptualist Audun Mortensen (fig. 4.1).[10] There was another expanded version, which was published by Flamme Forlag in an edition of three hundred copies.[11]

In the *Guardian*'s review of this exceptional book, Irvine begins by admitting some confusion as for the (sacrificed) seriousness of such a unique intervention. Similar to the Abercrombie & Fitch catalog intervention, this does not shed an academic intellectual light on Žižek.[12] Yet it creates what could be referred to as collectibles, which as such increase the value of the performer. *The Essential Žižek*—a compilation of Žižek's four seminal books—and a special set edition of *Living in the End Times* in Chinese, English, and Slovenian (which was produced as a limited triple edition for Expo Shanghai 2010), are examples of such collectibles. This kind of public exposure also comes at the price of the media-academia trade-off, as demonstrated by Irvine's confusion and suspicion of the book of jokes: "There's certainly no shortage of incredible nonsense written about [Žižek] on the web. Remember the widely reported story of his romantic tryst with Lady Gaga?"[13] Tellingly, in 2014, a more official collection of *Žižek's Jokes*—containing 150 pages, no less—was published serially for MIT Press. It was classified under "philosophy." On the back cover a reference to Wittgenstein states that a serious philosophical work would be written consisting entirely of jokes. The introduction (at the end of the book) recalls that for Žižek, jokes are amusing stories that offer a shortcut to philosophical insight. Situating the joke as a philosophical device has ironically taken seriousness away from Žižek while presenting him as a more likable, identifiable, and enjoyable public intellectual.

Žižek's repetitive performance, in the form of second editions, also facilitated his positioning. Creating continuity between performances, second editions are also opportunities for crucial revisions that keep ideas fresh and updated. Verso's republication of *Enjoy Your Symptom!* in 2001, *The Plague of Fantasies* in 2008, and *The Sublime Object of Ideology* in 2009 are such examples. The collected essays of *Repeating Žižek* also performs such continuity, just as Blackwell's second edition of *The Žižek Reader*.[14] Other forms of Žižek's successful interventions received sequels as well. The 2012 movie *The Pervert's Guide to Ideology* succeeded *The Pervert's Guide to Cinema* from 2006. Continuing the same analysis of popular culture and particularly of cinema, the second film popularized Žižek's performance even more by embedding him in major feature films and relating them to general public affairs in an entertaining and relevant way (fig. 4.2).

In 2012 *Foreign Policy* listed Žižek on its list "Top 100 Global Thinkers," calling him "a celebrity philosopher," the same year he published a (second) magnum opus. A magnum opus centers a series of interventions around itself as a massive, effectively powerful intervention, akin to a sun for the planets. In this case, the magnitude of this one is signified first and foremost by its length. With a page count of 1,038, *Less Than Nothing: Hegel and the Shadow in*

Figure 4.2: Žižek in *The Pervert's Guide to Ideology*, directed by Sophie Fiennes (2012), embedded in *They Live* by John Carpenter (1988), 05:20.

Dialectical Materialism is both metaphorically and literally a heavy, lengthy performance, or rather an intellectual tour de force.[15] Indeed, it seems as if the book itself is the statement beyond the many statements in it. Resembling an "anti-book,"[16] it is an unusual performance that almost deliberately invites astonishment, not only by the unending writing but also by the fact that he was actually able to get it published. In a highly competitive literary market, threatened consistently by the digital press looming in the ever-growing background, the mere publication of such a lengthy and expensive book is bizarre. In the era of "too long; don't read," it would seem that such a venture would be financially risky. However, precisely because the market is so competitive and flooded with new texts each day, Žižek's intervention is unique. It stands out, signaling that at least someone, the publisher, found it worthy of being published. In times of converging commercial standardization, when most products are reduced to the same form—a 200-page book to be exact— the 1,038-page book creates the capitalist bargain effect: five for one. And this intervention also promises to have it all—theory and practice—from beginning to end of Žižek's thought. He thus combined in one superintervention the two strands of his performances: the philosophico-psychoanalytical and the sociopolitical. However, as today is not the great era of/for reading, it is not enough to just publish a very long book and expect an audience, even for a book by Žižek. Thus the publisher organized a book launch in the form of a twenty-four-hour public reading of the book that took place in London at Cafe OTO on June 15, 2012. This unconventional book launch mirrors the very structure of *Less Than Nothing*. The American philosopher Robert Pippin explains: "The structure of the book is unusual. It is based on the adage that the second and third most pleasurable things in the world are the drink before and the cigarette after. Hence we get 'the drink before,' the pre-Hegelian context needed to understand Hegel's option (a lot of attention is devoted to Plato's Parmenides, Christianity, the death of God, and Fichte); 'The Thing Itself' (twice! once with Hegel, once with Lacan); and 'the cigarette after' (Heidegger, Levinas, Badiou, and a concluding chapter on 'the ontology of quantum physics')."[17] In his introduction, Žižek relates the work to the classical reference of Newton's *Eppur Si Mouve* while also superpositioning his intervention: "The present book is thus neither *The Complete Idiot's Guide to Hegel*, nor is it yet another university textbook on Hegel (which would be for morons, of course); it is something like *The Imbecile's Guide to Hegel*—Hegel for those whose IQ is somewhere close to their bodily temperature (in Celsius), as the insult goes."[18] By distancing this intervention from its commonplace competitors—the textbook and popular science—Žižek creates a third, unique superposition for his book; Žižek brings the ivory tower to the masses while also pulling the masses up to heights of the most difficult of philosophers. Popularizing Hegel and Lacan also popularized Žižek—as their popularizer.

The sold-out book launch was framed as "a collective event of reading and performing philosophy, bringing into play the questions around language, subjectivity and experience explored in the book."[19] As was reported for *Prospect Magazine*, intellectuals, radicals, and others gathered for the Žižekian event. One of the attendees reported "that she's never read any of his books, but she did see him on a panel about Greece." As the reporter recalls:

> [Žižek is] introduced to whoops and hollers, and opens with a familiar refrain: "What do you expect?" I worry that Žižek suffers from a perennial and self-inflicted problem—that he appeals to a wide variety of people for very different reasons, and that none of them ever forgive him for refusing to speak only to them. Nonetheless, he opens his talk in an admirably Hegelian fashion by trying to marry the two apparent extremes that have opened up in his audience, between the abstract and concrete. He points to the microphone, which someone has wisely equipped with a pop filter. For Marx and Hegel, he explains, the microphone is not "concrete"; it, too, is an abstraction. It is endlessly mediated, by developments in technology, the mining of metals, popular music.[20]

In this report Christofi sums up many of the positioning tactics carried out by Žižek's performance: first, the rhetorical question at the beginning; then, the array of differential receptions of Žižek's performance; his superpositioning of opposing positions; and his routine exemplification using whatever is in front of him, in this case a microphone. The reporter continues emphasizing what is unique in Žižek's performance, including the jokes and style: "Onstage, Žižek is magnetic. Constantly returning to phrases like 'you know,' 'of course,' 'that famous story,' 'and so on,' he gives the listener the impression that he really believes you know as much as him. He also knows his audience, raising the roof with a reference to a recent Guardian article which recounted his son making an oral sex joke, and eliciting knowing titters with references to Jacques Lacan, who crops up in every talk he has ever made. Many of his pronouncements border on observational comedy. Try agreeing, he suggests, when someone says their parents are jerks."[21] Žižek's theory is woven in his practice, and this is almost more noteworthy than his actual work. This unique performance is based on superpositioning the level of referencing using both classical and cutting-edge references; the level of claiming using both general and specific claims; the level of tone, which is spoken both objectively and subjectively; the level of form, which is at once formal and informal; and last, the level of metaphor using both facts and fiction. After talking to some of the attendees, the reporter discerns: "This seems to be the way Žižek himself works for most people. His readers claim to have honorable intentions towards understanding his cultural theory, but really we're all waiting for that moment when he turns his attention on something we are already interested in. Leading figures on the political left meet with him regularly, with people like Alexis Tsipras of Greek party Syriza involving him in their discussions. Film students love *The Pervert's Guide to Cinema*. We all know he's a genius. We're just waiting for him to come into our frame."[22] The wide array of public issues in the present with which Žižek engages—through referring back to past events or figures and providing novel readings of the future—allows for many different publics to "take" from Žižek whatever attracts them, be it culture, politics, or philosophy. Also, his endorsement by public figures (like Yanis Varoufakis and Julian Assange) shares and propagates his renowned status as a global public intellectual. This unusual book launch of such an unusual book, signals the growth of Žižek's popularization as a sociological phenomenon. In an era when most (of what there is, intellectually and materially) is more of the same, Žižek was able to speak same-same (as he repeats himself) but different (from other intellectuals).

Less Than Nothing was also reviewed by the *Guardian*, which introduced this "mega-book" to the wider public.[23] Rée explains that Žižek "is a gifted speaker—tumultuous, emphatic, direct and paradoxical—and he writes as he speaks."[24] This imposition of writing and speaking diverts from the common distanced academic writing that is expected of intellectuals. This superpositioning made Žižek "the saint of total leftism: a quasi-divine being, than whom none more radical can ever be conceived. Of course he relies on a formula: to be Žižekian is to hold that Freudian psychoanalysis is essentially correct, and that its implications are absolutely revolutionary."[25] This relation between a firm (practical) political position and the (intellectual) theory of the unconscious is thus seen as a formula or receipt for the Žižekian performance throughout several decades. As my survey of his followers indicates, Žižek's "political position" (49 percent) and his "entertaining performance" (49%) are equally important. However, considered against the more traditional "purpose" of a book, Rée argues:

> *Less than Nothing* ... won't give much pleasure even to his fans. His talent for brief intellectual entertainments does not carry over into longer literary forms – let alone this "mega-book," as he calls it, which goes on considerably longer than *War and Peace*. He does not seem to realize that the purpose of a long book is to build steadily to a culminating revelation, rather than to go on and on until it stops, leaving the argument exactly where it was at the beginning. In the past I have found it hard to dislike Žižek, but after a month's forced march through *Less Than Nothing* it seems to be getting easier.[26]

While admitting the pleasure one gets in interacting with a Žižek intervention, Rée's concluding thought indicates the contradiction in popular performers. It is akin to a real art performance, perhaps of one's favorite musician on stage. There is no purpose to this performance other than the enjoyment it produces in that very moment. Hence the crowd's demand for encore, to have a bit more, and more, and more. Resonating with this desire for more, Žižek's 1,038-page book provides the long performance that, from the reader's perspective, is unending. But the distance between the fans and the critics is well known; not many critics think highly of popular performers and tend to look down on them and their mass culture. It is this tension that will drastically affect Žižek's positioning.

Too Good to Be True: Gray, Chomsky, and Dabashi Debate Žižek

In his review of *Less Than Nothing* for the *New York Times,* John Gray, professor at the London School of Economics and a regular contributor to the *Guardian,* criticizes Žižek for his offensive and obscene writing, including the "regular recourse to a laborious kind of clowning wordplay."[27] He positions this in line with the Sokal affair, when physicist Alan Sokal "submitted a spoof article to a journal of postmodern cultural studies. Equally, it is hard to read this and many similar passages in Žižek without suspecting that he is engaged—wittingly or otherwise—in a kind of auto-parody."[28] Again, this positioning of Žižek as jokester or jester is very much due to his performative superpositioning. Gray continues to "condemn Žižek as a philosopher of irrationalism whose praise of violence is more reminiscent of the far right than the radical left."[29] While most leftist positions are associated with peace, pacifism, and are generally against violence, Žižek's support of (a certain, symbolic) public violence, has made his leftist position problematic.[30] Thus, while he recognizes Žižek as one of the world's best-known public intellectuals, Gray also finds Žižek's position to be an effect of the capitalist context in which he performs (his critical gestures):

> The role of global public intellectual Žižek performs has emerged along with a media apparatus and a culture of celebrity that are integral to the current model of capitalist expansion. . . . In a stupendous feat of intellectual overproduction Žižek has created a fantasmatic critique of the present order, a critique that claims to repudiate practically everything that currently exists and in some sense actually does, but that at the same time reproduces the compulsive, purposeless dynamism that he perceives in the operations of capitalism. Achieving a deceptive substance by endlessly reiterating an essentially empty vision, Žižek's work—nicely illustrating the principles of paraconsistent logic—amounts in the end to less than nothing.[31]

Gray finds in Žižek's performance no real essence, though perhaps neglecting the notion that performance precedes essence. This search for essence amounts to positioning Žižek as a result of today's capitalist mode of production (and enjoyment) that can turn anything—including events, people, and feelings—into exchangeable commodities at a growing rate. On the one hand, Žižek can be seen as a brand that requires an emotional and financial investment of its followers: there are many books to buy, and even other merchandise and collectibles to show one's support. On the other hand, having mostly digitally circulated material, such as recorded lectures and talks, Žižek also requires very little investment. This allows his consumers to enjoy (the identity and experience of) having the knowledge, without really acquiring it. Gray also distances Žižek's imposturous position from that of Marx: "to criticize Žižek for neglecting these facts is to misunderstand his intent, for unlike Marx he does not aim to ground his theorizing in a reading of history that is based in facts."[32] Žižek's superposition of facts and fiction has intensified the media-academia trade-off by which he has sacrificed his position as a serious intellectual.[33] Žižek is thus a living reminder that media "provide not only the facts but also the formats, norms, and rhetorics that citizens employ to develop their opinions and enter wider public discussion."[34] Thus, in his examination of Žižek's reception apropos of Gray's critique, Paul Taylor argues: "If Gray's denunciation itself means anything, [it's a] demonstration of a cynical aspect of contemporary culture.... Thus, Gray knows that Žižek is explicit about the position from which he makes his subjective enunciations about the world, and that this provides the reader with the basis from which to gauge its value. But he proceeds as if he didn't know this and rhetorically caricatures Žižek's method as the generation of ideas from an arbitrary basis."[35] Taylor's analysis alludes to the current fetishist position of facts. In a context of "fake news" there is a concerted effort to strip performances of their very performativity, and to "report the evidence" in the natural scientific way. Mistaking the public intellectual and the scientist leads to an expectation of apathetic interventions, as objective as possible, without sentiments (or jokes). Taylor generalizes the problematic status of facts, and by extension their defenders, by linking it with the Žižek-Chomsky controversy that occurred in 2013. He explains: "the latest manifestation of knee-jerk emotionality directed at Žižek can be seen in his quarrel with Chomsky, predictably portrayed by the media in fighting terms—'The Slavoj Žižek vs. Noam Chomsky spat is worth a ringside seat' and 'Chomsky vs. Elvis in a Left-Wing Cage Fight.'"[36] Memes and videos proliferated and circulated in response to the event, stressing the same counter-positioning (fig. 4.3). "Chomsky" became the third most frequent search item related to Žižek according to Google Trends.[37]

It all started in December 2012, when Chomsky was interviewed by the Michigan-based political radio program *Veterans Unplugged*. When asked about Žižek, Lacan, and Derrida and their theories, he accused them, and especially the former, of using theory and jargon-ridden language as a form of posturing. Once published and circulated online by the *Leiter Reports*, "The world's most popular philosophy blog, since 2003," this dispute became a basis for intellectual positioning.[38] As later chronicled by *Open Culture*, the "best free cultural & educational media on the web," it quickly escalated to an indirect correspondence between the two famous intellectuals over the status of facts.[39] In that sense it became the current iteration of Chomsky's old debates with Lacan (in 1966) and Foucault (in 1971).[40]

In this debate over theory and facts there is on the one hand the Anglo-Saxon empiricist position focused on facts, and on the other the Continental Franco-German speculative position with its focus on theory. Žižek superpositioned them both into provocative yet catchy slogans such as: "Fuck the starving children in Africa, theory matters more; only this attitude will save

Figure 4.3: Visual rendition of the Žižek-Chomsky controversy, 2013. Source: Katerina Daugel-Dauge, https://www.flickr.com/photos/d_d_d_d/9646285783/in/photostream/.

the starving children in Africa." These shocking formulations argue against the common cultural-capitalist injunction to enjoy the suffering of others, materialized through "understanding them" and engaging in charity, thereby obfuscating the real causes of their suffering. Therefore, while relying more on theory (than on facts, always selected subjectively), Žižek increases his sacrificial intellectual position as he distances himself further from the acceptable and even civil academic performance based on facts.[41]

On Chomsky's part, he had already written *The Responsibility of Intellectuals* in a *New York Review of Books* intervention in 1967, where he argued that "Intellectuals are in a position to expose the lies of governments, to analyze actions according to their causes and motives and often hidden intentions."[42] His positioning of intellectuals, including himself, is that of whistleblowers, who use facts to discredit and debunk the common State ideology.[43] However, with his experiences in Yugoslavia, Žižek holds a contrarian position, arguing that today's ideology is precisely this idea of exposing a lie. Žižek's repetitive definition of ideology—"they do not know it, but they are doing it"— performatively superpositions Jesus' remark on the Cross, Marx's critique, and Freud's unconscious. Žižek also updates this motto to our postideological era, where the public belief is actually a gross cynical disbelief: today, "we know it, and we still do it" (acting as if we do not know it). So, for example, Žižek's superpositioning of fact and fiction is rendered palpable by the fictitious way we relate to the facts we know about climate change, repressing some of them and keeping others.[44] According to Žižek, exposing the lies by sheer facts is not enough since it does not take into account the act (and art) of stating (and selecting) the facts. This view proposes that it is not only some outliers who deny climate change explicitly, but rather we all deny it in our common everyday practices. Under this light, critiquing Žižek for not being factual is missing his point; for Žižek what should be addressed is the sociopolitical (and therefore unconscious for the individual) mechanism that selects some facts and represses others.[45] Thus, from the Žižekian superposition, what is neglected by those fetishizing facts is the libidinal or emotional way by which humans (precisely as speaking-beings) relate to the facts. Commenting on that position, Chomsky claims, "I'm not interested in theory . . . , I'm not interested in posturing. . . . Žižek is an extreme example of this."[46] In his article *Bewildered Clarifications*, Žižek published his response: "To avoid a misunderstanding, I am not advocating here the 'postmodern' idea that our theories are just stories we are telling each other, stories which cannot be grounded in facts; I am also not advocating a purely neutral unbiased view. My point is that the plurality of stories and biases is itself grounded in our real struggles. With regard to Chomsky, I claim that his bias sometimes leads him to selections of facts and conclusions which obfuscate the complex reality he is trying to analyze."[47] As Taylor notes regarding this passage, "This is the counterintuitive insight misinterpreted by critics like Gray and Chomsky as a clownish indifference to facts. Consequently, Žižek may be dismissed as a joker but this characterization ignores the very serious historical role court jesters played in delivering the bad news to those in power that nobody else dared utter."[48] The point is as revealing about contemporary society as it is of Žižek's performance: today's relegation of theory to a joke, a thing done by jokers, is part of society's (or rather the state ideology's) defense mechanism against those attempting to change it. Again, Žižek's public success comes at the price of his serious intellectual position. Taylor links this trade-off to "the notion that [Žižek] adopts positions in order to impress," arguing that "the reasons why Žižek has impressed such a relatively large audience are more likely to be found in the characteristics of contemporary culture than his own deliberate strategies."[49] More precisely, both Žižek's and Chomsky's interventions are performed against a certain political, public context, and it is that relation that shapes much of their perceived and received interpretation and positioning. Thus, "opposed to Žižek's self-reflexive commitment to revolution, Chomsky's political project is based on an ultimate belief in the persuasive power of facts."[50] But as notions such as post-truth, fake news, and alternative facts illustrate more vividly than ever, facts are not enough to change minds and actions, or "to overcome the ideological component of the context from which they are derived."[51] In this sense, Taylor shows how Chomsky is actually demonstrating Žižek's analysis of the fetishist disavowal, as he knows full well that facts alone will not change the media's bias, yet he acts as if they would. Chomsky represses the limitation of facts while Žižek returns (to) it.

Far from being a performative empty gesture, then, Taylor finds a complex mechanism of repression involved in the reception (or rather rejection) of Žižek's position on and positioning by theory: first, the objective rejection of a subjective position—glorifying objective facts; second, a general (media-sponsored) rejection of speculative thought; third, the subjective rejection of objective thought—that the media is actually ignoring fact-based analysis; fourth, the "return of the repressed such that Žižek is seen and enjoyed as an entertaining oddity;"[52] and last, the repression of the uncomfortable or "unscientific" fact about the (selection of) facts. Against the ideological positioning of true facts versus false ones, Žižek's superpositioning brings to light, and on stage, the unconscious beliefs that underline and root any knowledge. By including unconscious beliefs in his analyses, he creates the effect of an unscientific discourse, yet as such it is more attractive for the general public; not so much because of the content (which is reduced to stupidities), but because of the form, which is more inviting and exciting. Hence Taylor's finding is that the real empty posture is seeking to impress "by establishing the credentials of [Gray's and Chomsky's] purportedly higher-order, more scientific mode of thinking."[53] Žižek's interventions in and through popular culture reveal their double-edged nature: they made him a global public intellectual, yet they also stripped his seriousness away from him. The framing of digital and social media tends to reduce his complexity level to a minimum. Thus, Žižek's media performance, according to Taylor, "involves a balancing act between his desire to break through the media's standard thought-screening procedures . . . and having his message drowned in the media's ocean of trivial detail and ideological disavowal."[54] This complex performative positioning is captured in an interview Žižek gave for the *New Statesman* in 2013: "Žižek has previously said [in the *Guardian*] that while the concept of 'humanity' is fine by him, that '99 per cent of people are idiots.' I ask him if *The Pervert's Guide to Ideology* is in some way an attempt to communicate theory to 'idiots.'"[55] Žižek's response was: "Yeah, but who are the idiots? I didn't mean so-called poor, uneducated, ordinary people. If anything, most of the idiots that I know are academics. . . . I do feel some kind of stupid responsibility, as a public intellectual, and then I ask myself, sincerely, what can I do? It would be bluffing to claim that I can give answers. As I always repeat, what we philosophers can do is just correct the questions."[56] In such public performances we see how Žižek distances himself from the common academic position while maintaining the position of a public intellectual, on the side of the public. He shifts the image of an intellectual from the problem-solving engineer to the Socratic skeptic thinker, with a superpositioning that is demonstrated repeatedly in his Hegelacanese. Intellectually, Žižek superpositions the opposition between Chomsky (pro language) and Foucault (against language) when he is asked to choose between them and says: "Er, you know this classical answer 'Coffee or Tea? Yes please;' 'Foucault or Chomsky? No thanks.'"[57] It is not surprising, then, that Žižek's interventions, performed in his unique nonacademic language and repertoire, created a distinct space in the intellectual as well as in the public arena.

It is as if Žižek constantly constructs his positions by relating them (critically) to others. Sometimes this is done professionally, as with Habermas in *The Sublime Object of Ideology*, and sometimes it is more personal, as with Chomsky. The debate with the Columbia professor Hamid Dabashi falls into this latter category. While Chomsky related Žižek's position to Lacanian posturing, Dabashi criticized him for his European (or rather, Eurocentric) identity.[58] As we shall see, in articles such as "Fuck You Žižek!" Dabashi positions his own intervention by making a relation between the theoretical deadlock of the postcolonial condition in academia (specifically about understanding or appropriating Frantz Fanon) and the practical deadlock of race and Eurocentrism.[59]

The Dabashi-Žižek affair began with a 2012 *Al Jazeera* piece entitled "Žižek and the Role of the Philosopher."[60] It argued that philosophers who become public intellectuals are those whose thoughts are drawn by events such as May 1968, the Eichmann trial, or the Iranian Revolution. Zabala described Žižek's superpositioning, claiming that his interventions disrupt ideological structures and change the role of the philosopher, along the lines of Edward Said's, since he writes *as if* he were "unemployed, in exile, and at the margins of society."[61] Practically, although Žižek (and Said) could be considered the elite, theoretically, his thinking was from the position of the subaltern. Dabashi's counterintervention was his article "Can the Non-European Think?," published a few weeks after Zabala's. In it, he attacked Žižek as part of Eurocentric hegemony over practicing theory. This sparked a fierce debate among intellectuals about public legitimacy, including Walter Mignolo, who responded with his own "Yes, We Can: Non-European Thinkers and Philosophers."[62]

Mignolo positioned himself with relation to Žižek's repeated master narrative of the present but opted for another reading of the future: the narrative being today's capitalistic deadlocks of ecology as outer nature, biogenetics as inner nature, inappropriateness of intellectual property, and new social apartheids. But as he put it, "Communism is only one way to move toward [a desirable global future]."[63] By particularizing Žižek's universal communist position, which stands for an international global left, Mignolo argued: "In the non-European World, communism is part of the problem rather than the solution. Which doesn't mean that if you are not communist, in the non-European world, you are capitalist."[64] Disregarding Žižek's own problematic relation to communism from Slovenia, where he was positioned as a radical democrat against the communist regime, Dabashi included this whole correspondence in his 2015 book (eponymous to his article), which he opened with the following alleged claim: "'Fuck you, Walter Mignolo!' With those grandiloquent words and the gesture they must have occasioned and accompanied, the distinguished and renowned European philosopher Slavoj Žižek begins his response to a piece that Walter Mignolo wrote in conversation with my essay 'Can Non-Europeans Think?'"[65] Žižek explained his own position in the two-part article "A Reply to My Critics" and the introduction to his *Agitating the Future* for the *Philosophical Salon*, the online channel of the *Los Angeles Review of Books*. His responses were both personal and professional: "In a public talk in which I responded to Mignolo's attack on me, I did use the words 'fuck you,' but they did not refer to Mignolo: his name was not mentioned in conjunction with them; they were a general exclamation addressed (if at anyone) at my public. From here, it is just one step to elevating my exclamation into 'Slavoj Žižek's famous "Fuck you, Walter Mignolo."'"[66] Professionally, with relation to his position as a communist, and against Dabashi's and Mignolo's position that conflates communism and Eurocentrism, Žižek argues that "Mignolo relies here on an all too naïve distinction between problem and solution.... His goal—harmony, plenitude of life—is a true Abstract Universal if there ever was one."[67] Personally, because of his robust relation to concrete change, rather than to mere abstract (pseudo)solutions, Žižek's positioning is dynamically changing within and across the global intellectual and public arenas. This dynamism digitally spread his ideas by different relay points, as the public debaters Gray, Chomsky, and Dabashi. Each of them critiqued Žižek and denounced his position of a real intellectual. Instead, they saw him as a mere jokester or charlatan and positioned him as a Eurocentric and not a global thinker. Together with a fierce critique of his recent political interventions, Žižek even started to question himself as a philosopher, and along the way the role of philosophy.

Superpositioning Philosophy and Antiphilosophy

Disciplinarily, Žižek's position as a philosopher has never been comfortably secured. Although being active in the field of philosophy for years, his position oscillates between philosophy and antiphilosophy. This oscillation includes many middle-range positions, indicated by the varied classification of his many books as cultural studies, politics, critical theory, film, and religion, in addition to philosophy. That is also why some follow Žižek's work on film, education, media, law, literature, politics, and even (back to) clinical psychotherapy. Thus, besides his interventions in various fields, Žižek's way of performing philosophy while undermining the authoritative position of the master as the subject supposed-to-know (all the answers to all questions) created a superposition of at once being and not being a philosopher. That is, not performing the usual academic philosopher's show, but still addressing the "hard core" of philosophy. In this regard, Bakke is right to note that "Žižek's trick is in being X and not-X *and* recognizable as such. . . . So assiduous, so consistent, so concerted is Žižek in this—the 'all in onceness'—that only a fool would think he is just another continental philosopher."[68] This is why, as she points out, "one can pull him into a role (philosopher), but . . . he makes it impossible—to do this with any perduring sense of purity. The nonphilosopher, the man at play, is always also there."[69]

As a form of "strategic self-marginalization," the ambiguity and fluidity of his position, taken by some as a serious philosopher and by others as a charlatan and jokester, prompted Žižek to respond to this questioning through an intervention entitled "Am I a Philosopher?"[70] In this keynote lecture of the 2016 International Žižek Studies Conference, which was later published as a paper, Žižek addressed the (perhaps rhetorical) question regarding his self-positioning as a philosopher. After reviewing some of the critiques raised against him, he associated his public persona with his performance and intellectual position: "I find these critiques of my work problematic on more than one count, even if I dis-count the—to put it mildly—very problematic 'grounding' of my bodily tics (incidentally, the result of an organic disease for which I am taking medicines!) in my anxiety about being excluded from academic apparatuses and not recognized as a 'serious' philosopher. (Can one even imagine the Politically Correct outcry if another thinker—who is, say, a lesbian feminist—were to be 'analyzed' at such a level?)."[71] My survey of his followers also captured Žižek's ambivalent position, as less than a third of responders (32 percent) consider him "a philosopher" and even less "an academic" (6 percent). Indeed, almost half (49 percent) of responders consider his most significant social role "public intellectual." The questioning of Žižek's position as a philosopher was even posed by other reputable philosophers and friends such as Alain Badiou, who remarked that "Žižek is not exactly in the field of philosophy."[72] Nonetheless, Kenneth Reinhard argued that Badiou, together with the Slovenian troika of Žižek, Dolar, and Zupančič, are "perhaps *the*—contemporary philosopher[s] of our time."[73] This complex superpositioning largely results from Žižek's interventions in various contexts: he edited the *Analecta* book series in Slovenia, launched the *Wo Es War* series with Verso to facilitate Dolar's and Zupančič's English publications,[74] edited the *sic* series for Duke University Press, *Short Circuit* for MIT, *Insurrections* for Columbia University Press, and *Lacanian Explorations* for the Berlin-based August Verlag; second, he introduced and vouched for Badiou's significance for contemporary philosophy, thus initiating his translation process to English.[75] Therefore, albeit his problematic position as a philosopher, Žižek has been successful in intervening effectively in the field of philosophy.

Yet the public and academic positioning of philosophy itself suffers from extreme devaluations that affect Žižek's own positioning as a philosopher. All across the West, philosophy departments are caught between being kept barely alive on the margins of public relevance and being shut down altogether. Also among academics philosophy is devalued. Stephen Hawking's 2011 remark that "philosophy is dead" is exemplary of this antiphilosophical position.[76] Even among his public of followers, "philosophy" is the least attractive topic of Žižek's work. According to my survey, only a tenth (10 percent) of responders view philosophy as the most attractive topic of Žižek. The most attractive topics are "culture/art" (64 percent), followed by "politics" (62 percent), "critique of neoliberalism" (58 percent), "psychoanalysis" (54 percent), "communism/Marxism" (51 percent), "critique of postmodernism" (47 percent), and "religion" (28 percent). Therefore, as a philosopher, Žižek had to re-*act* differently and to enact a different philosophical position, taking into account the contextual poor connection and relation of intellectuals and publics to philosophy. In doing so, he superpositioned philosophy and antiphilosophy, accepting its current death while proposing its rebirth. To understand this fully, we have to take a short detour into the realm of antiphilosophy and elucidate its current relation to philosophy.

Reinhard notes that although antiphilosophy shares with sophistry and religion critical stances toward philosophy, its methods and ends are distinct. According to him, "anti-philosophy is not the antithesis of philosophy, but a transhistorical mode of thinking and doing that is both *critical* of one or more key philosophical concepts (such as truth or the good) and proposes a kind of *act* that it regards as in excess of philosophy's conceptual horizon."[77] In his repetitive performances, Žižek intervenes by superpositioning philosophy and antiphilosophy, theory and practice; his very act or show, with his characteristic use of language, is itself part of his critique of conventional, academic philosophy. For this move he pays the price of sacrificing his proper philosophical position as well as his position as a proper philosopher. Moreover, this (anti)philosophical sacrifice bears intellectual and political, theoretical and practical meanings. By attempting to psychoanalyze the whole globalized world, Žižek includes himself in the picture of the world and demonstrates his global views on it, views that we can all share locally. With his articulation of Hegelacanese, Žižek also superpositions the Hegelian lesson that a philosophical system cannot be totally separated from the method by which it is presented, and the Lacanian lesson that "the aim of psychoanalysis is not self-understanding, but for the subject to 'traverse' into a new position in the topology of the Other, the position of the object in its fundamental fantasy, in an act which involves the 'destitution' of the subject itself."[78]

Žižek's continuous positioning of/by Lacan "as a way out" of the theoretical-intellectual (academic) and practical-political (public) deadlocks is explained by its very purpose: "psychoanalysis is not just a theory, but a practice, something that *takes place*, and as such it seems to constitute an *event* in the truth procedures of love."[79] Thus, whereas most antiphilosophers would champion the local and contingent practices of meaning making against the philosopher's certainty and global knowledge, Žižek's psychoanalytic antiphilosophy aims at the singular act (called "pass") that traverses any particularity-universality or local-global dualisms. Hence, says Reinhard, "The philosopher who rejects the finitism and relativism of today's dominant ideology . . . will find guidance and inspiration in . . . anti-philosophy," a contextual position that is facilitated by the Žižekian project.[80] This is why some have positioned Žižek not as a master but as a ("wild") analyst.[81] This positioning again brings Žižek closer to a Socrates (of the digital age), who, according to Badiou, was "the first philosopher but also the first analyst."[82] While Socrates sacrificed himself physically for corrupting the youth, Žižek paid a metaphysical sacrifice for his position through the media-academia trade-off. The following 2015 letter to the editor of the Missouri newspaper the *Daily Events*, "Who Is Žižek and Why Is He Corrupting My Son?," shows this problematic:

The End of Žižek 163

Dear Igor,

My son came home for winter break with a new culture hero—Slavoj Žižek. Žižek had taken his university by storm, giving two sold-out lectures and sitting for an online interview that lasted hours. "He's a post-modern ironist," my son said. It was nice to hear him use words I didn't think he knew. It was great that he went to hear a philosopher—any philosopher—give a lecture. But then I read some of Zizik's [sic] essays and I was appalled. Zizik [sic] says that Islamic terrorists are not fundamentalists or even revolutionaries, but the casualties of global capitalism. That on 9/11 a paranoid America got what it had been fantasizing about for decades. That Mohammad Atta and his terrorist hijackers represented the "good as the spirit of and actual readiness to sacrifice in the name of a higher cause." That when prisoners were tortured in Guantanamo they were really being initiated into the true essence of American culture. And if Americans really believed in Democracy they would not vote themselves, but would let the rest of the world choose their leader. My son says I should lighten up. It's just a big joke—"postmodern, dad"—meant to make people question conventional assumptions. But then I read an article which calls Žižek "the most dangerous philosopher in the west." Is this paranoia or fact?

60's Liberal,
Shaker Heights, Ohio[83]

The letter reveals the audience which is most receptive to Žižek's interventions: the youth. This generational context has been influential for Žižek since his early support of the Slovenian punk movement, through the success of his 1989 book among graduates rather than professors, to the above example. Yet this transition from the intra- to the extraintellectual arena comes at the price of being lost in translation. Although quite adamantly against postmodernism, Žižek is still occasionally associated with this position because of his provocative performance and French-Lacanian basis, already considered dubious since the Sokal affair of 1996.[84] Prior to that, and more locally, the effects of Žižek's intellectual corruption can also be found in Zupančič's recollection as a second generation and youngest member of the troika:

I was very efficiently corrupted. If you're looking for the origins of this affliction of corrupting the youth, this is a true story, extremely funny: first I came across Žižek's Slovene book *History and the Unconscious*. And the book begins with the inscription "at the beginning there was . . ." and then on the next page it's written—"phallus." And I didn't know the word. I mean, the Latin word, I didn't know it. So I remember checking, looking up in the dictionary of foreign words, saying "oh! This is really interesting!" So I just kept on reading, [and] the more you read, the easier it gets. But there was something powerful in this sense. So yes, corruption was definitely there.[85]

Thus negating its common pejorative de-meaning, corruption is considered here in the positive meaning of introducing the limits of the existing social order. And that meaningful change affects both the public and academia. Since Lacan's death in 1980 there has been a fierce dispute among Lacanians over the relationship between clinical practice and theory. Badiou describes this debate as ultimately "the 'You're not a clinician,' on the one hand, and the 'You're giving way on the theory,' on the other."[86] Žižek's superpositioning of this duality echoes Badiou's rejection of any kind of confusion, since "this distinction [of theory and practice] undermines the whole [Lacanian] edifice."[87] Conversely, Badiou claims that "act and matheme cannot be grasped in a divided figure that would refer, in its turn, to the opposition between clinical practice and theory . . . , since at the heart of the act there is the desire for the matheme."[88]

Žižek's intellectual interventions are performed as a psychoanalytic analysis, except with the social rather than individual subject; instead of analyzing individuals, Žižek analyzes societies, first the Slovenian and then the global. He applies or directs the same psychoanalytic method, being attentive to the social subject's forms of (mishap) speech. He listens to global society's speech through its production of popular culture. Žižek turns to psychoanalysis to occupy the antiphilosophical position. Its core is the idea that truth is outside language, and thus cannot be represented or talked about. Yet Žižek also enacts the philosophical position via Hegel's dialectic, claiming that post-Kantian philosophy had already integrated the aforementioned antiphilosophical lesson.

Therefore, Žižek's superpositioning of philosophy and antiphilosophy is achieved by juxtaposing Hegel and Lacan, identifying their similar approach to the positioning of truth outside language. As this outside is immanently understood, speaking is necessary for analysis to take place and for the form of speech to emerge and change. In the clinic, this translates to having two individuals in a room, the analyst and the analysand (patient). Outside of the clinic, this translation is less clear. What does it mean to analyze the social subject? By focusing on popular culture, Žižek is not only performing a publicity stunt for public attraction; rather, he identifies the popularity of some cultural production, such as films, commercials, and novels, to be prime sites for speaking with the social subject.[89]

In that speech engagement—analyzing cultural production and writing about it both in academic journals and in public media—the social form of speech emerges through the normal psychoanalytic method of repetition, metaphor, and metonym. Moreover, just like in the clinic, the (dis)position of the analyst is crucial for the success of the interventional analytic treatment. But even if we consider cultural production as society's speech, what is the body on which its "signifying stress" is inscribed? Who is the social body that suffers the burden of the signifier? Here, Žižek uses his own "experience as a device" and performs—like a "method actor"—the analytic method with regard to the social body, in which he is included.[90] What he experiences is considered common enough for many to share and follow his analysis of it, becoming an analysis of "us." A closer look on the analytic treatment will make Žižek's superpositioning of the analyst's and analysand's positions clearer.

As mentioned earlier, the analyst should actively denounce the position of the subject supposed-to-know and let the analysand create his or her own knowledge by him- or herself. The analytic treatment that culminates in the act or pass, as the termination of analysis, is defined by Badiou as a "demonstration of the Subject's real."[91] Now, if Žižek has taken Lacan outside the clinic in his attempt to socioanalyze the whole world (as a subject), then his interventions are equivalent to demonstrations of the real of the world. This corresponds to Žižek's compulsive and repetitive writing based on a frequent use of cultural examples and everyday exemplifications. "Demonstration," as Badiou defines it, "means that the real is not what is shown or monstrated but what is de-monstrated, hence that it's the undoing of the showing. This also means, approximating formalism, that that to which a Subject's real, insofar as it is demonstrated, can be linked is writing."[92] Žižek's writing is unique not only quantitatively but also in its quality and style, its structure and affect. Its adaptability to the internet age is related to its formality and visuality. His writing is so repetitive that it actually—as some commentators have noted for better or worse—eliminates his subjective position and creates the illusion that there is no author, that his numerous and enormous books are written by a robotic generator repeating the same algorithm.

In this way Žižek performs writing that is as close as possible to formal writing, for it blurs the border between presentability and re-presentability. As Badiou explains, "Only writing as such de-monstrates without monstrating. This writing cannot be a symbolization, which is tantamount to saying that it escapes the question of knowledge . . . 'demonstration' means that, in the very space where the real will insist, there must be the impasse of a symbolization, but this symbolization must contain the constraint that creates the impasse."[93] Žižek's performance is a psychoanalytic de-monstration in which what is shown is not a symbolic content but the real (as an) impasse inherent to any such content (indeed, there are no "answers" in Žižek). His interventions do not yield the common academic product, that is, knowledge resulted from a linear argumentation. Rather, they practically and emotionally instruct our thought process to encounter, indeed experience, beyond any argument, its formal and social conditions of (im)possibility.

This performative strategy at once evokes and fails the common expectation by the public for the intellectual, nonsubjective intervention. In doing that, Žižek resonates with the current capitalistic mode of production, whereby newness must be supplied repetitively. Žižek does not have anything specific to show or say, but his continuous commentary becomes a process of narrativization of the present, and since the present is always changing, so does Žižek's writing on it. This is why Dolar has remarked that Žižek has been writing a single book throughout his lifetime; a book composed of hundreds of others, all part of a phenomenon that encompasses videos, ideas, books, politics, film, and so on, and marketed, reproduced, and repeated by many different agents, friends such as followers and foes such as critics.[94]

The Beginning of the End? The Effects of Žižek's Superpositioning

Žižek and his troika's home journal, *Problemi*, launched its international English version in 2017. It introduced the broader Ljubljana School to the global (and digital) public and created an extended readership around key editorial figures such as Žižek, Dolar, and Zupančič. In addition, Žižek's performance, and specifically his Hegelacanese, received its own intellectual space with the publication of *The Žižek Dictionary*.[95] With this intervention, Žižek's performative language was recognized as unique, worthy of a defining source for its various users, thus joining Žižek to a lineage of great thinkers' dictionaries: Kant, Hegel, Lacan, and more recently, Badiou.[96]

Žižek's dictionary is a collaborative project of sixty-four terms covered by sixty-two professors, students, and researchers from various places and disciplines. The dictionary was edited by Rex Butler and includes a contribution by Žižek. As the back cover indicates, "Žižek is undoubtedly the most popular and discussed philosopher in the world today. . . . *The Žižek Dictionary* brings together leading Žižek commentators from across the world to present a companion and guide to Žižekian thought." Butler also notes that as a "master-thinker," Žižek should not be measured against the conventional academic norms. Rather, the merit of his work lies in questioning these very standards and replacing them. Therefore, Butler finds that "it is this paradox that Žižek dramatizes in an extraordinary way in his work."[97] On the one hand, "Žižek himself is absolutely to be identified with his work, which he does not perform but strictly enunciates . . . yet, on the other hand, there is a certain radical disjunction between Žižek and his work."[98] Whereas with Žižek there is the notion of "what you see is what you get," and thus he should not be judged by external criteria, there is also the notion that what is seen is a big joke and should not be taken seriously at all. This performative ambiguity, akin to an actor denouncing his act on stage, unsettles and brings uneasiness to the ordinary performative framework. By performing a different kind of performance altogether, Žižek is actively superpositioning the authentic and the fake, yielding a dynamic mode of intervention that plays on and appeals to both sides.

In addition to the more intellectual (read: long and heavy) books that Žižek continued to publish, such as *Absolute Recoil*, *Disparities* and *Incontinence of the Void*, he also published more popular interventions through which his global position as public intellectual was reinforced.[99] Such popular(izing) interventions are both textual and oral: the textual include the *Introducing Žižek* graphic guide, which tells the story and theory of Žižek in a comics form, as well as a pocket-sized, short and accessible Penguin book *Event*, intended for mass consumption.[100] Orally we find his repetitive and frequent performances on various popular news and social media channels like *Vice* Magazine (with over three million views) or the BBC (with around one million views).[101] Such interventions expose him and his thought in a public, popular form, both visually and textually.

In recent years, as Žižek's position became established, controversy grew as a result, compelling him to publish replies and clarifications. In other words, once he became an intellectual emblem, other aspiring or rising intellectuals could position themselves with relation and in opposition to Žižek. One such incident occurred during the New York Left Forum Conference on May 22, 2016. During Žižek's closing plenary, an academic-activist named Taryn Fivek heckled him, stepped onto the stage, grabbed the microphone, and started reading a flyer that accused him of racism and sexism (fig. 4.4). The heckler, Dr. Taryn Fivek, used Žižek's own provocative quotes, presumably as testimonials for his wrongdoings. This public incident evolved into a debate between the heckler and the audience regarding the context of Žižek's statements, and it was later covered and circulated digitally by *Russia Today*, which exposed this critique of Žižek globally.[102]

With that kind of global, public, and fierce critique, Žižek's position became less attractive and outdated. He explained that there was a series of is-

Figure 4.4: Anti-Žižek flyer circulated in the Left Forum in New York City on May 22, 2016. Source: Taryn Fivek.

sues that caused his negative positioning, as indicated by his decrease in citation indexes (fig. 4.5).

It began with relation to Žižek's position on ex-Yugoslavia, when parts of the European left redeemed Milošević from his contribution to the Balkan Wars.[103] Then, his marginalization continued with relation to his superpositioning (being neither for nor against) Greece's exit from the European Union, or "Grexit," while most (critical) intellectuals merely supported it. This negative positioning intensified with relation to the refugee (and migrant) crisis, whereby the common intellectual position was to support opening Europe and the acceptance of refugees. Instead, Žižek doubted this openness without

The End of Žižek 169

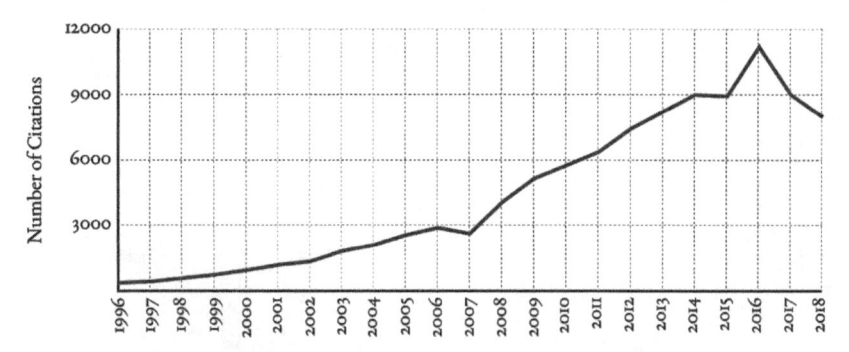

Figure 4.5: Žižek's citations per year, 1996–2018, indicating his decline after 2016. Source: Google Trends Search, January 3, 2019.

rejecting it.[104] Last, in relation to women's and LGBTQ movements, Žižek was criticized for questioning a movement's discursive affectivity as a means for real political change. In all these contextual fronts, which are among today's most burning global public issues, Žižek's superpositioning has been creating new positions, beyond the existing pro and against (the Serbs, Grexit, refugees, and political correctness). Also, these public fronts draw the intellectual and political front lines that affect both hiring and publishing. By 2017, Žižek had described the effects of those relations on his positioning:

> Now I'm limited in the US to very, extremely marginally media. It's that leftist bi-weekly *In These Times*, and then the digital *Los Angeles Review of Books*, which are very marginal. In Europe, did you notice that up until, I think two years ago, I was almost every month, sometimes more, on the *Guardian*, but [now] I'm out, prohibited. I annoyed all of them, the left and the liberal-center-right. *Le Monde* published me much more, invited me, now they more or less ignore me. Even now *Der Spiegel* no longer . . . they don't even answer; and this censorship was done very brutally.[105]

These contextual relations affected Žižek's performance. Thus, when counting his written public media interventions in the past twenty years (fig. 4.6), four points are clear: (1) there is an increasing rate of interventions; (2) there is a shift in the outlets of these interventions; (3) there is a noticeable surge after 9/11, the Arab Spring, and the Trump election; and (4) there is an average of more than one piece per month for twenty years. While such steady performance exported and established Žižek's position and work, it also exposed him to an expanding critique. Framed around deadlocks such as the #MeToo movement and ongoing refugee crisis, Žižek's positions on race and

170   CHAPTER FOUR

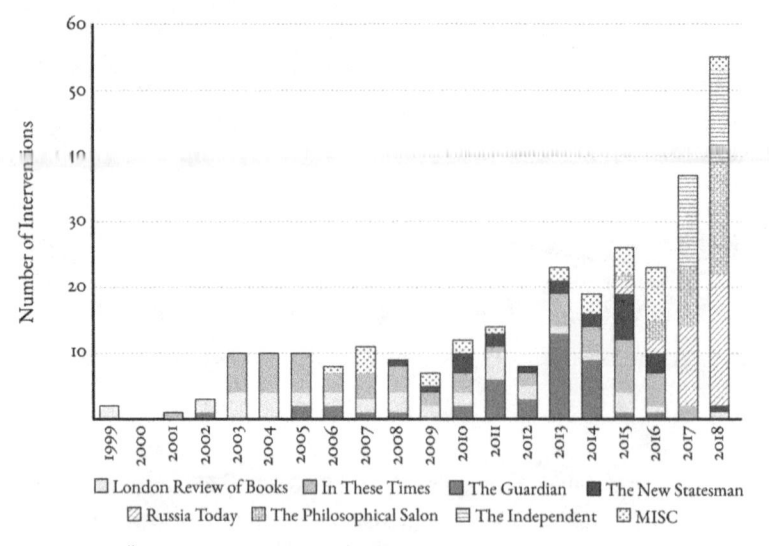

Figure 4.6: Žižek's public media interventions in English (total = 288), 1999–2018, indicating an increase after 9/11 (2001), the Arab Spring (2011), and the Trump election (2016).

sex were grounds for attacking and repositioning him as a "conservative" leftist. Yet in line with the media-academia trade-off, the less Žižek was hailed by the public media, the more he was still positioned as a worthy academic. Differently put, the critique of Žižek was differential as was the reception of his work. For example, in their edited volume *Traversing the Fantasy: Critical Responses to Slavoj Žižek*, Boucher, Glynos, and Sharpe argue against the popular trend of "Enjoy your Žižek!" that reduces his ideas to his performance, and instead argue that Žižek's performative style is inherently related to his politics: "Žižek's interventions are foremost a form of writing, one that produces certain political effects in the theoretical arena. This writing has the density of poetry, and deserves nothing less than a close literary analysis."[106]

Through this perspective, which links style and politics, the French sociologist Razmig Keucheyan positioned Žižek differently than a "conservative" leftist. In his *Mapping Critical Theory Today*, Keucheyan located Žižek along his ideal-typical typology, as an "innovator" leftist. Unlike other types of critical intellectuals—converts, pessimists, resisters, leaders, and experts—what makes "innovators" unique is their ability to achieve hybridization. As he puts it, "Žižek is a veritable machine for hybridizing theories."[107] His description of Žižek as "Lenin meets Lacan" echoes his superpositioning of theory and practice as the hallmark of his intellectual interventions.

Like Keucheyan, McKenzie Wark emphasized Žižek's contribution to novel readings of the future and positioned him as a thinker who will shape it. Wark argued that in today's contemporary global context, it is wrong to expect a singular figure of the public intellectual to challenge and inform the public. Instead, as indicated by the title and on the back cover, it is the general intellects "whose writing could, if read collectively, explain our times."[108] She defined general intellects as "people who are mostly employed as academics, and mostly pretty successful at that, but who try through their work to address more general problems about the state of the world today."[109] As especially clear in Žižek's superpositioning, Wark positioned such global public intellectuals as those who "do theory of the middle-range: not pure philosophy, but not case studies either."[110] However, given his insistence on the subject, within the "Marx-field" Wark positioned Žižek in the zone of high theory, "which subordinates labor and science to metaphors from its own past."[111] She contrasts this with his low-theory position, which "experimentally plays between metaphorical extensions from various forms of labor and science as they relate to world right now."[112] Therefore, her conclusion is that, although "Žižek's high theory Marxism of the bourgeois subject has little to say about the times," it "may . . . be of interest as the last form in which the bourgeois subject sings of itself—in the negative, as destined for the Void."[113] Nonetheless, Žižek's team and network relations have extended his reception and sustained his interest, carrying it to new fertile grounds. In many respects, these relations were constitutive of the Ljubljana School. Zupančič recalls how that relationally created label became the (real) school: "It was always a funny thing to hear, 'Ljubljana School.' There is no 'school,' this is really something that came to Ljubljana from elsewhere. People started to talk about it in terms of school, and even some people coming here trying to locate the school, which of course, does not exist. But then you see actually the effect of this collaboration."[114] These constitutive network relations were sustained by strong team relations of the troika members, which cut across divides such as personal-professional or old-young. As the second-generation troika member, Zupančič recalls: "I think there is a kind of a clearly philosophical, or theoretical, conceptual complicity, and also some kind of personal complicity. We meet at least once per week just to discuss both theory and also what is happening in our lives. So this has been growing stronger and stronger ever since the beginning, around 2000."[115] Also Dolar puts it this way: "I profoundly believe in extramural communities, people across disciplines, across institutions actually forming a group; an intellectual group which does things for the sake of that thing. It doesn't have to wait for an institutional commission, or any benefits, career or anything—you do your thing for the sake of it."[116] In terms of the school's relational effects, these are clear from its generational continuity. Stressing the openness of the school, Zupančič explains, "If we recognize young people that we immediately feel some kind of complicity with, they immediately become part of the network."[117] And here is how Dolar describes the generational effects of such relations:

> There are many generations who were formed from this school. Most of the people in the next generation were my students in the university, most come from philosophy. We have a dozen. And some of them have published in *Problemi*, Like Samo Tomšič with his work on Lacan and Marx, which is now going around in big waves, after the Verso book. You have Jure Simoniti who just published a book. You have Gregor Moder, whose book is coming out, on *Hegel and Spinoza*, which was a PhD here with me, with Northwestern University Press. You have Simon Hajdini, who is currently in Chicago and also was a student of mine. The next generation is taking advantage of this established relationship. And you have a number of people who first made their name here, and now published internationally. There is some in the US. There's a Polish extension, a Danish extension. The School has no limits. It's wrong to think we have limits.[118]

Notwithstanding his position being undermined, questioned, and put at stake, Žižek still managed to leave real effects behind him. So while in academia there seem to be a lasting effect of the relations built and sustained by Žižek over the years, public matters are more fluid and malleable. As political relations infiltrate intellectual ones, allowing some and blocking others, having the ability to publish publicly beyond the nonlasting internet pages is largely shaped by finding the right agents; namely, by establishing network relations with others in the same context and being able to shift them to new ones as contexts and positions change. As Žižek explains such conflicts in reference to his longtime publisher Verso Press: "There are young guys who are actually running things. But then there is the old gang of three people. They are Perry Anderson, Tariq Ali, and Robin Blackburn. It's really a kind of a secret committee, they meet once a month and they decide everything. And there I'm in a regular conflict . . . , it's this old conflict which is very much alive, Trotskyites vs. Maoists."[119] Having multiple relations in academia but also in the publishing industry is thus effectively useful in overcoming such political hurdles, as well as other ones, such as publishing time in the post-codex era of compressed temporality and spontaneity of event and response. Žižek eventually moved away from MIT Press, as "Roger Conover is basically against Lacan, and too much for this Art book-line."[120] He also stopped publishing with Northwestern University Press so as not to interfere with the existing work of his friend Adrian Johnston. Third, he moved away from Duke University Press for its slow publishing process. Therefore, in today's relational conditions, Žižek admits: "I moved my theoretical books to Bloomsbury. They do it fast, I have good relations there, they are very serious, they have good distribution. And for political books with Penguin, because they do it fast. So this is now my situation, basically. OK, Bloomsbury, Penguin. But, the basic thing, I'm doing now, again, it's Bloomsbury, philosophical books. I want to die doing this."[121] We see again how the dynamism of intellectual interventions brings about material effects. In Žižek's case, they oscillate between positive and negative effects. On the one hand, he suffered from an immense critique since becoming a public intellectual phenomenon; he was questioned as a philosopher and a leftist; and he was shunt from various publishing outlets. On the other hand, aside of the poisoning itself, another effect concerns the dissemination of ideas. And in this respect, Žižek's relations and connections in academia (Dolar, Miller), politics (Varoufakis, Assange), and culture (NSK, Pussy Riot), helped him to facilitate his positioning, disseminate his ideas, circulate his performances, and distribute his interventions. They show clearly that although Žižek is typically considered a one-man show, given his successful intellectual individualization, the effective dissemination of his ideas is hardly a "one-man job."

Through his team relations—of collaboration and cooperation—his troika founded the Ljubljana School for Theoretical Psychoanalysis, and with his personal friends and wives—especially his first wife, Renata Salecl, and the currently third, Jela Krečič—he intervened frequently in public affairs. Using his network relation, with Miller and Laclau, but also with other esteemed and established intellectuals such as Fredric Jameson, Joan Copjec, and Eric Santner—Žižek formed a network of Lacanian-oriented thinkers from various states, universities, and disciplines.

These relations were organized into book series, conferences, and even posts and positions.[122] They also materialized in the form of books, articles, and digital lectures. Via these relations, Žižek's ideas reached a global and diverse audience, public and intellectual alike. As his interventions were published with more than a dozen publishers, they were also translated to Spanish, French, German, Portuguese, Italian, Japanese, Korean, Russian, and Chinese—so their reach grew even wider.[123] And with a symposium list of over twenty-five countries—Žižek's presence is as widespread as it is challenged, intellectually and publicly.

In summary, this chapter explored the process and outcomes of the media-academia trade-off. It showed what happened when an intellectual intervenes in the public domain that turned digital. This turn created the conditions in which Žižek's performance became a hit. Like the internet culture, he too ignored the conventional forms of writing and speaking, and in this way he made himself an easy target for senior and conventional academics. In what follows, we will draw some general conclusion about the present age and its intellectual condition.

Conclusion

In line with the global internet age and its concern for the psychological self, Žižek engages with public and practical issues (from sexuality to faith to politics) while theorizing them as problems of the subject, at once individual and collective. His performative language of Hegelacanese, and the repetitive repertoire of rhetorical questions, jokes, and examples, have resonated with the general public toward creating the Žižekian effect; namely a readership which consumes and recycles his intellectual points while bypassing their theoretical origin. His characteristic mode of intellectual intervention, superpositioning, emphasized the performative gap between who and what he is (intellectual and philosopher) and why he says what he does—against the common intellectual and philosophical positions, thus self-undermining his authoritative position. Analogous to Socrates, he has become the sacrificial intellectual of the digital era.

The claim that Žižek is a living contradiction is not only metaphorical or rhetorical but also dialectical: by embodying contradiction and ironically performing it through opposing positions, Žižek shows that contradiction and irony (X and ¬X simultaneously) are not only parts of language, but as such also belong to the world that language represents: everything can be what it is and what it is not at the same time. In doing so, Žižek is positioned with Hegel and against Aristotle's law of noncontradiction by performing what Hegel said of Socrates: "The irony of Socrates has this great quality of showing how to make abstract ideas concrete and effect their development, for on that alone depends the bringing of the Notion into consciousness . . . and we may call this [dialectic] the universal irony of the world."[1] As I have shown with regard to the effects of Žižek's sacrificial positioning—the media-academia trade-off—in our contradictory, ironic times, "To know one's limit is to know how to sacrifice oneself."[2]

Knowledge Production in Knowledge Societies

The shifts from the codex to the post-codex era and from the production regime of the typewriter to that of the computer have together drastically changed the conditions of intellectual activity. These changes, whereby intellectual work is largely done on screen and not exclusively by intellectuals, include the general shift from scarcity and hierarchy of knowledge to its abundance and diversity. Specifically, there are fewer restrictions on knowledge in the digital public sphere, which leads to massive access to, and popularization of, knowledge. Other changes are the widespread emergence of the social sciences and higher education, the blurring boundaries between laypersons and professionals, the weakening influence of philosophical systems, and the rise of social media. This digital public sphere is dramatically different from the common context of intellectual intervention that relied on the position of the authoritative intellectual. Until the first half of the twentieth century, intellectual and cultural capital was exclusive to the elite. Despite this concentration, the public at large valued intellectual life.

At this time, education was more hierarchical, providing limited access to independent resources of information. Typical authoritative intellectuals had to rely on their high cultural capital (like being a philosopher) to establish their public position. This allowed them to intervene in a wide array of subjects from an elevated position, as if speaking from above. In the digital era, this is no longer the case. As Marshall and Atherton argue, "Online culture has spawned a number of avenues for the presentation of ideas by intellectuals that produce a different constellation of how ideas move, and perhaps a quite different idea of what constitutes an intellectual."[3] They explain that online culture is not defined by its medium and thus allows ideas to move more freely across texts, images, and videos. Indeed, "In this new online space, we are seeing a new generation of public intellectuals who have some facility in producing and presenting themselves," which is "a different constellation of experts as celebrities that match the exigencies of online attention economy."[4]

In addition to the new intellectual categories that have emerged—the expert intellectual that relies on empirics, and the dialogical that relies on equality with the public—there has also been the emergence (again) of the sacrificial intellectual. Putting on a show that undermines the expected (academic) intellectual position, Žižek constantly signals that he is *not* an authoritative intellectual and that there is nothing more hypocritical than to think that one is. Thus, his performance problematizes the particularity of the expert public intellectual and puts into question even this bounded expertise while it also rejects any kind of a real dialogue with the public, which again is put into question. In this kind of performance, Žižek superpositions the intellectual and anti-intellectual positions, reformulating their very opposition by critically shifting the debate from official credentials to unofficial practices (of thought). But as was shown across this book, this puts into question his very own intellectual position that is sacrificed. Having a superposition thus runs the risk of not having a standard, common, and expected position. As Taylor notes, "Žižek's reception is dominated by two opposing, but both essentially uncritical, distortions: i) Uncritical fixation upon the curiosity and entertainment value of a celebrity thinker. ii) Hypercritical knee-jerk condemnation . . . from dogmatically empiricist commentators for whom Žižek's speculative philosophy acts a 'postmodern' plessor."[5] Being too critical and not too critical at once, or in Eagleton's words, a "modern thinker and a postmodern writer," Žižek's sacrificial position is the price he pays for his performative superpositioning. His role as the sacrificial intellectual is a testament that today, against the declinist thesis, it is not the public intellectual per se who has declined but its authoritative form.[6]

As social contexts change so do the conditions for public intellectualism and, as argued, intellectuals such as Žižek use superpositioning to intervene in such contexts, which encourage some forms of intellectual interventions and discourage others. As Berlatsky claims in the *New Republic* regarding intellectual substance in the digital public space, "to do intellectual work [according to those hailing it] means to tell other people that they're not as smart as you are. If that's what the public intellectual is, maybe it's time to reinvent the title—if not kill it entirely."[7] Today's public intellectuals, those who intervene outside the formal university setting, should therefore reflect on the new digital conditions for intellectual activity:

1. *Democratization* of knowledge—caused by fewer media restrictions, leading to massive public access to knowledge.
2. *Popularization* of knowledge—caused by increased intellectual production, leading to low longevity and status of knowledge.

If modernism created the conditions for the move from oral to scriptural economy, then postmodernism set the stage for the move from the scriptural to the digital. The ability to perform in all these ways is paramount for the contemporary intellectual. However, this implies more than having an online presence; it rather means making the ideas themselves, and the way they are packaged, digitally ready. In the internet culture through which digital performance is circulated, ideas are to be made visual if they are to become viral. Therefore, literally better than a thousand words, an online image of Žižek sitting on a toilet renders his material analysis of ideology, his image lying in bed renders his weird openness to the public gaze, and his many memes circulate his famous quotes. The digitally popular circulation of his interventions paralleled Žižek's own repetitive repertoire and performative style. His adaptability to the digital, post-codex context is key to his positioning process and its effects. Among the effects of his interventions is a vast readership that was able to develop quickly in the past few years. Thus, for instance, when asked, "How long have you been following Žižek?," the responses to the survey I conducted with Žižek's followers in three Facebook groups suggest that by the end of 2018, most (69 percent) had been doing so for "a few years," whereas less than a third reported doing so for "more than a decade" (12 percent) or "less than a year" (15 percent).

In Žižek's recent short and popular intellectual intervention, *Like a Thief in Broad Daylight: Power in the Era of Post-Humanity*, he continues to provide global society with a narrative of the present. The title of the introduction delivers his superpositional diagnosis: "First the Bad News, Then the Good News . . . Which May Be Even Worse."[8] Just like his inaugural global intervention, *The Sublime Object of Ideology* in 1989, almost thirty years later Žižek still positions himself with oppositional relation to Habermas as a state philosopher, *the* thinker of normalization as suppression of social struggles: "Habermas is effectively the ultimate philosopher of (re)normalization, desperately working to prevent the collapse of our established ethico-political order: 'Could it be that Jurgen Habermas' corpus will be one day of the first in which simply nothing at all prodding can be found any more? Heidegger, Wittgenstein, Adorno, Sartre, Arendt, Derrida, Nancy, Badiou, even Gadamer, everywhere one stumbles upon dissonances. Normalization takes hold. The philosophy of the future—integration brought to completion.'"[9] As per his usual tactic and antic, Žižek casts a wide net of recognizable intellectuals, using them as entry points, with a name-dropping that attracts everyone to his point. That such (state) thinkers attempt to eliminate current struggles prevents the change they may bring. In fact, he diagnoses, the change is already here, yet we do not notice or register it. Hence change occurs like a thief in broad daylight. To illustrate this point, Žižek again brings classical references from the past so as to make sense of the present. He cites St. Paul to show how radical social transformation, such as the one the world is experiencing at the moment, does not happen while we are ready for it but rather under our noses: "Capitalism is openly disintegrating and changing into something else. We do not perceive this ongoing transformation because of our deep immersion in ideology."[10] This form of unforeseen yet obvious change is more common than we think, as it is found also in the psychoanalytic treatment as well as in political revolutions. Superpositioning the individual and the social on the one hand, and theory and practice on the other, Žižek argues that "miracles can happen."[11]

The example he uses is the 2017 UK general election campaign that was directed against Jeremy Corbyn. Although a coordinated character assassination targeted Corbyn, he had emerged even stronger, not in spite but because of it (at least until 2019 elections): "A character trait—Corbyn's accentuated ordinary decency—may be an argument for him (for the voters tired of the Conservative media blitz) or an argument against him (for those who think that a leader should be strong and charismatic)"; this, according to Žižek in his Hegelacanese, demonstrates that "undecidability is a feature of symbolic determination which cannot be accounted for in terms of simple linear determinism."[12] This exemplary form of superpositioning the for and against (as other) positions allows Žižek to move from the intraintellectual to the extraintellectual public arena, and from the local to the global. The book's conclusion is yet another rhetorical question: "For How Long Can We Act Globally and Think Locally?," which is followed by another, more concrete and interventional question: "What can we learn from Hegel about Donald Trump and his liberal critics?" To answer these questions, Žižek refers to the past to make sense of the present. He recalls that back in the 1960s, the motto of the early ecological movements was "Think globally, act locally!" Today, however, Trump's shameless breaking of liberal taboos reverses this motto to "Act globally, think locally!" (i.e., turn the United States into a global power for extremely local interests). Bringing Hegel and Trump together to draw conclusions for the global future is precisely the signature move of Žižek's intellectual interventions. By crossing both time (past to future) and space (intra- to extraintellectual), superpositioning right and left, Žižek repeats the point he made on BBC Channel 4 on November 3, 2016 when he was asked "If you were American who would you vote for?" His answer was shocking and raised many brows: "Trump. I am horrified at him. I'm just thinking that Hillary is the true danger."[13] In contradistinction to the common rightist (Trump) and leftist (Clinton) positions, Žižek argued for a break with the left in order to revive a truer, better left (à la Bernie Sanders). Two years later, the American writer and broadcaster Mike Crumplar argued that "Žižek was right in 2016."[14] And two months prior to that article, he published another piece, "Slipping Slavoj," in which he described his declining position: "It's hard to believe, but just in 2011, Slavoj Žižek was speaking at Occupy Wall Street to excitement and acclaim. Žižek was still a respected leftist academic. Fast forward seven years and the situation couldn't be more different. Leftists recoil at his name.

Academics think he's made himself into a factory of lazy, watered-down philosophy for bite-sized consumption. Activists think he's betrayed the left on political correctness and made overtures to fascism. Žižek has become a neo-reactionary philosopher."[15] As discussed before, Žižek has lost his appeal among both leftist academics and activists. Crumplar explains this development through referencing Žižek's repositioning:

> Žižek always was speaking to the Left. The Left was able to tolerate his objections to their general consensus positions, particularly regarding nationalism and political correctness, by considering him a sort of jester. He was a quirky celebrity with a funny accent and lots of things to say about classic movies. But once these objections to left-liberal consensus positions came to pass and were affirmed in a way that they could no longer ignore whatsoever (by nationwide popular democratic votes for candidates and positions that absolutely rejected this, across the western world), Žižek had to be jettisoned—CANCELLED.[16]

By revealing the left's ideological blind spots, Žižek was positioned as one who undermines conventional positions not only of the right, which is more obvious, but also and perhaps even more so of common leftist positions as they appear in popular media. For example, in the case of Trump, Žižek explained why the liberal left's attacks on "Trump's vulgar racist and sexist outbursts, factual inaccuracies, economic nonsense and so on" missed the point and ended up strengthening him:[17] "They missed how identification works: we as a rule identify with others' weaknesses, not only, or even principally, with their strengths; so the more Trump's limitations were mocked, the more ordinary people identified with him and perceived attacks on him as condescending attacks on themselves."[18] This superpositioning, in which both sides of the binary are "upset" with the Žižekian position, earned Žižek his role as both a global public intellectual and a sacrificial intellectual. Crumplar suggests some irony in these circumstances: "There is, of course, a certain Hegelian significance to [Žižek's] cancellation. Is Žižek himself not the 'vanishing mediator' here in the conflict between the theoretical abstraction of the neoliberal late capitalist world order and its empirical negation in the political upheaval that has thrown everything into question? If anything, shouldn't this cancellation be nothing other than a sign of the TRUTH of the position?"[19] He summarizes four issues that according to him Žižek was right about: the need for a leftist populism; the rising antagonisms of borders and migration; the fundamentality of political correctness as a site of tension, particularly in sexual politics and multiculturalism; and the fascism that fills the conceptual void left by neoliberal late capitalism. Then, Crumplar relates these concerns to Trump's election while asking, rhetorically, "Are these issues not the defining issues of our time? Shouldn't this be the takeaway of the Left from 2016?"[20] As recent research has shown, "cancel culture" is intimately related to academia. Broadly understood as ostracizing someone for violating social norms, especially concerning racism and sexism, the activist practice is akin to consumer boycott of perceived unethical brands and corporations. Yet in the digital public sphere this is done online, using social media, with the aim of preventing individuals from appearing in certain public domains. What this sort of critique against Žižek misses, is that in and through his breaching experimental performance, he is "always making the normative social field evident."[21]

More evidence to this can be found in Ben Burgis's critique of the contemporary left as it ties to Žižek and cancel culture. In his recent *Canceling Comedians While the World Burns*, Burgis suggests that as a cluster of cultural trends, cancel culture actually has an impact on different parts of society to varying degrees. The problem with it, as he puts it, "*is not that it's so effective.*"[22] Rather, it lies deeper in this culture's logic that equates every self-critical perspective with a support of the opposition. For example, he recalls: "The anti-war left in the Bush era didn't have any trouble understanding that when people like Noam Chomsky and Glenn Greenwald pointed out that a lot of terrorism was caused by blowback from US interventions around the world and that this is a reason to oppose such interventions they weren't expressing sympathy for Al Queda [sic]. Somehow, though, all these comrades thought my advocacy of *taking away the lockdown protestors' best recruitment pitch by providing better solutions to the economic grievances they were articulating* amounted to 'support' for the protests."[23] His other example is the debate held in Toronto in 2019 between Žižek and Jordan Peterson.[24] In this "debate of the century," the two public intellectuals came together to perform live in front of a full house at the Sony Center and online on YouTube.[25] However, as Burgis argues in his analysis of the debate, many viewers and participants left disappointed. This is because Žižek's response did not match their expectations, which was more along the lines of a brutal fight (Benjamin Studebaker laid out some of what that might have looked like in a *Current Affairs* piece called "How Žižek Should Have Replied to Jordan Peterson"). Instead, they witnessed how Žižek "gently corrected a few of Peterson's many misinterpretations of Marx and Marxism and—almost as an afterthought—gave Peterson a quick recommended reading list, but he never went in for the kill."[26]

What eventually contributed to Žižek's "cancellation" among left wingers was that he seemingly agreed with Peterson on the critique of political correctness. Yet as explained by the Canadian writer Clifton Mark, "While both are critical of political correctness... Peterson attacks it from the right, Žižek from the left." According to Mark, Žižek's tempered response to Peterson was due to their asymmetrical expertise. Hence, "Despite the collegiality, the exchange was unequal. Peterson's expertise is in clinical psychology, not in politics, philosophy, or economics. Žižek's expertise was directly related to the topics of discussion. This made the evening feel like an office hours session between a professor and an earnest but misguided student."[27]

The relation between academia and cancel culture is explained by a combination of factors, including a perceived liberal hegemony in academia that silences other, conservative voices. This is added to shifting cultural values among American and European postindustrial societies over issues such as identity politics.[28] And, of course, digital technology is responsible for the expanding collective expression as well as the filter bubbles and echo chambers that reinforce politics of outrage. Therefore, social media is "thought to have amplified the reach, and accelerated the pace, of the cancel culture spreading on college campuses and beyond."[29] However, according to Žižek, cancel culture and political correctness more broadly take part in "fake radicalism":[30] these sorts of cancellations, which often times target him, ignore the true causes for racism and sexism while merely focusing on (his) speech and performance.

Intellectual Work in the Age of Digital Reproduction

The changes that reading and writing are undergoing, of which Žižek is a part, were grasped already by Michel de Certeau in his *The Practice of Everyday Life*. In everyday common practices (and tactics) such as eating, walking, reading, writing, and dwelling, which are hardly the exclusive practices of scientists, experts, leaders, and other elites, one can find both the shared repetitive social form that governs these practices and the singular ways in which practitioners of life—readers and consumers—subvert and maneuver that form. According to de Certeau's early and prophetic contextualization of this intellectual activity, while both the expert and the philosopher perform the position of mediators between society and a body of knowledge, a crucial difference is worth noting: "It is true that the Expert is growing more common in this [technocratic] society, to the point of becoming its generalized figure, distended between the exigency of a growing specialization and that of a communication that has become all the more necessary. He blots out (and in a certain way replaces) the Philosopher, formerly the specialist of the universal. But his success is not so terribly spectacular. In him, the productivist law that requires a specific assignment (the condition of efficiency) and the social law that requires circulation (the form of exchange) enter into contradiction."[31] As demonstrated throughout the book, Žižek avoids this contradiction by superpositioning both the philosophical and antiphilosophical positions. This blurs the boundaries between the intraintellectual arena and the public, extraintellectual arena; it is rather a bridge-building exercise between the ivory tower and the streets. By undermining his own intellectual-philosophical position, Žižek also challenges the philosophical authority as such, denying it (and himself) of the knowledge usually ascribed to it by the public, and enacts what Alvin Gouldner called "a culture of critical discourse."[32] That is a "form of speech and writing which emphasizes that all assertions—particularly those in the political sphere—are open to challenge."[33] As Giddens explains, "Whereas most other groups in society are prepared to accept the invocation of someone's authority as a basis for evaluating ideas, intellectuals reject any such viewpoint."[34] In Žižek's case this rejection of the (academic) philosophical authority is performed by the oral and textual "breaking of the fourth wall." It is rather that in today's digital context Žižek plays a timely part in breaking—rather than completely rejecting—the traditional dramaturgical academic rules, and in doing so, he responds to the current shift in the foundation of intellectual authority. This response is performed in his frequent manipulations of letters, words, and sentences, and his broad array of topics that usually includes popular culture; all are signals for the reader that this is not an intellectual intervention of the regular (noninterventional) way. Thus Žižek brings back the subjective tone precisely as a performative self-sacrifice. In this way he negates the common academic asubjective tone that excludes rhetoric from the scientific discourse. However, for his superpositioning to work, Žižek takes into account the recent public tendency, termed "post-truth," of a cynical starting position toward any general assertion. Almost an a priori (and hence pseudo)critical gesture, the public today does not start with Giddens's conforming position, which is later challenged by the intellectual. Today, when the public's starting position on knowledge, and especially philosophy, is to challenge it, Žižek's critical move is to reassert philosophy's authority but from a different (psychoanalytic) position. De-monstrating its theoretical and practical updated relevance, Žižek reasserts the value of philosophy in an antiphilosophical (or, rather, post)philosophical manner. In his performances, Žižek resonates with the changed relations between practices of writing and reading in the digital context. Again, de Certeau had already noted this fundamental change in the conditions of knowledge in 1980s: "From TV to newspapers, from advertising to all sorts of mercantile epiphanies, our society is characterized by a cancerous growth of vision, measuring everything by its ability to show or be shown and transmuting communication into a visual journey.... Thus, for the binary set production-consumption, one would substitute its more general equivalent: writing-reading."[35] Describing the formal structure of such a common practice as reading, de Certeau explicitly turned to popular culture, arguing that it, "as well as a whole literature called 'popular,' take on a different aspect: they present themselves essentially as 'arts of making' this or that, i.e., as combinatory or utilizing modes of consumption."[36] Žižek followed this insight in his analyses of popular culture as a source for social (and by extension individual) enjoyment as libidinal investments. This enjoyment is incited by Žižek's texts and talks, which eventually led internet users to do the digital popularization for him. According to today's digital mode of knowledge production and consumption, the public no longer reads but rather watches. Consequently, what is publicly considered watchable is measured by different criteria than the readable, especially in the highly competitive times of the information inflation. So instead of clarity of writing, oral and visual performativity is the publicly attractive form of argumentation. Together with this changed intelligibility, "rules of public speech are undergoing an important transformation as our sensibility for injury and hurt augments."[37] As Žižek himself is not officially "on" any kind of social media, and does not manage any kind of internet presence by himself (besides email, that is), his enormous public of followers is doing the digital writing (and work) for him. A readership without actual readers, the digital internet culture enjoys Žižek and capitalizes on his eccentric showmanship.

De Certeau thus envisioned the blurring of three borders: between theory and practice, production and consumption, and writing and reading. Today, in the internet age and the "recited" or "cybernetic" society, writing has lost its original legitimacy and holy foundation. Today's form of writing promotes short articles and tweets, as the time for reading is shrinking drastically. In parallel, the will to know translates to an ever-growing pressure to read as much as (im)possible. As a result, reading is more active than ever, with the rapid evolution of new forms of reading, such as skimming and speed reading. Hence the open debate about how to read or not read Žižek.[38] Considering reading as "poaching," de Certeau claimed that this "misunderstood activity" should not be taken as a passive reception or consumption, but rather a productive activity. As we see today, reading is not an "activity reserved for the literary critic, that is, once again, for a category of professional intellectuals (*cleres*),"[39] but one that can be extended to all cultural practitioners. Arguing against the passive consideration of reading (and consumption), de Certeau claimed: "In reality, the activity of reading has on the contrary all the characteristics of a silent production. [The reader] insinuates into another person's text the ruses of pleasure and appropriation: he poaches on it, is transported into it, pluralizes himself in it like the internal rumblings of one's body."[40]

In his contribution to *Repeating Žižek*—a book published in Žižek's sic series that includes contributions by close students and followers—Benjamin Noys addresses Žižek's "reading machine" to argue that "Žižek has a method of reading, and this method of reading can also help us grasp how we should read Žižek."[41] First, he defines Žižek's reading, particularly his reading of other philosophers, as a method "to read philosophy as a site for ontological questioning, but a site that can only be understood through Lacanian psychoanalysis."[42] Then, Noys goes on to define the (public) method of reading Žižek, which requires "an effort to trace how Žižek is a writer of beginnings."[43] He locates the truth of Žižek (and his work) not in his content but in his act. By constantly undermining the authoritative, totalizing position of philosophy and the philosopher, Žižek reveals philosophy's incompleteness by supplementing it with what seems to be secondary, exemplary topics such as culture. However, relating Žižek's performance to his superpositioning, Noys claims that "it is the short circuit... that opens the field of philosophy again. This is the point where Žižek is a philosopher. This is also the moment of [the Hegelian] negativity."[44] As he puts it while linking the past-present-future movement with the sacrificial positioning, "at this moment a displacement takes place that generates a torsion in the field of philosophy and that places it within a 'new topology' of the world."[45]

In and through his performances Žižek practically acknowledges that reading is today situated at the point where social stratification (access to information) and poetic operations (textual encoding and decoding) intersect. His writing goes against the "social hierarchization [that] seeks to make the reader conform to the 'information' distributed by an elite (or semi-elite); ... insinuating their inventiveness into the cracks in a cultural orthodoxy."[46] Žižek's frequent participation in public debates (in universities, art galleries, cafés, organizations) that then get uploaded to the internet, not so much to promote Žižek's ideas but rather the institutions or mediators themselves, allowed the public to see (at their own volition and convenience) his thought in action and observe how body language accentuates and reverberates his ideas as the spoken word takes over the written. Žižek debunks the "fiction of the 'treasury' hidden in the work, a sort of strong-box full of meaning, [which] is obviously not based on the productivity of the reader, but on the social institution that overdetermines his relation with the text. By its very nature available to a plural reading, the text becomes a cultural weapon, a private hunting reserve, the pretext for a law that legitimizes as 'literal' the interpretation given by socially authorized professionals and intellectuals."[47] Taken in its active rather than passive form, reading "has no place," but it is a space for "games and tricks," what we today call memes and GIFs. And while reading is becoming more and more active, writing is becoming less and less authoritative, bringing down with it intellectual authority. De Certeau thus anticipated the blurred border between writing and reading common to the internet age, to which Žižek is reacting with his Hegelacanese and its textually performed language games (such as italicization and capitalization). These rhetoric and performative practices are Žižek's ways of, as he puts it, "torturing language to tell the truth." He deviates from the common academic language and performs a sacrificial positioning maneuver that situates him on the side of the public rather than that of intellectuals. Žižek's move thus empowers the reader by moving away from the locus of power enacted in the common *academic* intellectual reading. Instead, Žižek favors the *public* intellectual reading and writing—that is, from the perspective of the public. This is contrary to how the modern practice of writing was developed through the concentration of power. As de Certeau traced this development, he defined modern writing as "the concrete activity that consists in constructing, on its own, blank space—the page—a text that has power over the exteriority from which it has first been isolated."[48] Consequently, the practice of writing has gained much power, principled social hierarchy, and organized educational systems. In other words, writing was a strategy aimed at fixating the law as its proper space, so its arbitrariness is hidden and represented as natural.

While in the previous codex era subjects were less aware of the (less transparent) ways they were manipulated, or they were so only through their conscious or unconscious subversive actions, in today's post-codex era writing is unable to hide its lacking credentials, namely the lack of the holy speech that was used to found the original scriptural economy. Modern writing has lost some of its strategic abilities and has returned to being a practical tactic; in other words, it blurs the strategy-tactic distinction. Moreover, one of modernity's main features is the spread of literacy among all classes of society. Yet writing has always been thought of as the active part of which reading—a newspaper, a book, or a blog—is the passive counterpart. Today we have the same conception regarding watching television, which is frequently criticized for its passivity. But theoretical developments such as the concept of interpassivity,[49] complementing interactivity, have allowed Žižek, and de Certeau before him, to counter this common positioning. Arguing for the active role of reading (or viewing), the latter suggested that readers become active as they do not just receive but participate and interpret the message. This is especially true in the internet age of comments, likes, shares, and retweets.

Not having a proper (place) at all, the internet encourages a *glocal* language, which is at once common and uncommon, allowing its users to play linguistic games as a way of subverting established meanings and forms. As the game, the rebellion, and the subversion characterize best the email, the chat, the talkback, and the like, reading and writing are upgraded into novel tactical practices. But what is the strategic proper against which they act? Is it Facebook, Twitter, or Google? Perhaps it is Saudi Arabia and China, with their digital censorship, or the United States, which tries to block digital leaks and pirating? Are nation-states, those old-time dinosaurs, still the proper of our digital times, creating better strategies for recruiting the internet to their uses with the help of private corporations? In such questions we see the related political dimension of reading and writing in the internet age.

For example, in his examination of Žižek and digital culture, Burnham positions Žižek as an "internet philosopher." He finds Žižek's self-plagiarizing to be "technique par excellence of writing in the age of the Internet."[50] Against the main, common critique of Žižek, that he cuts and pastes whole sections from one book to another, Burnham argues that what is noticeable is Žižek's method of making writing—what intellectuals usually abhor—disappear. Skipping from note taking directly to editing, this collage or patchwork method characterizes much of Žižek's writing or intellectual activity. According to Burnham,[51] it is useful to look at three aspects of Žižek's performance and positioning as internet philosopher: methodology: construction of texts; reception: consumption of Žižek; and theory: obscene underside of the law. Regarding Žižek's performative methodology, Burnham quotes his understanding of the internet to note that, "indeed, such a panoply of references while utterly typical of post-1980s cultural studies ... is, Žižek argues, a hallmark of the Internet age: 'In cyberspace ... are we not again with Eisenstein's dream of "intellectual montage"—of filming *Capital*, of producing the Marxist theory out of the clash of concrete images? Is not hyper-text a new practice of montage?'"[52] From here we can take two structuring principles of Žižek's performance that made his positioning different from that of other global thinkers: first, the (Freudian) compulsion to repeat, all the way to self-plagiarism; and second, the hypertextuality of his intellectual interventions, in content and form.

These two principles resonate with the spatial contexts of the internet age and the production regime of the computer; but they also relate to the changed temporal context, namely that of compressed time. Today more than ever, the public feeling as well as that of the individual is of extreme rapidity, what some have termed "accelerationism."[53] As if every second matters most, and everyday something new happens. Be it true or false, as a character of our time, Žižek has reacted to it with a lightning-fast publication rate. It seems that he had recognized early on today's impossibility of effectively intervening through the publication of only one book per decade. This timing of Žižek's global intellectual interventions reverberates his superpositioning of event and response, very much attuned to the internet immediacy of real-time performance. This is how Oltarzewska describes this aspect of timing as a performative strategy: "Žižek's engagement with major world events as well as the minor cultural artifacts of contemporary life is febrile, immediate and intensely voluble: no sooner has the dust settled than a commentary hits the Internet, its swift revisions, earnest capitalizations and colloquial tone generating a climate of urgency. The quasi-simultaneity of event and response creates a sense of temporal compression and theatre heightened by the vestiges of *énonciation*—a Žižekian trademark—that linger in his online submissions, and, increasingly, in his published work, jarring with the carefully edited norms of the standard academic *énoncé*."[54] In this way Žižek's reactions to the changing context of intellectual activity were more adequate than others', and effectively created his online presence for him. Becoming an internet phenomenon with memes, clips, and paraphernalia—Žižek the "cybercommunist" surely entertains, and in our digital public space, this enjoyment-producing entertainment makes his performance unique.[55] His suitability and adaptability to the internet age is emphasized in Gunkel's characterization of Žižek's performance as the "art of the mash-up." That is, as a Žižekian "'short-circuit' or 'parallax' that connects two disparate traditions."[56] For example, in music he superpositions the Beatles and Jay-Z; in literature he superpositions eighteenth-century German idealism with contemporary Scandinavian detective stories; and in cinema he superpositions Hitchcock and *Kung Fu Panda*. Ultimately, his superpositioning of popular culture and high theory created a welcoming path (of Hegelacanese) for both intellectuals and publics to engage with these contents. And his repetitive performance resonated with the internet form of writing using such contents differently. Žižek literally demonstrates this short circuit and codifies it in the naming of his MIT Press series.

In terms of effects, Žižek's interventions are viral and are thus more widely circulated and distributed than most intellectual interventions. Indeed, as "the philosopher of cyberspace" Michael Heim wrote in his *Electric Language*, "Digital writing turns the private solitude of reflective reading and writing into a public network."[57] So it is possible to find his varied interventions—from books to lectures—digitalized en masse, as e-books, and scanned PDFs on digital book reservoirs such as AAAAArg.org or b-ok.org. Moreover, there are several dedicated websites acting as internet mediators to his bibliography and cinematography, such as Lacan.com, TheoryLeaks.com, ZizekianInstitute.org, and ZizekAnalysis.wordpress.com, as well as YouTube channels and podcasts such as that of Birkbeck Institute for the Humanities. But what makes Žižek's production and consumption, branding and marketing, really unique, is the high-low signification it has embraced from the very beginning of his continuous local public intellectualism since the 1980s. In both content and form, including linguistic and rhetorical devices such as the level of referencing, claiming, tone, affect, style—Žižek's performances attract both a high and a low range of audiences and reactions. So, for example, his quasi tics are as discussed as the consistency of the communist hypothesis. Such high and low strata coexist in an intellectual way that is typical both for Žižek's own intellectual production and the blogosphere's consumption.

By referring to Freud's "talking cure," La Berge suggests looking at Žižek's textual performance as *The Writing Cure*. As part of the collected volume *The Truth of Žižek*, he defines Žižek's textual performance as writing as transference and argues that he "has constructed a transferential relationship by positioning his readership as his readership-as-analyst."[58] Therefore, La Berge claims: "To keep reading/critiquing Žižek is to be trapped in this dichotomy, which has all the structure of a stalemated threat: either you destroy the analysis or I will, is always, in a sense, the analysand's ultimate threat. The discursive analysis he has constructed between himself and his readership provides the circuit of sustaining this dialectic: his projective assaults on the postmodern serve to reaffirm his own ego (unconscious) as modern. Once this interpretation has been offered in the service of his writing cure, it seems we should then rest with the classically modern response: analytic silence."[59] According to La Berge's speculation, Žižek bombards us with his critical interventions because he hates us—the readers and viewers who consume his so many interventions—so much so that he cannot stop telling us in and through his endless writing. This is complementary with his indictment that those who love to hate him, are thus unable to resist attending his performances. As in the psychoanalytic treatment, it will perhaps be over when there is nothing left to say or read; until then, his performance goes on. Clearly, for now, this global public intellectual is not going down without a sacrificial fight.

Acknowledgments

This book is based on research undertaken at Darwin College, University of Cambridge, in the years 2015–2019. I would like to thank all those who have supported me during that period, without whom this book would have never been written.

I arrived at Cambridge after studying and working at Tel Aviv University under supervisors Yehouda Shenhav and Shaul Mishal, who initiated me into sociology as an academic discipline and a way of life. While in Cambridge, my PhD supervisor, Patrick Baert, provided insurmountable guidance and advice on the research for this book. In this regard, I also received highly valuable feedback from my examiners, Marco Santoro of the University of Bologna and Darin Weinberg of King's College, University of Cambridge. In Ljubljana, Slavoj Žižek, Mladen Dolar, and Alenka Zupančič generously hosted me, providing their time and insight which greatly contributed to the research of this book. I am also grateful for insights gained through conversing with scholars such as Kaitlyn Tucker Sorenson of the University of Chicago and Ori Goldberg of Tel Aviv University.

Ideas cannot just float in thin air. Therefore, I am sincerely lucky to have my extraordinarily devoted parents, Roman and Shoshana, and late sister, Chen Bar-El (1987–2012), who facilitated my time in Cambridge and supported me in ways that go beyond words. Similarly, my dearest partner, Dena Qaddumi, has been gracious enough to offer her ears for my talking, her brains for my picking, and her shoulders for my crying. The illustrations in the book are much improved thanks to her! I also thank my Cambridge friends—Merve Sancak, Benjamin Ferschli, Stefanos Roimpas, and Girish Nivarti—who have all provided both sage advice and great encouragement. Udi Aloni deserves a thanks for helping in his own way. Elizabeth Branch Dyson and her wonderful team at the University of Chicago Press have been extremely supportive during the review and production process and I thank them for that.

The following material has appeared in print before, and I would like to thank the publishers for the permission to reprint it: An earlier version of chapter 2 was previously published in the *British Journal of Sociology* 72, no. 2 (2021), and is reprinted with the permission of the London School of Economics and Political Science. Portions of chapter 3 were previously printed in the following publication: Eliran Bar-El and Patrick Baert "'The Fool' Revisited: The Making of Žižek as Sacrificial Public Intellectual," *Cultural Sociology* 15, no. 4: 539–57. Copyright © 2021 (Eliran Bar-El and Patrick Baert). DOI: 10.1177/17499755211007243.

Notes

INTRODUCTION

1. The *Žižek* nightclub, record label, and "eclectic collective of musicians and DJs . . . [n]amed in honor of contemporary Slovenian philosopher," has operated in Buenos Aires since the early 2000s. See Brian Byrnes, "Argentina's New Dance Music goes Global," *CNN*, November 5, 2009, http://edition.cnn.com/2009/SHOWBIZ/Music/11/04/argentina.craze/index.html. In early 2019, the Tokyo-based brand Poliquant launched a Žižek-inspired fashion collection. See HB Team, "POLIQUANT Delivers FW19 Lookbook 'AWKWARDNESS' Inspired by Slavoj Zizek," February 2, 2019, *Hyperbeast*, https://hypebeast.com/2019/2/poliquant-fw19-awkwardness-lookbook.
2. The *International Journal of Žižek Studies* launched in 2007; see its website at http://zizekstudies.org. For Žižek's dictionary, see Rex Butler, ed., *The Žižek Dictionary* (Durham, UK: Acumen, 2014). For his impressionist clip, see Klemen Slakonja, "*Slavoj Žižek in The Perverted Dance (Cut the Balls)*," YouTube, 2013, https://www.youtube.com/watch?v=80X0pbCV_t4.
3. See Robert C. Smith, *The Ticklish Subject? A Critique of Žižek's Lacanian Theory of Subjectivity, with Emphasis on an Alternative* (Holt, UK: Heathwood Press, 2013); Steve Fuller, "Why Slavoj Žižek Is a Waste of Space for the Social Scientifically Literate Left," *Sociological Imagination*, 2013, http://sociologicalimagination.org/archives/13940; Nikos Mottas, "An Apologist of Imperialism: Slavoj Žižek and NATO's War in Yugoslavia," *In Defense of Communism*, 2017, https://www.idcommunism.com/2017/03/an-apologist-of-imperialism-slavoj.html.
4. At the time, Yugoslavia was a Socialist Federal Republic composed of Bosnia and Herzegovina, Croatia, Macedonia, Montenegro, Serbia, and Slovenia. The term "Eastern Bloc" referred to a group of communist states from Asia and Europe led by the Soviet Union.
5. Žižek's 1982 (second) PhD dissertation was published as *The Most Sublime Hysteric: Hegel with Lacan* (Cambridge, UK: Polity Press, 2014). In addition to such events, this book traces back the Slovenian context to events prior to 1982.
6. Gretchen Bakke, *The Likeness: Semblance and Self in Slovene Society* (Oakland:

University of California Press, 2020), 112. Perceptively, she recalls how one professor reacted to Žižek's 2016 lecture at the University of Vermont: "It isn't enough to hear him; you must see him or, at least, his gyrating gesticulations and snarling, spitting visage seem to command your gaze. I think this part of his performance is crucial because he is not only one of our most preeminent dialectical thinkers, but he actually embodies the tensions/tortures of that mode of thinking, literally showing the audience what it's like to have two opposing ideas in your mind at the same time." See Bakke, *Likeness*, 121n21.

7   Decca Aitkenhead, "Slavoj Žižek: 'Humanity Is OK, but 99% of People Are Boring Idiots,'" *The Guardian*, June 10, 2012, https://www.theguardian.com/culture/2012/jun/10/slavoj-zizek-humanity-ok-people-boring.

8   Adam Kirsch, "The Deadly Jester," *New Republic*, December 2, 2008; "Disputations: Still the Most Dangerous Philosopher in the West," *New Republic*, January 7, 2009, https://newrepublic.com/article/64692/disputations-still-the-most-dangerous-philosopher-the-west.

9   For example, see Elizabeth Wright and Edmond Wright, *The Žižek Reader* (Oxford, UK: Blackwell, 1999); Sarah Kay, *Žižek: A Critical Introduction* (Cambridge: Cambridge University Press, 2003); Tony Myers, *Slavoj Žižek* (London: Routledge, 2003).

10 See Broderick Chow and Alex Mangold, *Žižek and Performance* (London: Palgrave Macmillan, 2014); Matthew Flisfeder and Louis Willis, eds., *Žižek and Media Studies: A Reader* (London: Palgrave Macmillan, 2014).

11 For a particular discussion on the globalism of intellectuals, see Michael Desch, ed., *Professors or Pundits? Public Intellectuals in the Global Arena* (Notre Dame, IN: University of Notre Dame Press, 2016).

12 For an example of such an approach, see Marcus Morgan and Patrick Baert, *Conflict in the Academy: A Study in the Sociology of Intellectuals* (London: Palgrave Macmillan, 2015).

13 See Barbara A. Misztal, *Intellectuals and the Public Good* (Cambridge: Cambridge University Press, 2007).

14 Michael Keren and Richard Hawkins, eds., *Speaking Power to Truth: Digital Discourse and the Public Intellectual* (Athabasca, AB: Athabasca University Press, 2015), 2.

15 See Hannah Arendt, *Between Past and Future: Eight Exercises in Political Thought* (New York: Viking Press, 1961); Stefan Auer, "Public Intellectuals, East and West: Jan Patočka and Vaclav Havel in Contention with Maurice Merleau-Ponty and Slavoj Žižek," in *Intellectuals and Their Public: Perspectives from the Social Sciences*, ed. Christian A. Fleck and Andreas Hess (Farnham, UK: Ashgate, 2009), 89–106; Henry A. Giroux, "Public Intellectuals, Academic Violence and the Threat of Political Purity," *Media International Australia* 156, no. 1 (August 2015): 89–97, https://doi.org/10.1177/1329878X1515600111.

16 Keren and Hawkins, *Speaking Power to Truth*, 2.

17 The terms "intellectual" and "philosopher" are used interchangeably, for the moment. The emphasis here is on persons of intellect, truth, or knowledge.
18 Whereas Plato's dialogues emphasized oral and spontaneous intellectual interventions, epitomized in Socrates's engagements with his fellow men, in modernity the emphasis shifted toward authorship and trained intellectualism, leading to the present distinction between "intellectual" and "public intellectual." For a focused elaboration on this shift in intellectual life, see Zygmunt Bauman, *Legislators and Interpreters* (Ithaca, NY: Cornell University Press, 1987); Russell Jacoby, *The Last Intellectuals: American Culture in the Age of Academe*, 2nd ed. (New York: Basic Books, 2000); Paul A. Rahe, "The Idea of the Public Intellectual in the Age of the Enlightenment," in *The Public Intellectual: Between Philosophy and Politics*, ed. Arthur M. Melzer et al. (New York: Rowman & Littlefield, 2003), 27–52.
19 Neil McLaughlin and Eleanor Townsley, "Contexts of Cultural Diffusion: A Case Study of 'Public Intellectual' Debates in English Canada," Canadian Review of Sociology 48, no. 4 (November 2011): https://doi.org/10.1111/j.1755-618X.2011.01268.x.
20 Julian Benda, *The Treason of the Intellectuals* (1928; New York: William Morrow & Company, 2006), 27.
21 Benda, *Treason of the Intellectuals*, xxv.
22 Jeffery C. Alexander, "Public Intellectuals and Civil Society," in *Intellectuals and Their Public: Perspectives from the Social Sciences*, ed. Christian A. Fleck and Andreas Hess (Farnham, UK: Ashgate, 2009), 19.
23 Gil Eyal, "Plugging into the Body of the Leviathan: Proposal for a New Sociology of Public Interventions," *Middle East Topics & Arguments* 1, (May 2013), 14. For a critical assessment of boundary work in science, see Thomas Gieryn, *Cultural Boundaries of Science: Credibility on the Line* (Chicago: University of Chicago Press, 1999).
24 Arthur M. Melzer, Jerry Weinberger, and Richard M. Zinman, eds., *The Public Intellectual: Between Philosophy and Politics* (New York: Rowman & Littlefield, 2003), 11.
25 See Richard A. Posner, *Public Intellectual: A Study of Decline* (Cambridge, MA: Harvard University Press, 2001).
26 For a detailed review of these changes, see Patrick Baert and Alan Shipman, "Transforming the Intellectual," in *The Politics of Knowledge*, ed. Patrick Baert and Fernando Domínguez Rubio (London: Routledge, 2012), 179–204.
27 For focused analyses of the changes universities are undergoing from various perspectives, see Frank Furedi, *What's Happened to the University? A Sociological Exploration of its Infantilisation* (London: Routledge, 2016); Heather Fraser and Nik Taylor, *Neoliberalization, Universities and the Public Intellectual: Species, Gender and Class and the Production of Knowledge* (London: Palgrave Macmillan, 2016).
28 Keren and Hawkins, *Speaking Power to Truth*, 6.

29. Ronald N. Jacobs and Eleanor Townsley, *The Space of Opinion: Media Intellectuals and the Public Sphere* (Oxford: Oxford University Press, 2011), 10.
30. Clint Burnham, "Slavoj Žižek as an Internet Philosopher," in *Žižek and the Media: A Reader*, ed. Matthew Flisfeder and Louis Willis (London: Palgrave Macmillan, 2014), 201–10.
31. Keren and Hawkins, *Speaking Power to Truth*, 6.
32. See Gil Eyal, *The Crisis of Expertise* (Cambridge, UK: Polity Press, 2019); Tom Nichols, *The Death of Expertise: The Campaign against Established Knowledge and Why It Matters* (Oxford: Oxford University Press, 2017).
33. Henry Farrell, "The Tech Intellectuals," *Democracy* 30 (Fall 2013), https://democracyjournal.org/magazine/30/the-tech-intellectuals/.
34. Farrell, "Tech Intellectuals."
35. Jodi Dean, *Blog Theory: Feedback and Capture in the Circuits of Drive* (Cambridge, UK: Polity Press, 2010), 1.
36. Jonathan Beller, *The Cinematic Mode of Production: Attention Economy and the Society of the Spectacle* (Lebanon, NH: University Press of New England, 2006), 4.
37. Keren and Hawkins, *Speaking Power to Truth*, 7.
38. Keren and Hawkins, 8.
39. Keren and Hawkins, 5.
40. Bonnie Kristian, "We're All Public Intellectuals," *The National Interest*, January 24, 2017, https://nationalinterest.org/feature/were-all-public-intellectuals-now-19171.
41. Keren and Hawkins, *Speaking Power to Truth*, 7. See also Jennifer Cobbe, "Algorithmic Surveillance," *SSRN*, November 3, 2018, https://ssrn.com/abstract=3277966.
42. Liz Pirnie, "Creating the Conditions for an Intellectually Active People: What Today's Public Intellectual Can Learn from Anonymous," in *Speaking Power to Truth: Digital Discourse and the Public Intellectual*, ed. Michael Keren and Richard Hawkins (Athabasca, AB: Athabasca University Press, 2015), 94.
43. For a more positive use of the intellectual invention of a public, see Corey Robin, "How Intellectuals Create a Public," *Chronicle of Higher Education*, January 22, 2016, https://www.chronicle.com/article/How-Intellectuals-Create-a/234984.
44. For example, two of the most common typologies of intellectuals are Gramsci's "traditional" and "organic," and Foucault's "general" and "specific."
45. Jagna Oltarzewska, "'So Much Depends on Circumstances': Žižek in France," *Études Anglaises* 1, no. 58 (January 2005): 53.
46. See Charles Kurzman and Lynn Owens, "The Sociology of Intellectuals," *Annual Review of Sociology* 28 (August 2002): 63–90; Christine V. Wood, "The Sociologies of Knowledge, Science, and Intellectuals: Distinctive Traditions and Overlapping Perspectives," *Sociology Compass* 4, no. 10 (October 2010): 909–23.
47. Michèle Lamont, "How to Become a Dominant French Philosopher: The

Case of Jacques Derrida," *American Journal of Sociology* 93 no. 3 (November 1987): 584–622; Lamont, *How Professors Think* (Cambridge, MA: Harvard University Press, 2009); Charles Camic, "The Making of a Method: A Historical Reinterpretation of the Early Parsons," *American Sociological Review* 52, no. 4 (August 1987), 421–39; Camic, "Reputation and Predecessor Selection: Parsons and the Institutionalists," *American Sociological Review* 57, no. 4 (August 1992): 421–45; Neil Gross, "Becoming a Pragmatist Philosopher: Status, Self-Concept, and Intellectual Choice," *American Sociological Review* 67, no. 1 (February 2002), 52–76; *Richard Rorty* (Chicago: University of Chicago Press, 2008); Scott Frickel and Neil Gross, "A General Theory of Scientific/Intellectual Movements," *American Sociological Review* 70, no. 2 (April 2005): 204–32.

48 Charles Camic and Neil Gross, "The New Sociology of Ideas," in *The Blackwell Companion to Sociology*, ed. Judith R. Blau, 2nd ed. (Oxford, UK: Blackwell, 2001), 230–49; Charles Camic et al., *Social Knowledge in the Making* (Chicago: University of Chicago Press, 2011).

49 See also Lucile Dumont, "The Moving Frontiers of Intellectual Work: The Importation and Early Reception of Roland Barthes' Works in the United States (1960s–1980s)," *Sociologica* 1 (2017): https://doi.org/10.2383/86984.

50 Richard Rorty (1931–2007) was a renowned American pragmatist philosopher.

51 Charles Camic and Neil Gross, "The New Sociology of Ideas," in *The Blackwell Companion to Sociology*, ed. Judith R. Blau, 2nd ed. (Oxford, UK: Blackwell, 2001), 243.

52 Pierre Bourdieu, *Pascalian Meditations*, trans. Richard Nice (Stanford, CA: Stanford University Press, 2000), 131.

53 See Kauko Pietila, *Reason of Sociology: George Simmel and Beyond* (London: Sage, 2010), 64.

54 Thomas Medvetz, "Bourdieu and the Sociology of Intellectual Life," in *The Oxford Handbook of Pierre Bourdieu*, ed. Thomas Medvetz and Jeffery J. Sallaz (New York: Oxford University Press, 2018), 460.

55 See Pierre Bourdieu, "Intellectual Field and Creative Project," *Social Science Information* 8 (April 1969): 89–119; Bourdieu, *The Rules of Art: Genesis and Structure of the Literary Field*, trans. Susan Emanuel (Cambridge, UK: Polity Press, 1992); Bourdieu, *The Field of Cultural Production* (Cambridge, UK: Polity Press, 1993).

56 Göran Bolin, "The Forms of Value: Problems of Convertibility in Field Theory," *tripleC* 10, no. 1 (January 2012): 33.

57 Medvetz, "Bourdieu and the Sociology of Intellectual Life," 468.

58 Anthony King, "Thinking with Bourdieu against Bourdieu: A 'Practical' Critique of the Habitus," *Sociological Theory* 18, no. 3 (November 2000): 425.

59 See Pierre Bourdieu, "The Social Conditions of the International Circulation of Ideas," in *Bourdieu: A Critical Reader*, ed. Richard Shusterman (Oxford, UK: Blackwell, 1999), 220–28; Marco Santoro, "How 'Not' to Become a Dominant French Sociologist: Bourdieu in Italy, 1966–2009," *Sociologica* 2, no, 3 (2009): https://doi.org/10.2383/31372; Santoro, "From Bourdieu to Cultural Sociol-

ogy," *Cultural Sociology* 5, no. 1 (March 2011): 3–23; Marco Santoro and Marco Solaroli, "Contesting Culture: Bourdieu and the Strong Program in Cultural Sociology," in *Routledge International Handbook of the Sociology of Art and Culture*, ed. Laurie Hanquinet (New York: Routledge, 2015), 49–76; Marco Santoro et al., "Bourdieu's International Circulation. An Exercise In Intellectual Mapping," in *The Oxford Handbook of Pierre Bourdieu*, ed. Thomas Medvetz and Jeffery J. Sallaz (New York: Oxford University Press, 2018), 21–67.

60 See Randall Collins, *The Sociology of Philosophies: A Global Theory of Intellectual Change* (Cambridge, MA: Harvard University Press, 1998).

61 See, for example, Dyala Hamzah, ed., *The Making of the Arab Intellectual: Empire, Public Sphere and the Colonial Coordinates of Selfhood* (London: Routledge, 2012).

62 Jeffery C. Alexander, "Public Intellectuals and Civil Society," in *Intellectuals and Their Public: Perspectives from the Social Sciences*, ed. Christian A. Fleck and Andreas Hess (Farnham, UK: Ashgate, 2009), 21.

63 See Regis Debray, *Teachers, Writers, Celebrities: The Intellectuals of Modern France* (London: NLB, 1981); Antoine Lilti, *The Invention of Celebrity* (Cambridge, UK: Polity Press, 2017); Johannes Angermuller and Julian Hamann, "The Celebrity Logics of the Academic Field: The Unequal Distribution of Citation Visibility of Applied Linguistics Professors in Germany, France, and the United Kingdom," *Journal for Discourse Studies* 1 (2019): 77–93.

64 Peter William Walsh and David Lehmann, "Academic Celebrity," *International Journal of Politics, Culture, and Society* 34 (March 2021): 26.

65 Lewis Coser, "The Intellectual as Celebrity," *Dissent* 20, no. 1 (1973): 47.

66 Coser, 50.

67 Richard A. Lanham, *The Economics of Attention: Style and Substance in the Age of Information* (Chicago: University of Chicago Press, 2006).

68 Coser, "Intellectual as Celebrity," 53.

69 Olivier Driessens, "The Celebritization of Society and Culture: Understanding the Structural Dynamics of Celebrity Culture," *International Journal of Cultural Studies* 16, no. 6 (November 2013): 650.

70 Olivier Driessens, "Celebrity Capital: Redefining Celebrity Using Field Theory," *Theory and Society* 42 (September 2013): 543–60.

71 Jeffery C. Alexander, "Cultural Pragmatics: Social Performance Between Ritual and Strategy," *Sociological Theory* 22, no. 4 (December 2004): 527–73.

72 Jeffery C. Alexander, "Celebrity-Icon," *Cultural Sociology* 4, no. 3 (November 2010): 323–36.

73 Jeffery C. Alexander, "Dramatic Intellectuals," *International Journal of Politics, Culture, and Society* 29, no. 4 (December 2016): 343.

74 Bakke, *Likeness*, 123.

75 Paul A. Bové, "Celebrity and Betrayal: The High Intellectuals of Postmodern Culture," *Minnesota Review* 21 (Fall 1983): 83.

76 Geoffrey Galt Harpham, "Doing the Impossible: Slavoj Žižek and the End of Knowledge," *Critical Inquiry* 29, no. 3 (Spring 2003): 453–85.

77 For a specific discussion on positioning theory, see Patrick Baert, "Positioning Theory and Intellectual Interventions," *Journal for the Theory of Social Behavior* 42, no. 3 (April 2012): 304–24; Patrick Baert and Marcus Morgan, "A Performative Framework for the Studying of Intellectuals," *European Journal of Social Theory* 21, no. 3 (February 2017): 1–18; Simon Susen and Patrick Baert, *The Sociology of Intellectuals: After "The Existentialist Moment"* (London: Palgrave Macmillan, 2017).

78 Gil Eyal and Larissa Buchholz, "From the Sociology of Intellectuals to the Sociology of Interventions," *Annual Review of Sociology* 36, no. 1 (2010): 120.

79 For a review of performance in the digital age, see Martina Leeker, Imanuel Schipper, and Timon Beyes, eds., *Performing the Digital* (Bielefeld, Germany: Transcript, 2017).

80 See Jeffrey C. Alexander and Giuseppe Sciortino, "On Choosing One's Intellectual Predecessors: The Reductionism of Camic's Treatment of Parsons and the Institutionalists," *Sociological Theory* 14, no. 2 (July 1996): 154–71; Patrick Baert, *The Existentialist Moment: The Rise of Sartre as Public Intellectual* (Cambridge, UK: Polity Press, 2015), 161.

81 Pierre Bourdieu and Jean Claude Passeron, "Sociology and Philosophy in France since 1945: Death and Resurrection of a Philosophy without Subject," *Social Research* 34, no. 1 (Spring 1967): 162.

82 See Jeffrey C. Alexander, Bernhard Giesen, and Jason L. Mast, eds., *Social Performance: Symbolic Action, Cultural Pragmatics, and Ritual* (Cambridge: Cambridge University Press, 2006).

83 Baert, *Existentialist Moment*, 14.

84 Martina Leeker, Imanuel Schipper, and Timon Beyes, eds., *Performing the Digital: Performativity and Performance Studies in Digital Cultures* (Bielefeld: Transcript Verlag, 2017), 9.

85 Leeker, Schipper, and Beyes, 11.

86 According to Coser, for example, the power of ideas circulates and propagates through intellectual sects, that is, committed intellectuals who share fidelity to their tradition's founder, such as Marx or Freud, as well as the passion for spreading their world-changing ideas. See his *Men of Ideas* (New York: Free Press, 1965). Using a similar notion, Charles Kadushin noted that only "when intellectuals are well 'organized,' at least into informal circles, that the market place gives them considerable power over the production of books and journals." See his "Intellectuals and Cultural Power," *Media, Culture and Society* 4, no. 3 (July 1982): 262; and his *The American Intellectual Elite* (Boston: Little Brown, 1974).

87 Jacques Rancière, "A propos de l'etre et l'evénement d'Alain Badiou," 1989, http://horlieu-editions.com/textes-en-ligne/philosophie/ranciere-a-propos-d-etre-et-evenement-d-alain-badiou.pdf.

88 Jacobs and Townsley, *Media Intellectuals*, 70–71.

89 By "sacrificial intellectual" I do not necessarily mean that Žižek is a sacrificial intellectual per se, but that he acts and performs himself as one. This

Žižekian self-positioning is linked to the process which allowed him to attain various academic positions across the world, while, importantly, maintaining a self-portrayal of an academic pariah. However, this argument does not hold Žižek to be pathbreaking per se; rather, it emphasizes how his unconventional performance is perceived and received by other intellectuals and cultural critics, in a way that propagated his interventions.

90 The term "trade-off" could lead to the misinterpretation that academic recognition and media celebrity are only negatively correlated or mutually exclusive. Yet this trade-off feeds off today's intellectual conditions and is aligned with the "celebritization" of contemporary academic life. It does not mean that academic respectability and intellectual celebrity exclude each other, but in fact they are related to each other, as Žižek's case demonstrates.

91 According to Baert's distinction, each such type of public intellectual performs a specific public engagement: the "authoritative" is a general, elitist, position of speaking to the public from above, while the "expert" type is more confined to a field of expertise, and the "dialogical," which presents itself as equal to the public. See Baert, *Existentialist Moment*, 184–89.

92 For a discussion on archiving as a method, see Marlene Manoff, "Theories of the Archive across the Disciplines," *Libraries and the Academy* 4, no. 1 (January 2004): 9–25; Jacques Derrida, *Archive Fever: A Freudian Impression* (Chicago: University of Chicago Press, 1996).

93 On the use of new social media in social research, see Peter Adler, "The Sociologist as Celebrity: The Role of Media in Field Research," *Qualitative Sociology* 7 (December 1984): 310–26; Dhiraj Murthy, "Digital Ethnography: An Examination of the Use of New Technologies for Social Research," *Sociology* 42 (October 2008): 837–55; Charles F. Gattone, "The Social Scientist as Public Intellectual in an Age of Mass Media," *International Journal of Politics, Culture, and Society*, 25 (September 2012): 175–86; Patrick Baert and Josh Booth, "Tensions within the Public Intellectual: Political Interventions from Dreyfus to the New Social Media," *International Journal of Politics, Culture, and Society* 25 (September 2012): 111–26.

94 For this classification of work see UK SIC 2007, January 24 2022, Office of National Statistics, http://www.pgagroup.com/business-activity-classification.html. For the educational classification see Hildegard Brauns et al., "The CASMIN Educational Classification in International Comparative Research," in *Advances in Cross-National Comparison: A European Working Book for Demographic and Socio-Economic Variables*, ed. Jürgen H. P. Hoffmeyer-Zlotnik and Christof Wolf (New York: Kluwer Academic; Plenum, 2003), 221–44.

95 For a discussion on participant observations in social research, see Michael Burawoy, "The Extended Case Method," *Sociological Theory* 16, no. 1 (March 1998): 4–33; Robert K. Yin, *Case Study Research: Design and Methods*, 4th ed. (Thousand Oaks, CA: Sage, 2009).

96 See, for example, Daniel R. Huebner, *Becoming Mead: The Social Process of Academic Knowledge* (Chicago: University of Chicago Press, 2014).

CHAPTER ONE

1 Bakke, *Likeness*, 28, emphasis in original.
2 The symposium that marked the founding of the Society for Theoretical Psychoanalysis, also known as the Ljubljana School, took place on October 11–12, 1982. This event is chronicled in *Problemi—Razprave* 4–5 (1983).
3 Ian Parker, *Slavoj Žižek: A Critical Introduction* (London: Pluto Press, 2004), 11.
4 For example, see Tomaž Mastnak, "The Implosion of the Social: Beyond Radical Democracy," in *The Subject and Democracy*, ed. Tomaž Mastnak and Rado Rika (Ljubljana: Freedom Press, 1988), 113–25.
5 For a focused discussion on Slovenian civil society, see Tatjana Rakar, Tomaž Deželan, Senka Š. Vrbica, Zinka Kolarič, Mateja Nagode, and Andreja Črnak-Meglič, *Civil Society in Slovenia* (Ljubljana: Narodna in Univerzitetna Knjižnica, 2011).
6 Jeffery C. Alexander in Håkon Larsen, "Cultural Sociology as Social Research: A Conversation with Jeffrey C. Alexander," *Sosiologisk Tidsskrift* 22, no. 1 (January 2014): 77.
7 See Sabrina P. Ramet, *Balkan Babel: The Disintegration of Yugoslavia from the Death of Tito to the Fall of Milošević*, 4th ed. (London: Verso, 2002).
8 See Misha Glenny, *The Fall of Yugoslavia: The Third Balkan War* (New York: Penguin Books, 1992).
9 Mladen Dolar, personal interview by author, April 24, 2017, Le Petit Café, Ljubljana.
10 Jones Irwin and Helena Motoh, *Žižek and His Contemporaries* (London: Bloomsbury, 2014), 15.
11 Irwin and Motoh, 15.
12 Mladen Dolar, personal interview by author, April 24, 2017, Le Petit Café, Ljubljana.
13 Slavoj Žižek, personal interview by author, April 25, 2017, Ljubljana.
14 Slavoj Žižek, personal interview by author, April 25, 2017, Ljubljana.
15 Slavoj Žižek, personal interview by author, April 25, 2017, Ljubljana.
16 See also Federico G. Sicurella, "Intellectuals as Spokespersons for the Nation in the Post-Yugoslav Context: A Critical Discourse Study" (Ph.D. diss., Lancaster University, 2015).
17 Parker, *Slavoj Žižek*, 13.
18 See Adolf Bibič, "The Emergence of Pluralism in Slovenia," *Communist and Post-Communist Studies* 26, no. 4 (December 1993): 367–86.
19 Mladen Dolar, personal interview by author, April 24, 2017, Le Petit Café, Ljubljana.
20 Mladen Dolar, personal interview by author, April 24, 2017, Le Petit Café, Ljubljana.

21 Slavoj Žižek, "'Suture': Forty Years Later," in *Concept and Form*, vol. 2 of *The Cahiers pour l'Analyse and Contemporary French Thought*, ed. Peter Hallward and Knox Peden (London: Verso, 2012), 147.

22 Rastko Močnik, "Postmodernism and the Alternative," in *NSK from Kapital to Capital*, ed. Zdenka Badovinac et al. (1985, Ljubljana; Cambridge, MA: MIT Press, 2015), 118–34; Stina E. Lyon, "What Influence? Public Intellectuals, the State and Civil Society," in *Intellectuals and Their Public: Perspectives from the Social Sciences*, ed. Christian A. Fleck and Andreas Hess (Farnham, UK: Ashgate, 2009), 69–88.

23 The first wave of such translations was done in the 1960s with the translations of still partly controversial existentialist authors Sartre and Camus. The most important wave of translations, however, followed from 1970, with texts by Horkheimer, Marcuse, Althusser, Husserl, Heidegger, Saussure, Derrida, as well as Orwell's *Animal Farm* and the first post–World War II translation of Nietzsche's *Birth of Tragedy*. Later came those of Foucault, Deleuze, Guattari, Adorno, Gramsci, Balibar and a whole range of translations of Freud, Lacan, and Alain-Miller. See Boris Vezjak, "Hegelianism in Slovenia: A Short Introduction," *Bulletin of the Hegel Society of Great Britain* 17, no. 2 (1996): 1–12; Helena Motoh, "'Punk Is a Symptom': Intersections of Philosophy and Alternative Culture in the 80's Slovenia," *Synthesis Philosophica* 54, no. 2 (January 2012): 285–96.

24 Mladen Dolar, personal interview by author, April 24, 2017, Le Petit Café, Ljubljana.

25 Mladen Dolar, personal interview by author, April 24, 2017, Le Petit Café, Ljubljana.

26 Ian Parker, *Slavoj Žižek*, 12.

27 See Rastko Močnik, "From Nation to Identity," *School Field* 13, no. 6 (2002): 81–98.

28 Slavoj Žižek, personal interview by author, April 25, 2017, Ljubljana.

29 Slavoj Žižek, personal interview by author, April 25, 2017, Ljubljana.

30 Slavoj Žižek, personal interview by author, April 25, 2017, Ljubljana.

31 Slavoj Žižek and Glen Daly, *Conversations with Žižek* (Cambridge, UK: Polity Press, 2004), 29.

32 Slavoj Žižek, personal interview by author, April 25, 2017, Ljubljana.

33 Radio Študent, established in 1969, played a significant role in the dissemination of ideas in Slovenia. See also Tomaž Mastnak, "Civil Society in Slovenia: From Opposition to Power," *Studies in Comparative Communism* 23, nos. 3–4 (Autumn–Winter 1990): 305–17. *Mladina* is a weekly magazine for young readership established after World War II, which during the mid-1980s became a forum for democratic civil society.

34 Mladen Dolar, personal interview by author, April 24, 2017, Le Petit Café, Ljubljana.

35 Slavoj Žižek, personal interview by author, April 25, 2017, Ljubljana.

36 Žižek and Daly, *Conversations with Žižek*, 24.

37 Tony Myers, *Slavoj Žižek* (London: Routledge, 2003), 8.
38 Mladen Dolar, interview by author, 2017. Močnik was indeed a key figure in the shaping of the Ljubljana School's position and specifically Žižek's positioning. He studied in Paris in 1969–1970, and again in 1975 (for a PhD under the semiotician Algirdas J. Greimas). As noted by Kaitlyn Tucker, "Močnik brought certain French Structuralist and semiotic texts to Slovenia and certain Slovene thinkers to Paris. Most notably, Močnik introduced Žižek to Derrida, an event which in itself comprised another critical moment in the history of the Ljubljana School." See Kaitlyn Tucker Sorenson, "Experience as Device: Encountering Russian Formalism in the Ljubljana School," *Slavic Review* 79, no. 1 (Spring 2020): 91–114.
39 Žižek and Daly, *Conversations with Žižek*, 28–29.
40 Mladen Dolar, personal interview by author, April 24, 2017, Le Petit Café, Ljubljana.
41 Slavoj Žižek, "Civil Society, Fanaticism, and Digital Reality: A Conversation with Slavoj Žižek," interview by Geert Lovink, *Ctheory* (1996): https://journals.uvic.ca/index.php/ctheory/article/view/14649/5529.
42 Žižek, "Civil Society, Fanaticism, and Digital Reality," 1996.
43 Slavoj Žižek, personal interview by author, April 25, 2017, Ljubljana.
44 Žižek's MA thesis was published in Serbo-Croatian the next year in 1976, under the title "Znak, Oznacitelj, Pismo" (Sign, Signifier, Letter).
45 Tucker Sorenson, "Experience as Device."
46 Mladen Dolar, personal interview by author, April 24, 2017, Le Petit Café, Ljubljana.
47 Mladen Dolar, personal interview by author, April 24, 2017, Le Petit Café, Ljubljana.
48 Niilo Kauppi, *French Intellectual Nobility: Institutional and Symbolic Transformations in the Post-Sartrian Era* (New York: State University of New York Press, 1996).
49 Mladen Dolar, personal interview by author, April 24, 2017, Le Petit Café, Ljubljana.
50 Mladen Dolar, personal interview by author, April 24, 2017, Le Petit Café, Ljubljana.
51 Mladen Dolar, personal interview by author, April 24, 2017, Le Petit Café, Ljubljana.
52 See Raphael Sassower, *The Price of Public Intellectuals* (London: Palgrave Macmillan, 2014).
53 For example, Žižek and Dolar's PhD supervisor, Božidar Debenjak, was a charismatic lecturer on Hegel's phenomenology of spirit, using his own translation of it.
54 Mladen Dolar, personal interview by author, April 24, 2017, Le Petit Café, Ljubljana.
55 *Tel Quel* (As Is) was a group and a journal based in Paris (published 1962–1980), dealing with avant-garde literary critique associated with structural-

ism and deconstruction. See Niilo Kauppi, *The Making of an Avant-Garde: Tel Quel* (New York: Mouton de Gruyter, 1994).

56   Tucker Sorenson, *"Experience as Device."*

57   Žižek and Daly, *Conversations with Žižek*, 30.

58   Slavoj Žižek, personal interview by author, April 25, 2017, Ljubljana.

59   See Slavoj Žižek, "The Inherent Transgression," *Cultural Values* 2, no. 1 (March 1998): 1–17; Jason Glynos, "Self-Transgression and Freedom," *Crispp* 6, no. 2 (June 2003): 1–20; Glynos, "Self-Transgressive Enjoyment as a Freedom Fetter," *Political Studies* 56 (October 2008): 679–704.

60   Mladen Dolar, personal interview by Kaitlyn Tucker Sorenson, January 7, 2016, Ljubljana.

61   Making this positioning even more explicit, Žižek maintains: "This is why I insist so much on the split between Foucault and Derrida, on the one hand (despite all their differences), and Lacan. If we understand modernism in terms of the urge to demask an illusion, etc., then deconstruction is itself a most extreme form of modernism. At this general level, despite all *their* differences, Habermas and Lacan move in the same direction in accepting certain limits and renouncing certain utopian conditions on the possibility of freedom. The way these divisions have been made should be reformulated.... But I disagree with the way in which Habermas understands this in relation to the postmodernism debate. For me, it is modernism which insists on the utopian idea of disalienation, while postmodernism is precisely the recognition that you accept a certain division as the price of freedom. In this specific sense, Habermas is a postmodernist without knowing it." See Peter Dews and Peter Osborne, "Lacan in Slovenia," *Radical Philosophy* 58 (Summer 1991): 26.

62   Žižek and Daly, *Conversations with Žižek*, 33–34.

63   Žižek and Daly, 36.

64   Published in Belgrade by the Institut za Filozofiju i Društvenu Teoriju.

65   Jure Simoniti, "The Slovene Re-Actualization of Hegel's Philosophy," *Filozofija i Društvo* 26, no. 4 (2015): 783.

66   See Slavoj Žižek, "Eastern Europe's Republics of Gilead," *New Left Review* 183 (September–October 1990): 50–62.

67   Mladen Dolar, personal interview by author, April 24, 2017, Le Petit Café, Ljubljana.

68   More recently Žižek used the same framework again in his coauthored publication with student Agon Hamza, in their *From Myth to Symptom: The Case of Kosovo* (Pristina: Kolektivi Materializmi Dialektik, 2013). See also Sean Homer, *Slavoj Žižek and Radical Politics* (London: Routledge, 2016), 3–10.

69   Parker, *Slavoj Žižek*, 27.

70   Sean Sheehan, *Žižek: A Guide for the Perplexed* (London: Continuum, 2012), 9.

71   See also Tomaž Mastnak, "On the Soul of Social Movements: A Few Remarks from Up Close on Žižek's Letter from Afar," in *NSK from Kapital to Capital*, ed. Zdenka Badovinac et al. (1987, Ljubljana; Cambridge, MA: MIT Press, 2015),

177–82; "From the New Social Movements to Political Parties," in *Yugoslavia in Turmoil: After Self-Management*, ed. James Simmie and Jose Dekleva (New York: Pinter Publishers, 1991), 32–58; "Civil Society and Fascism," in *NSK from Kapital to Capital*, ed. Zdenka Badovinac et al. (2014, Ljubljana; Cambridge, MA: MIT Press, 2015), 280–89.

72 See Scott Frickel and Neil Gross, "A General Theory of Scientific/Intellectual Movements," *American Sociological Review* 70, no. 2 (April 2005): 204–32.

73 See George Konrad and Ivan Szelenyi, *The Intellectuals on the Road to Class Power: A Sociological Study of the Role of the Intelligentsia in Socialism*, trans. Andrew Arato and Richard E. Allen (New York: Helen and Kurt Wolff, 1979); Kennedy D. Michael, "The Constitution of Critical Intellectuals: Polish Physicians, Peace Activists and Democratic Civil Society," *Studies in Comparative Communism* 23, nos. 3–4 (Autumn-Winter 1990): 281–301; George Konrad and Ivan Szelenyi, "Intellectuals and Domination in Post-Communist Societies," in *Social Theory for a Changing Society*, ed. Pierre Bourdieu and James S. Coleman (New York: Russell Sage Foundation, 1991), 337–72.

74 Irwin and Motoh, *Žižek and his Contemporaries*, 29. For a focused examination of the third trend of Laibach/NSK, see Alexei Monroe, *Interrogating Machine: Laibach and NSK* (Cambridge, MA: MIT Press, 2005); Ian Parker, "Žižek, NSK, Marxism, Psychoanalysis and the State: Cynicism and Resistance to Capitalism and Bureaucracy in Europe," *International Journal of Žižek Studies* 6, no. 1 (2012): 1–21; and Simon Bell, "Laibach and the NSK: Aestheticising the East/West Nexus in Post-Totalitarian Europe," *Культура/Culture* 4 (November 2014): 105–14.

75 Tomaž Mastnak, "Civil Society in Slovenia: From Opposition to Power," *Studies in Comparative Communism* 23, nos. 3–4 (Autumn–Winter 1990): 306.

76 See Slavoj Žižek, "History and Repetition: How 'Truth Arises out of Misrecognition,'" in *NSK from Kapital to Capital* [1982], 35–49; "Ideology, Fascism, Punk," in *NSK from Kapital to Capital* [1984], 96–113.

77 See Mladen Dolar, "O Nekaterih Vprašanjih in Protislovjih v Marksističnih Analizah Fašizma," *Problemi—Razprave* 16, no. 177/180 (1978): 49–111; Dolar, *Struktura Fašističnega Gospostva: Marksistične Analize Fašizma in Problem Teorije Ideologije* (Ljubljana: DDU Univerzum, 1982).

78 Motoh, "'Punk Is a Symptom,'" 290.

79 Mladen Dolar, "Psychoanalysis in Power: On Fascism, Marxism and the Poster Scandal," in *NSK from Kapital to Capital* [1987], 168–71; Mladen Dolar, "From Structuralism to Lacan—Interview with Mladen Dolar," in *Žižek and his Contemporaries*, ed. Jones Irwin and Helena Motoh (London: Bloomsbury, 2014), 93–112.

80 Phil Cohen, "Subcultural Conflict and Working-Class Community," *CCCS Working Papers* 2 (1972): 5–53.

81 See Maple Razsa and Andrej Kurnik, "The Occupy Movement in Žižek's Hometown: Direct Democracy and a Politics of Becoming," *American Ethnologist* 39, no. 2 (May 2012): 238–58.

82 Motoh, "'Punk Is a Symptom,'" 288.
83 Mastnak, "Civil Society in Slovenia," 310.
84 Irwin and Motoh, *Žižek and His Contemporaries*, 32.
85 "The poster scandal" refers to the 1987 winning race poster, made by the design division of the Neue Slowenische Kunst (NSK, new Slovenian art), which assumed the position of "state artists" to reveal the regime's true face. It caused a national scandal, ultimately leading to the decision to discontinue the race, for it pseudo-Nazi insignia supposed to critique Tito's personality cult. Dušan Nećak, "A Chronology of the Decay of Tito's Yugoslavia 1980–1991," *Nationalities Papers* 21, no. 1 (Spring 1993): 178.
86 Stuart Jeffries, "A Life in Writing: Slavoj Žižek," *The Guardian*, July 15, 2011.
87 Renata Salecl (b. 1962) was Žižek's first wife. She is a Slovenian philosopher, sociologist, and legal theorist. She holds research and teaching positions in Ljubljana and elsewhere. Together with Žižek and Dolar, she is a founder of the Society for Theoretical Psychoanalysis. See Salecl, in Dews and Osborne, "Lacan in Slovenia," 26.
88 Tomaž Mastnak, "On the Soul of Social Movements," 178.
89 Žižek, "Civil Society, Fanaticism, and Digital Reality."
90 Žižek, "Civil Society, Fanaticism, and Digital Reality."
91 Rastko Močnik, "How We Were Fighting for the Victory of Reason and What Happened When We Made It," in *A Non-veteran Reflection*, ed. Jones Irwin (Piran, Slovenia: Obalne Galerije Piran, 1993), 88.
92 See Slavoj Žižek, "Why Are Laibach and NSK Not Fascists?" in *NSK from Kapital to Capital* [1993], 202–4; "The Enlightenment of Laibach," in *NSK from Kapital to Capital* [1994], 205–12.
93 Pavel Gantar, "Discussions on Civil Society in Slovenia," in *Civil Society, Political Society, Democracy*, eds. Gigi Graziano and Adolf Bibič (Ljubljana: Slovenian Political Science Association, 1993), 350–65.
94 Mladen Dolar, personal interview by author, April 24, 2017, Le Petit Café, Ljubljana.
95 Alenka Zupančič, personal interview by author, April 26, 2017, Slovenian Academy of Sciences and Arts, Ljubljana.
96 Alenka Zupančič, personal interview by author, April 26, 2017, Slovenian Academy of Sciences and Arts, Ljubljana.
97 Aleš Erjavec, *Postmodernism and the Postsocialist Condition: Politicized Art under Late Socialism* (Berkeley: University of California Press, 2003), 96.
98 Motoh, "'Punk Is a Symptom,'" 299.
99 Slavoj Žižek, "Editorial," in *Problemi* 19, no. 205–6 (1981): 27.
100 Žižek, in Irwin and Motoh, *Žižek and his Contemporaries*, 132–35.
101 Parker, *Slavoj Žižek*, 32.
102 See Geoff Boucher, *The Charmed Circle of Ideology: A Critique of Laclau and Mouffe, Butler and Žižek* (Melbourne: Re.Press, 2009).
103 Peter Sloterdijk (1947–) is a contemporary German philosopher, a public in-

tellectual, and a long-time critic of liberal democracy. Notwithstanding this right-wing tendency, Žižek's frequently refers to his works.
104 Motoh, "'Punk Is a Symptom,'" 292.
105 Žižek, "Ideology, Fascism, Punk," 113.
106 Slavoj Žižek, "Why Are Laibach and NSK Not Fascists?" in *NSK from Kapital to Capital*, ed. Zdenka Badovinac et al. (1993; Ljubljana; Cambridge, MA: MIT Press, 2015), 202–4.
107 Parker, *Slavoj Žižek*, 32; see also Parker, "The Truth about Over-identification," in *The Truth of Žižek*, ed. Paul Bowman and Richard Stamp (London: Continuum, 2007), 144–60.
108 Parker, *Slavoj Žižek*, 32.
109 Slavoj Žižek, *Filozofija skozi Psihoanalizo* (Ljubljana: DDU Univerzum, 1984), 124.
110 Slavoj Žižek, *Interrogating the Real* (London: Continuum, 2005), xiii.
111 Žižek, *Interrogating the Real*, xv.
112 Žižek, xv.
113 Dušan Nećak, "A Chronology of the Decay of Tito's Yugoslavia 1980–1991," 176.
114 International Crisis Group, *ICG Kosovo Spring Report*, March 1, 1998, https://www.refworld.org/docid/3ae6a6ec4.html.
115 Parker, *Slavoj Žižek*, 25.
116 Attila Ágh, "The Parliamentarization of the East Central European Parties: Party Discipline in the Hungarian Parliament, 1990–1996," in *Party Discipline and Parliamentary Government*, ed. Shaun Bowler, David M. Farrell, and Richard S. Katz (Columbus: Ohio State University Press, 1999), 167–88.
117 Žižek and Daly, *Žižek and His Contemporaries*, 49.
118 Žižek, "Civil Society, Fanaticism, and Digital Reality," 1996.
119 Žižek, in Dews and Osborne, "Lacan in Slovenia," 28.
120 Salecl, in Dews and Osborne, 29.
121 Žižek, in Dews and Osborne, 32.
122 Žižek, in Dews and Osborne, 50.
123 On his part, and alluding to Freud's key "Signorelli" incident and to Lacan's structural maxim of it, Dolar applied this framework to analyze Yugoslavia's disintegration. See Mladen Dolar, "The Unconscious Is Structured as Yugoslavia," *Mladina*, September 29, 1989, 15–30.
124 In a previous article from 1989, "The Undergrowth of Enjoyment: How Popular Culture Can Serve as an Introduction to Lacan," Žižek extended this Lacanian framework to analyze and criticize pop-culture ideology in addition to the political one. Subsequently, Žižek's "theft-of-enjoyment" idea was picked up by political scientists in the study of nationalism. See Jason Glynos, "The Grip of Ideology: A Lacanian Approach to the Theory of Ideology," *Journal of Political Ideologies* 6, no. 2 (2001): 191–214; Yannis Stavrakakis and Nikos Chrysoloras, "(I Can't Get No) Enjoyment: Lacanian Theory and the Analysis of Nationalism," *Psychoanalysis, Culture & Society* 11 (July 2006): 144–63.

125 Žižek, "Eastern Europe's Republics of Gilead," 54.
126 Žižek, in Dews and Osborne, "Lacan in Slovenia," 30.
127 See Johanna Bockman and Gil Eyal, "Eastern Europe as a Laboratory for Economic Knowledge: The Transnational Roots of Neoliberalism," *American Journal of Sociology* 108, no. 2 (September 2002): 310–52.
128 Parker, *Slavoj Žižek*, 28.
129 Žižek, in Dews and Osborne, "Lacan in Slovenia," 25–26.
130 Parker, *Slavoj Žižek*, 28.
131 Žižek, in Dews and Osborne, "Lacan in Slovenia," 26.
132 Mladen Dolar, personal interview by author, April 24, 2017, Le Petit Café, Ljubljana.
133 Dušan Nećak, "A Chronology of the Decay of Tito's Yugoslavia 1980–1991," 173.
134 Žižek, "Civil Society, Fanaticism, and Digital Reality," 1996.

CHAPTER TWO

1 Clint Burnham, "Slavoj Žižek as an Internet Philosopher," in *Žižek and the Media: A Reader*, ed. Matthew Flisfeder and Louis Willis (London: Palgrave Macmillan, 2014).
2 Žižek, in Dews and Osborne, "Lacan in Slovenia," 25.
3 See Jamil Khader and Molly A. Rothenberg, eds., *Žižek Now* (Cambridge, UK: Polity Press, 2013), 5.
4 Mladen Dolar, personal interview by author, April 24, 2017, Le Petit Café, Ljubljana.
5 This is because there are many more second-language English speakers (and translators) than native speakers.
6 Oltarzewska, "'So Much Depends on Circumstances,'" 55.
7 Mladen Dolar, personal interview by author, April 24, 2017, Le Petit Café, Ljubljana.
8 Mladen Dolar, personal interview by author, April 24, 2017, Le Petit Café, Ljubljana.
9 Slavoj Žižek, personal interview by author, April 25, 2017, Ljubljana.
10 See Robert S. Boynton, "Enjoy your Žižek," *Lingua Franca* 8, no. 7 (October 1998): 1–10.
11 Oltarzewska, "'So Much Depends on Circumstances,'" 55.
12 I rely here on Genette's distinction, according to which "if the addressee of the text is indeed the reader, the addressee of the title is the public.... If the text is an object to be read, the title ... is an object to be circulated—or, if you prefer, a subject of conversation." See Gérard Genette, *Paratexts: Thresholds of Interpretation* (Cambridge: Cambridge University Press, 1997), 75. Also, Thoburn noted that "a book's title serves a dual function. It introduces readers to the text's theme ... but it also helps place the book in a market." See Nicholas Thoburn, *Anti-Book: On the Art and Politics of Radical Publishing* (Min-

neapolis: University of Minnesota Press, 2016), ix. See also Filipe Carreira da Silva and Monica Brito Vieira, *The Politics of the Book: A Study on the Materiality of Ideas* (University Park: Pennsylvania State University Press, 2019), 10. On Hegel in France, see Michael Kelly, *Hegel in France* (Birmingham, UK: University of Birmingham Press, 1992).

13 See Slavoj Žižek and Mladen Dolar, eds., *Hitchcock* (Ljubljana: DDU Univerzum, Analecta, 1984).

14 Žižek and Glen, *Conversations with Žižek*, 40–41. The volume on Hitchcock, *Tout ce que vous avez toujours voulu savoir sur Lacan, sans jamais oser le demander a Hitchcock*, was published in Paris by Navarin in 1988.

15 Žižek and Daly, *Conversations with Žižek*, 40.

16 Oltarzewska, "'So Much Depends on Circumstances,'" 58.

17 See Jeremy Ahearne, *Intellectuals, Culture and Public Policy in France: Approaches from the Left* (Liverpool, UK: Liverpool University Press, 2010).

18 See François Cusset, *French Theory: How Foucault, Derrida, Deleuze, & Co. Transformed the Intellectual Life of the United States* (Minneapolis: University of Minnesota Press, 2008); Niilo Kauppi, *Radicalism in French Culture: A Sociology of French Theory in the 1960s* (Surrey, UK: Ashgate, 2010); Andrew Cole. *The Birth of Theory* (Chicago: University of Chicago Press, 2014); Johannes Angermuller, *Why There Is No Poststructuralism in France: The Making of an Intellectual Generation* (London: Bloomsbury, 2015).

19 Tony Myers, *Slavoj Žižek*, 8; see also Laurent Jeanpierre and Sebastien Mosbah-Natanson, "French Sociologists and the Public Sphere of the Press: Thought Based on a Case Study (*Le Monde*, 1995–2002)," in *Intellectuals and Their Public: Perspectives from the Social Sciences*, ed. Christian A. Fleck and Andreas Hess (Farnham, UK: Ashgate, 2009), 173–92.

20 Paul A. Taylor, "Žižek's Brand of Philosophical Excess and the Treason of the Intellectuals: Wagers of Sin, Ugly Ducklings, and Mythical Swans," *International Journal of Žižek Studies* 8, no. 2 (2014): http://www.zizekstudies.org/index.php/IJZS/article/view/829/834.

21 Oltarzewska, "'So Much Depends on Circumstances,'" 57–58.

22 See Laurent Jeanpierre, "D'un communisme qui viendrait...," afterword to Slavoj Žižek, *Actualité du Manifeste du Parti Communiste* (Paris: Fayard, 2002), 214.

23 Oltarzewska, "'So Much Depends on Circumstances,'" 58.

24 Oltarzewska, 58.

25 Sean Homer, "It's the Political Economy, Stupid! On Žižek's Marxism," *Radical Philosophy* 109 (July–August 2001): 8.

26 *The Essential Žižek* is a compilation of Žižek's four major early works, put together into a set by Verso Press. See the website for this series at https://www.versobooks.com/series_collections/10-the-essential-zizek.

27 Slavoj Žižek, personal interview by author, April 25, 2017, Ljubljana.

28 See Agnes Heller, "Death of the Subject," *Thesis Eleven* 25, no. 1 (February 1990): 22–38.

29 For a specific evaluation of Žižek's analysis of the cynical position, see Adrian Johnston, "The Cynic's Fetish: Slavoj Žižek and the Dynamics of Belief," *Psychoanalysis, Culture & Society* 9, no. 3 (November 2004): 259–83.
30 Ernesto Laclau, in Slavoj Žižek, *The Sublime Object of Ideology* (London: Verso, 1989), ix.
31 Oltarzewska, "'So Much Depends on Circumstances,'" 57.
32 Laclau, in Žižek, *Sublime Object of Ideology*, ix.
33 Incidentally, this rejection of the clinical Lacan from psychology or psychoanalysis to literary circles is not without a cause, given Lacan's attack on what he called "ego-psychology" (assuming a united self), referring to the dominant psychological orientation in the United States. In fact, already in 1987, two years before the publication of *The Sublime Object of Ideology*, Žižek had published a paper, in his usual rhetorical question form, distancing Lacan from poststructuralism.
34 Catherine Liu and Devan Bailey, "The Apprentice in Theory: Fan, Student, Star," *Los Angeles Review of Books*, October 5, 2018, https://lareviewofbooks.org/article/the-apprentice-in-theory-fan-student-star/.
35 Stephen Hersh, "Lacan: A Radical Return to Freud," *Michigan Daily*, January 22, 1978, 3, https://digital.bentley.umich.edu/midaily/mdp.39015071754498/156.
36 Liu and Bailey, "The Apprentice in Theory."
37 See also David R. Shumway, "The Star System in Literary Studies," *PMLA* 112, no. 1 (January 1997): 85–100.
38 Slavoj Žižek, "Slavoj Žižek and Donald James in Conversation: Talking Ideas," *Institute of Contemporary Arts*, April 3, 1992, https://sounds.bl.uk/Arts-literature-and-performance/ICA-talks/024M-C0095X0843XX-0100V0.
39 Rod Stoneman, "When Channel 4 Was Radical," *Tribune Mag*, June 3, 2020, https://tribunemag.co.uk/2020/06/when-channel-4-was-radical.
40 For a specific analysis of the Lacanian genealogy, see Lorenzo Chiesa, ed., *Lacan and Philosophy: The New Generation* (Melbourne: Re.Press, 2014).
41 Laclau, in Žižek, *Sublime Object of Ideology*, x, emphasis in original.
42 Laclau, in Žižek, x.
43 Laclau, in Žižek, xi.
44 Laclau, in Žižek, xii.
45 Laclau, in Žižek, xii.
46 Laclau, in Žižek, xi.
47 Laclau, in Žižek, xii.
48 Laclau, in Žižek, xii.
49 Laclau, in Žižek, xii.
50 Laclau, in Žižek, xii.
51 Laclau, in Žižek, xii.
52 Laclau, in Žižek, xii.
53 Laclau, in Žižek, xiii.
54 Laclau, in Žižek, xv.

55 Jacob and Townsley, *Media Intellectuals*, 167. For a concise comparison of Žižek's reception in France and England, see Eliran Bar-El, "'If at First You Don't Succeed': Why Žižek Failed in France but Succeeded in England," *British Journal of Sociology* 72, no. 2 (March 2021): 412–25.
56 Slavoj Žižek, personal interview by author, April 25, 2017, Ljubljana.
57 With 10,273 citations, this work amounts to a fifth of Žižek's overall citations. It should be noted that citations are more fruitful than sales figures when describing impact. The reason is that academic books are exorbitantly expensive and therefore circulate through other means that are not reliably quantifiable (e.g., scans, PDFs, libraries, borrowing).
58 Žižek, *Sublime Object of Ideology*, xxiii.
59 As the acknowledgments section concedes, most the material of the book was already presented between 1987 and 1989 in a series of (noticeably) American Lacanian conferences or local newspapers (e.g., *Vestnik IMS*). See Slavoj Žižek, "'Pathological Narcissus' as a Socially Mandatory Form of Subjectivity," in *The Culture of Narcissism*, ed. Christopher Lasch (Zagreb: Naprijed, 1986); "The Subject before Subjectivation," *Vestnik IMS* 1, (1988): 86–96.
60 Žižek, *Sublime Object of Ideology*, 1.
61 Žižek, 1.
62 Matthew Specter, *Habermas: An Intellectual Biography* (Cambridge: Cambridge University Press, 2011), 1.
63 Žižek, *Sublime Object of Ideology*, 2.
64 Žižek, 2.
65 Žižek, 2.
66 Žižek, 2, emphasis in original.
67 See Daniel Bell, *The End of Ideology* (Cambridge, MA: Harvard University Press, 1960); Francis Fukuyama, "The End of History?," *National Interest* 16 (Summer 1989): 3–18.
68 Žižek, *Sublime Object of Ideology*, 2–3.
69 Žižek, 4.
70 Žižek, 5–6.
71 Žižek, 6.
72 Žižek, 6.
73 Žižek, 7.
74 We will see shortly how Žižek adds another space for his unique position in the form of the fourth element, beyond the triadic structure.
75 Žižek, *Sublime Object of Ideology*, 7.
76 Other instances where Žižek used the rhetorical question form are his articles: "Why Lacan Is Not a Post-Structuralist," "How Popular Culture Can Serve as an Introduction to Lacan," "Why Should a Dialectician Learn to Count to Four?," and "From Desire to Drive: Why Lacan Is Not Lacanian."
77 Rex Butler and Scott Stephens, preface to Slavoj Žižek, *The Universal Exception* (London: Continuum, 2006), 1–12.

78 Slavoj Žižek, in Ernesto Laclau, *New Reflections on the Revolutions of Our Time* (London: Verso, 1990), 249.
79 Žižek in Laclau, 302.
80 Žižek in Laclau, 302.
81 Žižek in Laclau, 302.
82 One such collaboration is *Contingency, Hegemony, Universality: Contemporary Dialogues on the Left*, coauthored with Judith Butler and Ernesto Laclau (London: Verso, 2000). Incidentally, Žižek recalls what pushed him to further advance his own series with Verso: after publishing the "triple-orgy book," "Laclau's dream was to bring us all together, Judith Butler, me and him, under his domination, that we would see him. But then when it was clear that we remain at our positions, it was over." Slavoj Žižek, interview by author, 2017.
83 Although some of the chapters of these books were published before in an article form, being guarded behind paywalls made it harder for them to reach public circulation. Books, especially by widely known publishers like Verso or Routledge, do not face such a problem and circulate more easily. Yet journal articles, even if harder to get, are more digestible than a long book, especially in a capitalist context when (reading) time is scarce. Thus, having *both* outlets means increasing public accessibility and intellectual affectivity.
84 Žižek and Daly, *Conversations with Žižek*, 40–41.
85 Slavoj Žižek, *For They Know Not What They Do: Enjoyment as a Political Factor* (London: Verso, 1991), 1.
86 Žižek, 1–2.
87 Žižek, 2.
88 Žižek, 3–4.
89 Helen Brown, "Slavoj Zizek: The World's Hippest Philosopher," *The Telegraph*, July 5, 2010, https://www.telegraph.co.uk/culture/books/authorinterviews/7871302/Slavoj-Zizek-the-worlds-hippest-philosopher.html.
90 Tim Dean, "Art as Symptom: Žižek and the Ethics of Psychoanalytic Criticism," *Diacritics* 32, no. 2 (2002): 20–41.
91 See Immanuel Kant, *Critique of Pure Reason* (1787; Cambridge: Cambridge University Press, 1998), 174–267; Theodor Adorno, *Introduction to Dialectics* (Cambridge, UK: Polity Press, 2017), 68–70.
92 Todd McGowan, "The Priority of the Example: Speculative Identity in Film Studies," in *Žižek and Media Studies: A Reader*, ed. Matthew Flisfeder and Louis Willis (London: Palgrave Macmillan, 2014), 71.
93 McGowan, 70.
94 McGowan, 73.
95 See Richard Stamp, "'Another Exemplary Case:' Žižek's Logic of Examples," in *The Truth of Žižek*, ed. Paul Bowman and Richard Stamp (London: Continuum, 2007), 171–76; Thomas Biebricher, "The Practices of Theorists: Habermas and Foucault as Public Intellectuals," *Philosophy and Social Criticism* 37, no. 6 (July 2021): 709–34; Bent Flyvbjerg, "Habermas and Foucault: Think-

ers for Civil Society?," *British Journal of Sociology* 49, no. 2 (June 1998): 210–33; *Making Social Science Matter* (Cambridge: Cambridge University Press, 2001), 66.
96   See Slavoj Žižek, *Mapping Ideology* (London: Verso, 1994).
97   Žižek and Daly, *Conversations with Žižek*, 40–41.
98   For Freud, the goal of a psychoanalysis—in theory and practice—was to make us conscious of the workings of the unconscious, and this goal is branded by the slogan "Wo Es war, soll Ich werden" (Where It was, shall I be), that is, to replace the It (id as unconscious) with the I (as conscious self).
99   Slavoj Žižek, *The Metastases of Enjoyment: On Women and Causality* (London: Verso, 1994), series preface, emphasis in original.
100 See Carsten Bagge Lausten and Henrik Jøker Bjerre, *The Subject of Politics: Slavoj Žižek's Political Philosophy* (Penrith, CA: Humanities-ebooks, 2015).
101 Žižek, *Metastases of Enjoyment*, 170.
102 This line of thought will be expanded later to critically analyze more recent phenomena such as political correctness.
103 Žižek, *Metastases of Enjoyment*, 208.
104 Slavoj Žižek, *The Indivisible Remainder: An Essay on Schelling and Related Matters* (London: Verso, 1996), 198–208.
105 Slavoj Žižek and F. W. J. von Schelling, *The Abyss of Freedom/Ages of the World* (Ann Arbor: University of Michigan Press, 1997).
106 Renata Salecl and Slavoj Žižek, eds., *Gaze and Voice as Love Objects* (Durham, NC: Duke University Press, 1996).
107 Salecl and Žižek, front matter.
108 Salecl and Žižek, front matter.
109 Slavoj Žižek, *The Plague of Fantasies* (London: Verso, 1997).
110 Žižek, 56.
111 Žižek, 56.
112 Slavoj Žižek, *The Ticklish Subject: The Absent Centre of Political Ontology* (London: Verso, 1999), 1.
113 Žižek, 4.
114 See Slavoj Žižek, "Multiculturalism, or, The Cultural Logic of Multinational Capitalism," *New Left Review* 1, no. 225 (September–October 1997): 34–51; "Against Human Rights," *New Left Review* 34 (July–August 2005): 115–31.
115 See Slavoj Žižek, "The Matrix, or, The Two Sides of Perversion," paper presented at the International Symposium at the Center for Art and Media, Karlsruhe, Germany, October 28, 1999, http://www.lacan.com/Žižek-matrix.htm; Žižek, "The Matrix, or, Malebranche in Hollywood," *Philosophy Today* 43 (1999): 11–26; Žižek, "The Matrix, or, The Two Sides of Perversion," in *The Matrix and Philosophy*, ed. William Irwin (Peru, IL: Open Court, 2002), 240–66.
116 Žižek, "The Matrix, or, The Two Sides of Perversion," 240.
117 Robert Samuels, "Žižek's Rhetorical Matrix: The Symptomatic Enjoyment of Postmodern Academic Writing," *JAC* 22, no. 2 (Spring 2002): 339.

118 Žižek, "The Matrix, or, The Two Sides of Perversion," 240.
119 Žižek, 244.
120 See Žižek's intervention in the American *In These Times, Ideology Reloaded* (2003), which repeats the second Matrix's title of *The Matrix Reloaded* (2003), http://www.lacan.com/zizekloaded.htm.
121 See Slavoj Žižek in *Laibach: A Film from Slovenia* (directed by Daniel Landin Peter Vezjak, 1993); *Predictions of Fire* (directed by Michael Benson, 1996).
122 Slavoj Žižek in *Liebe Dein Symptom wie Dich selbst!* (directed by Claudia Willke, Katharina Höcker, 1996), 0:00:50–0:01:36.
123 Žižek in *Liebe Dein Symptom wie Dich selbst!*, 2:35.
124 One of Žižek's most repeated jokes in his repertoire is that he indeed loves dialogues but specifically of the late Plato kind; namely when one side speaks all the time, and every so often the other side intervenes with an affirmative remark (i.e., not a "real" dialogue).

CHAPTER THREE

1   Fredric Jameson, *The Political Unconscious: Narrative as a Socially Symbolic Act* (London: Methuen, 1981). See also Gérard Genette, *Narrative Discourse: An Essay on Method* (Ithaca, NY: Cornell University Press, 1980).
2   James S. Hurley, "Real Virtuality: Slavoj Žižek and 'Post-Ideological' Ideology," *Postmodern Culture* 9, no. 1 (1998): https://doi.org/10.1353/pmc.1998.0036; Ian Parker, "Žižek: Ambivalence and Oscillation," *PINS* 30 (2004): 23–34.
3   Sarah Kay, *Žižek: A Critical Introduction* (Cambridge: Cambridge University Press, 2003); Tony Myers, *Slavoj Žižek* (London: Routledge, 2003); Ian Parker, *Slavoj Žižek: A Critical Introduction* (London: Pluto Press, 2004).
4   John B. Thompson, *Book Wars* (Cambridge, UK: Polity Press, 2021), 15.
5   See Michael Bhaskar, *The Content Machine: Towards a Theory of Publishing from the Printing Press to the Digital Network* (New York: Anthem Press, 2013), 5.
6   Thompson, *Book Wars*, 483.
7   Thompson, 466.
8   John B. Thompson, *Books in the Digital Age: The Transformation of Academic and Higher Education Publishing in Britain and the United States* (Cambridge, UK: Polity Press, 2005), 11. See also his *Merchants of Culture* (Cambridge, UK: Polity Press, 2010).
9   See Alfredo Joignant and Mauro Basaure, "Crisis and Public Intellectuals: From the Transnational Intellectual Field to the Digital Global Public Circuit," *Sociology Compass* 15, no. 5 (May 2021): https://doi.org/10.1111/soc4.12875.
10 On the formation of this distinction, see Kadushin, "Intellectuals and Cultural Power," 262.
11 Thompson, *Books in the Digital Age*, 11.
12 Mladen Dolar, interviewed by author, 2017.

13 Alenka Zupančič, interviewed by author, 2017.
14 The Open Syllabus Project (http://opensyllabusproject.org) aims to create a worldwide big-data corpus of university course syllabi, mainly from the past decade in the United States, for the purposes of research, teaching, and administration. Methodologically, it uses "teaching score" as a numerical indicator of the frequency with which a particular work is taught. It counts as "taught" any appearance (singular or multiple) of a work in a syllabus. An overall teaching score is based on "the rank of the text among citations in the total collection."
15 Elizabeth Wright and Edmond Wright, *The Žižek Reader* (Oxford, UK: Blackwell, 1999).
16 Wright and Wright, *Žižek Reader*.
17 Wright and Wright, vii.
18 Wright and Wright, vii.
19 Wright and Wright, viii.
20 Wright and Wright, viii.
21 Wright and Wright, viii.
22 Stuart Hall, "Encoding/Decoding," in *The Cultural Studies Reader*, ed. Simon During (London: Routledge, 1993), 101.
23 Hall, 102–3.
24 On academia as cult, see Andrew Marzoni, "Academia Is a Cult," *Washington Post*, November 1, 2018, https://www.washingtonpost.com/outlook/academia-is-a-cult/2018/10/31/eea787a0-bd08-11e8-b7d2-0773aa1e33da_story.html.
25 This review of Žižek became more widespread when it was republished in Eagleton's later book, which links intellectual and cultural figures, thus creating a mix of Yeats, Eliot, and Žižek but also David Beckham (who also appears on the front cover, of course). See Terry Eagleton, "Enjoy!," *London Review of Books* 19, no. 23 (November 1997): 7–9; Eagleton, *Figures of Dissent: Critical Essays on Fish, Spivak, Žižek and Others* (London: Verso, 2003).
26 Diane Elam, "Sublime Repetition," *Surfaces* 1 (1991): 6.
27 Elam, 9–10.
28 Denise Gigante, "Toward a Notion of Critical Self-Creation: Slavoj Žižek and the 'Vortex of Madness,'" *New Literary History* 29, no. 1 (Winter 1998): 153.
29 Edward R. O'Neill, "The Last Analysis of Slavoj Žižek," *Film-Philosophy* 5, no. 17 (2001): http://www.film-philosophy.com/vol5-2001/n17oneill, emphases added.
30 O'Neill, "Last Analysis."
31 John Lechte, "The Sublime Object of Ideology; Looking Awry: An Introduction to Jacques Lacan Through Popular Culture," *Thesis Eleven* 34, no. 1 (February 1993): 191.
32 Lechte, 195.
33 David R. Shumway, "The Star System in Literary Studies," *PMLA* 112, no. 1 (January 1997): 85–100.

34　Liu and Bailey, "The Apprentice in Theory."
35　Liu and Bailey, "The Apprentice in Theory."
36　Slavoj Žižek, "Lacan between Cultural Studies and Cognitivism," *Umbr(a): Science and Truth* 1 (2000): 9.
37　See Alan Sokal and Jean Bricmont, *Fashionable Nonsense* (New York: Picador, 1998).
38　Slavoj Žižek, "Cultural Studies versus the 'Third Culture,'" *South Atlantic Quarterly* 101, no. 1 (Winter 2002): 32.
39　Noah Horwitz, "Contra the Slovenians: Returning to Lacan and away from Hegel," *Philosophy Today* 49, no. 1 (2005): 25.
40　Christopher Hanlon, "Psychoanalysis and the Post-Political: An Interview with Slavoj Žižek," *New Literary History* 32, no. 1 (December 2001): 1.
41　Thomas Osborne, "On Mediators: Intellectuals and the Ideas Trade in the Knowledge Society," *Economy and Society* 33, no. 4 (2004): 430–47.
42　Derek Hook, "Slavoj Žižek, Meta-Theory and the Return to Politics," *PINS* 29 (January 2003): 67–70.
43　See Jeffery C. Alexander, "Cultural Pragmatics: Social Performance between Ritual and Strategy," *Sociological Theory* 22, no. 4 (December 2004): 527–73.
44　Jeffery C. Alexander, *Trauma: A Social Theory* (Cambridge, UK: Polity Press, 2012), 2.
45　Alexander, 17.
46　See Slavoj Žižek, "The Desert of the Real: Is This the End of Fantasy?" *In These Times*, October 29, 2001; Žižek, "Welcome to the Desert of the Real!," *South Atlantic Quarterly* 101, no. 2 (Spring 2002): 385–89; Žižek, *Welcome to the Desert of the Real: Five Essays on September 11 and Related Dates* (London: Verso, 2002).
47　Žižek, "Desert of the Real."
48　Žižek, "Desert of the Real."
49　Žižek, "Desert of the Real."
50　Žižek, "Desert of the Real."
51　Žižek, "Desert of the Real."
52　Žižek, "Desert of the Real," 2.
53　See Verso Books' 9/11 series, at https://www.versobooks.com/series_collections/34-9-11.
54　Tod Sloan, "Ideology Theory Tackles the Post-September 11 World," *Theory and Psychology* 14, no. 4 (2004): 564.
55　Sloan, 565.
56　Sloan, 565.
57　See Samuel P. Huntington, "The Clash of Civilizations?" *Foreign Affairs* 72, no. 3 (Summer 1993): 22–49.
58　Sloan, "Ideology Theory Tackles the Post-September 11 World," 566.
59　Loren Glass, "Terrorism, Inc.," *Historical Materialism* 16 (January 2008): 221.
60　See Slavoj Žižek, "Notes towards a Politics of Bartleby: The Ignorance of Chicken," *Comparative American Studies* 4, no. 4 (2006): 375–94.

61 Peter Lecouras, "9/11, Critical Theory, and Globalization," *Interdisciplinary Literary Studies* 12, no. 1 (January 2010): 82.
62 Lecouras, 82.
63 Lecouras, 81.
64 Lecouras, 82.
65 Glass, "Terrorism, Inc.," 220.
66 Glass, 221.
67 The quote was taken from a talk given by Žižek at the Westfield House, Cambridge, on May 12, 2017, celebrating the Reformation's five hundredth anniversary. The moderator presented Žižek by a collection of remarks about him made by several Cambridge scholars.
68 Richard Wolin, "Kant at Ground Zero," *New Republic*, February 9, 2004, https://newrepublic.com/article/104828/kant-ground-zero.
69 Wolin, "Kant at Ground Zero."
70 Chyatat Supachalasai, "A Trauma Revisited: Fanon, Žižek, and Violence," *International Journal of Žižek Studies* 8, no. 2 (2016): 11, http://www.zizekstudies.org/index.php/IJZS/article/view/768/773.
71 On his position for Lacan and Hegel: Tony Myers, *Slavoj Žižek* (London: Routledge, 2003). On his position against Foucault and Habermas: Fabio Vighi and Heiko Feldner, *Žižek: Beyond Foucault* (London: Palgrave Macmillan, 2007). On cultural studies: Paul Bowman, "Cultural Studies and Slavoj Žižek," in *New Cultural Studies: Adventures in Theory*, ed. Gary Hall and Clare Birchall (Edinburgh: Edinburgh University Press, 2006), 162–77. On literature: Shelly Brivic, *Joyce through Lacan and Žižek: Explorations* (New York: Palgrave Macmillan, 2008). On theology: Adam Kotsko, *Žižek and Theology* (New York: T & T Clark International, 2008); Frederiek Depoortere, *Christ in Postmodern Philosophy: Gianni Vattimo, Rene Girard, and Slavoj Žižek* (London: Routledge, 2008). On media: Paul A. Taylor, *Žižek and the Media* (Cambridge, UK: Polity Press, 2010). On philosophy: Adrian Johnston, *Žižek's Ontology: A Transcendental Materialist Theory of Subjectivity* (Evanston, IL: Northwestern University Press, 2008).
72 Adrian Johnston, *Badiou, Žižek, and Political Transformations: The Cadence of Change* (Evanston, IL: Northwestern University Press, 2009); Matthew Sharpe and Geoff M. Boucher, *Žižek and Politics: A Critical Introduction* (Edinburgh: Edinburgh University Press, 2010).
73 Matthew Beaumont and Matthew Jenkins, "An Interview with Slavoj Žižek," *Historical Materialism* 7, no. 1 (January 2000): 181–97.
74 Sarah Kay, *Žižek: A Critical Introduction* (Cambridge, UK: Polity Press), p. x.
75 Kay, *Žižek*, 157.
76 Kay, 157, emphasis in original.
77 See Slavoj Žižek, "Seize the Day: Lenin's Legacy," *The Guardian*, July 23, 2002, https://www.theguardian.com/books/2002/jul/23/londonreviewofbooks.
78 Slavoj Žižek, "Bring Me My Philips Mental Jacket: Slavoj Žižek Welcomes the

Prospect of Biogenetic Intervention," *London Review of Books* 25, no. 10 (May 2003): 3–5; Yanis Stavrakakis, *The Lacanian Left: Psychoanalysis, Theory, Politics* (Edinburgh: Edinburgh University Press, 2007).

79 See Slavoj Žižek, *Iraq: The Broken Kettle* (London: Verso, 2004); "What Rumsfeld Doesn't Know That He Knows about Abu Ghraib," *In These Times*, May 21, 2004; Slavoj Žižek, Eric L. Santner, and Kenneth Reinhard, *The Neighbor: Three Inquiries in Political Theology* (Chicago: University of Chicago Press, 2005); Slavoj Žižek et al., eds., *Hegel and the Infinite: Religion, Politics, and Dialectic* (New York: Columbia University Press, 2011).

80 Slavoj Žižek, *The Parallax View* (Cambridge, MA: MIT Press, 2006).

81 Admittedly, Žižek borrowed the concept of parallax from the Japanese Marxist intellectual Kojin Karatani, which is developed in his 2003 book, *Transcritique: On Kant and Marx*. This attempt to overcome dualisms is hardly unique to Žižek. For example, Giddens's structuration theory, Bourdieu's field theory, and Latour's actor-network theory are three renowned attempts to overcome the opposition of structure/subject in different ways. However, what is unique to Žižek is the identification with/by such a dynamic positioning, which does not rest at his theories but extends to his personal life and overall thinking and behavior. In other words, superpositioning is not just a component of the thinker's theory, but it is also a practiced and symbolic element of his performance; thus, Žižek became recognized through his dynamically shifting superpositioning.

82 Ted Smith, "Book Review: Slavoj Žižek, The Parallax View," *Political Theology* 10, no. 2 (2009): 365.

83 Fredric Jameson, "First Impressions," *London Review of Books* 28, no. 17 (September 2006): 8.

84 Terry Eagleton, "On the Contrary: Terry Eagleton on Slavoj Žižek's The Parallax View," *Free Library*, June 22, 2006, https://www.thefreelibrary.com/On+the+contrary%3A+Terry+Eagleton+on+Slavoj+Žižek%27s+The+Parallax+View.-a0147603538.

85 Adrian Johnston, "Slavoj Žižek's Hegelian Reformation: Giving a Hearing to *The Parallax View*," *Diacritics* 37, no. 1 (Spring 2007): 3–20.

86 See Short Circuits series, MIT Press, https://mitpress.mit.edu/books/series/short-circuits.

87 Slavoj Žižek, *The Puppet and Dwarf: The Perverse Core of Christianity* (Cambridge, MA: MIT Press, 2003).

88 Žižek, *Puppet and Dwarf*, 3.

89 Eugene Wolters, "That Time Žižek Wrote for Abercrombie & Fitch," *Critical-Theory*, March 19, 2013, http://www.critical-theory.com/that-time-zizek-wrote-for-abercrombie-fitch/.

90 Ella Riley-Adams, "The Rise and Fall of Abercrombie's Incredible, Risky Print Magazine," *Content Strategist*, January 21, 2016, https://contently.com/2016/01/21/the-rise-and-fall-of-abercrombies-incredible-risky-print-magazine/.

91 See Savas Abadsidis, ed., "Back to School," *A&F Quarterly* (Columbus, OH: Abercrombie and Fitch, 2003), 2.
92 Žižek in Abadsidis, 3.
93 Incidentally, Žižek was positioned in this exact way by Rebecca Mead in a May 5, 2003, article for the *New Yorker* entitled "The Marx Brother" (https://www.newyorker.com/magazine/2003/05/05/the-marx-brother).
94 See Abadsidis, "Back to School," 4.
95 Riley-Adams, "Rise and Fall."
96 Riley-Adams, "Rise and Fall."
97 See Abadsidis, "Back to School," 16, 61, 102.
98 Joshua Glenn, "The Examined Life: Enjoy Your Chinos!," *Boston Globe*, July 6, 2003, http://dev.autonomedia.org/node/2092.
99 Žižek interviewed by Jordan Richman, "Conversation on the Apocalypse," *Fantastic Man* 33 (Spring–Summer 2021).
100 Barry Nolan, "Interview with Slavoj Žižek," online video recording, YouTube, 2004, https://www.youtube.com/watch?v=KjEtmZZvGZA.
101 Jacobs and Townsley, *Media Intellectuals*, 68.
102 Nolan, "Interview with Slavoj Žižek," 0:01–0:34.
103 Žižek in Nolan, "Interview with Slavoj Žižek," 0:57–1:41.
104 Slavoj Žižek, *On Belief* (London: Routledge, 2001).
105 Slavoj Žižek, "Why Only an Atheist Can Believe: Politics between Fear and Trembling," lecture at (former) Calvin College, Grand Rapids, MI, November 10, 2006, http://žižekpodcast.com/2016/04/18/ziz056-why-only-an-atheist-can-believe/; Slavoj Žižek and Boris Gunjević, *God in Pain: Inversions of Apocalypse* (New York: Seven Stories Press, 2012); Creston Davis, John Milbank, and Slavoj Žižek, eds., *Theology and the Political: The New Debate* (Durham, NC: Duke University Press, 2005); Slavoj Žižek and John Milbank, *The Monstrosity of Christ: Paradox or Dialectic?* (Cambridge, MA: MIT University Press, 2009).
106 That (objective) dynamic of belief is canonized in Žižek's repertoire as the point that no one has to believe (subjectively) for belief to function. This point is demonstrated repeatedly by using common and scientific references and claiming that (1) both children and parents know that Santa Claus does not exist, yet they behave as if he does so to maintain the proper social ritual of transcendence, and (2) Niels Bohr's remark on superstitions, which work even if one does not believe in them.
107 Ted A. Smith, "Book Review: Slavoj Žižek, The Parallax View," *Political Theology* 10, no. 2 (2009): 368.
108 Karine Nahon and Jeff Hemsley, *Going Viral* (Cambridge, UK: Polity Press, 2013).
109 See Slavoj Žižek, "A Cyberspace Lenin: Why Not?" *International Socialism* 2, no. 95 (2002): https://www.marxists.org/history/etol/newspape/isj2/2002/isj2-095/Žižek.htm.
110 Slavoj Žižek, in *The Reality of the Virtual* (directed by Ben Wright, 2005); *Žižek!*

(directed by Astra Taylor, 2005); *The Pervert's Guide to Cinema* (directed by Sophie Fiennes, 2006).

111 See Rotten Tomatoes, "The Pervert's Guide to Cinema," 2006, https://www.rottentomatoes.com/m/the_perverts_guide_to_cinema.

112 Stephen Holden, "Sometimes Groucho's Cigar Is Not Just a Cigar," *New York Times*, January 15, 2009, https://www.nytimes.com/2009/01/16/movies/16perv.html.

113 Holden, "Sometimes Groucho's Cigar Is Not Just a Cigar."

114 Peter Bradshaw, "The Pervert's Guide to Cinema," *The Guardian*, October 6, 2006, https://www.theguardian.com/film/2006/oct/06/documentary.

115 Charles Andrews, "Failing to Fight for the Christian Legacy: Žižek!" *MoveableType* 3 (2007): 130. One can think of Lacan's *Television*, his televised introduction to psychoanalysis that aired in 1973 in France, as the first kind of this visual dissemination of French theory. Besides the mentioned 2002 film on Derrida, one can also think of Deleuze's 1996 *L'Abécédaire* as a form of cinematic intellectual intervention.

116 Nathan Lee, "Food for Thought in 'Slavoj Žižek: The Reality of the Virtual,'" *New York Times*, June 2, 2006, https://www.nytimes.com/2006/06/02/movies/food-for-thought-in-slavoj-zizek-the-reality-of-the-virtual.html.

117 Slavoj Žižek in Taylor, *Žižek!*, 1:00:22–1:01:06.

118 David J. Gunkel, "Recombinant Thought: Slavoj Žižek and the Art and Science of the Mashup," *International Journal of Žižek Studies* 6, no. 3 (2012): http://zizekstudies.org/index.php/IJZS/article/view/27/24.

119 Slavoj Žižek in Taylor, *Žižek!*, 1:00:22–1:01:06.

120 Slavoj Žižek, "Love beyond Law," *Journal for the Psychoanalysis of Culture and Society* 1 (1996): 160–61.

121 René Lemieux, "Recension-Žižek!," *International Journal of Žižek Studies* 2, no. 2 (2016): 2, http://zizekstudies.org/index.php/IJZS/article/view/115/115.

122 François Théron, "Slavoj Žižek: Un philosophe inclassable," *Le Nouvel Observateur*, special edition no. 57, 2004, 50.

123 For the Birkbeck Archive of podcasts and videos, see http://www.bbk.ac.uk/bih/podcasts.

124 See History and Mission of the EGS, 1994, at http://egs.edu/about.

125 Incidentally, Žižek admits that the EGS is "a stupid corrupted organization . . . I get cash. It's mafia. So this helps me a lot that I get non-taxed nontraceable money" (2017, interview by author).

126 See the *International Journal of Žižek Studies* home page at http://zizekstudies.org/index.php/IJZS.

127 See the *International Journal of Žižek Studies* home page at http://zizekstudies.org/index.php/IJZS.

128 Slavoj Žižek, "Language, Violence and Non-violence," *International Journal of Žižek Studies* 2, no. 3 (2008): https://zizekstudies.org/index.php/ijzs/article/viewFile/129/227; Žižek, *Violence* (London: Profile Books, 2008). The ques-

tion of violence has had, for a long time, a strong positioning value for intellectuals, as it touches upon the practical limit point of their thought. Especially in political and moral thought, the question of revolt, resistance, and revolution translates directly into human and civil prescriptions for action, namely what can a citizen or a person do and what they cannot. Thus intellectuals can be divided throughout history by their support of some forms of violence (whether it is symbolic or physical, individual or collective).

129 Slavoj Žižek, *First as Tragedy, Then as Farce* (London: Verso, 2009); Žižek, *Living in the End Times* (London: Verso, 2010); Žižek, "Use Your Illusions," *London Review of Books*, November 14, 2008, https://www.lrb.co.uk/the-paper/v30/n22/slavoj-zizek/use-your-illusions; John Thornhill, "Lunch with the FT: Slavoj Žižek," *Financial Times*, March 6, 2009, https://www.ft.com/content/06b42e32-09dd-11de-add8-0000779fd2ac.
130 See "First as Tragedy, Then as Farce," August 4, 2010, RSA Animate, https://www.thersa.org/discover/videos/rsa-animate/2010/08/rsa-animate---first-as-tragedy-then-as-farce-.
131 See Slavoj Žižek, "Don't Just Do Something, Talk" *London Review of Books*, October 10, 2008, https://www.lrb.co.uk/the-paper/v30/n19/slavoj-zizek/don-t-just-do-something-talk.
132 Žižek, "Don't Just Do Something, Talk."
133 Žižek, "Don't Just Do Something, Talk."
134 Thornhill, "Lunch with the FT."
135 See "Slavoj Žižek on Hardtalk," November 25, 2009, dstpfw, 8:07 mins., https://www.youtube.com/watch?v=w8cIagiKwkw; See also "Living in the End Times According to Slavoj Zizek," January 11, 2010, Vpro Tegenlicht, https://www.vpro.nl/programmas/tegenlicht/backlight/Living-in-the-end-times-according-to-slavoj-zizek.html.
136 Žižek, *First as Tragedy*, 15.
137 Žižek, 28–31.
138 Žižek, 69.
139 Žižek, 91.
140 See OccupyWallSt, "Today Liberty Plaza had a visit from Slavoj Žižek," October 9, 2011, http://occupywallst.org/article/today-liberty-plaza-had-visit-slavoj-zizek/.
141 See Slavoj Žižek in *The Possibility of Hope* (directed by Alfonso Cuarón, 2006); *The Pervert's Guide to Cinema* (directed by Sophie Fiennes, 2006); *Alien, Marx & Co.* (directed by Ein Porträt, 2006); *Terror! Robespierre and the French Revolution* (directed by Carl Hindmarch, 2009); *Examined Life* (directed by Astra Taylor, 2009); *Marx Reloaded* (directed by Jason Barker, 2011).
142 Slavoj Žižek, "For Egypt, This Is the Miracle of Tahrir Square," *The Guardian*, February 10, 2011, https://www.theguardian.com/global/2011/feb/10/egypt-miracle-tahrir-square.
143 Žižek, "For Egypt."

222   NOTES TO PAGES 141–146

144   Jean-Pierre Filiu, *The Arab Revolution: Ten Lessons from the Democratic Uprising* (Oxford: Oxford University Press, 2011); Jeffery C. Alexander, *Performative Revolution in Egypt* (London: Bloomsbury, 2011).
145   Žižek, "For Egypt."
146   Žižek, "For Egypt."
147   See Slavoj Žižek, *The Year of Dreaming Dangerously* (London: Verso, 2012).
148   This book was reviewed and popularized by Sean O'Hagan for *The Guardian*, who found that "Žižek is to today what Jacques Derrida was to the 80s: the thinker of choice for Europe's young intellectual vanguard. This fills him with dismay. Unlike Derrida, though, he is determinedly left wing, if not in the traditional sense." See his "Slavoj Žižek: Interview," *The Guardian*, June 27, 2010, https://www.theguardian.com/culture/2010/jun/27/slavoj-zizek-living-end-times.
149   This was due to interventions such as the series of books on *The Idea of Communism*, documenting the three international conferences of London (2010), New York (2013) and Seoul (2016).
150   Žižek, *The Year of Dreaming Dangerously*, back cover.
151   See Amy Goodman and Slavoj Žižek, "The Iraq War, the Bush Presidency, the War on Terror & More," *Democracy Now*, May 12 2008, https://www.democracynow.org/2008/5/12/world_renowned_philosopher_slavoj_Žižek_on.
152   See Rosanna Greenstreet, "Q&A Slavoj Žižek, Professor and Writer," *The Guardian*, August 9, 2008, https://www.theguardian.com/lifeandstyle/2008/aug/09/slavoj.zizek; Slavoj Žižek, "On 9/11, New Yorkers Faced the Fire in the Minds of Men," *The Guardian*, September 11, 2006, https://www.theguardian.com/commentisfree/2006/sep/11/comment.september11. See Slavoj Žižek, "A Very Dangerous Q&A," *ABC*, October 3, 2011, https://www.abc.net.au/qanda/a-very-dangerous-qa/10662062.
153   Žižek, "A Very Dangerous Q&A."
154   Mehdi B. Kacem, "A Tunisian Renaissance," *16 Beaver* (blog) 2011, http://16beavergroup.org/articles/2011/04/10/tunisie-badiou-et-zizek-passent-a-cote-de-lessentiel/.

CHAPTER FOUR

1   Gregg Lambert, "The Philosopher and the Writer: A Question of Style," in *Between Deleuze and Derrida*, ed. Paul Patton and John Protevi (London: Continuum, 2003), 120.
2   Jacques Derrida, *Points: Interviews 1974–1994* (Stanford, CA: Stanford University Press, 1995), 218.
3   Derrida, 218.
4   Michel de Certeau, *The Practice of Everyday Life* (Berkeley: University of California Press, 1984), 16.

5 Creston Davis, "Today's Psychotic Academy: Risking the Pedagogy of 'Žižek's 180,'" *Philosophy Today* 61, no. 2 (Spring 2017): 380; see also Irwin Feller, "Universities as Engines of R&D-Based Economic Growth: They Think They Can," *Research Policy* 19, no. 4 (1990): 335–48; Steve Fuller, *The Sociology of Intellectual Life: The Career of the Mind in and Around Academy* (London: Sage, 2009).
6 See Justin Clemens, "The Politics of Style in the Works of Slavoj Žižek," in *Traversing the Fantasy: Critical Responses to Slavoj Žižek*, ed. Geoff Boucher, Jason Glynos, and Matthew Sharpe (London: Routledge, 2005), 3–22.
7 Davis, "Today's Psychotic Academy," 381.
8 Lambert, "The Philosopher and the Writer," 125. On maximal and minimal, see Isaac A. Reed, "Cultural Sociology as Research Program: Post-Positivism, Meaning, and Causality," in *The Oxford Handbook of Cultural Sociology*, ed. Jeffery C. Alexander, Ronald N. Jacobs, and Philip Smith (Oxford: Oxford University Press, 2012), 27–45.
9 Lambert, 127.
10 Initially the work was self-published by Mortensen in 2011 as an artist's coffee-table book in a limited edition of one, as pictured in the exhibition *The Art of the Joke* (2012) at V1 Gallery in Copenhagen. The book was republished by the Norwegian publishing house Flamme Forlag in 2012, and later, in agreement with the author, sold to MIT Press, which published an edition titled *Žižek's Jokes* in 2014. The book has been translated into German, French, Russian, Turkish, Greek, Italian, Bengali, and several other languages, and has gained a worldwide readership.
11 See Audun Mortensen, "The Collected Jokes of Slavoj Žižek," 2012, https://shop.flammeforlag.no/products/dd.
12 Lindesay Irvine, "Slavoj Žižek's Jokes are No Laughing Matter," *The Guardian*, January 6, 2012, https://www.theguardian.com/books/booksblog/2012/jan/06/slavoj-zizek-jokes.
13 Specifically, the risk is that a book of jokes will turn into a joke of a book. For more on the Gaga-Žižek affair, see Uri Friedman, "No, Lady Gaga Is Not Friends with Marxist Philosopher Slavoj Žižek: A Story on Collaboration between the Two Has Been Discredited," June 22, 2011, https://www.theatlantic.com/entertainment/archive/2011/06/lady-gaga-and-marxist-slavoj-zizek-friendship-wasnt/352046/.
14 See Agon Hamza, ed., *Repeating Žižek* (Durham, NC: Duke University Press, 2015); Kelsey Wood, *Žižek: A Reader's Guide* (Chichester, UK: Wiley-Blackwell, 2012).
15 Slavoj Žižek, *Less Than Nothing: Hegel and the Shadow of Dialectical Materialism* (London: Verso, 2012).
16 Nicholas Thoburn, *Anti-Book: On the Art and Politics of Radical Publishing* (Minneapolis: University of Minnesota Press, 2016).
17 Robert Pippin, "Back to Hegel?" *Mediations* 26, nos. 1–2 (Spring 2013): 7–28.
18 Žižek, *Less Than Nothing*, 3.

19 See "History Is Made at Night: A 24-Hour Event to Launch Less Than Nothing," Verso Books, June 2012, https://www.versobooks.com/events/458-history-is-made-at-night-a-24-hour-event-to-launch-less-than-nothing.
20 Alex Christofi, "My Night with Žižek," *Prospect*, June 19, 2012, https://www.prospectmagazine.co.uk/arts-and-books/24-hour-zizek-less-than-nothing-hegel.
21 Christofi, "My Night with Žižek."
22 Christofi, "My Night with Žižek."
23 A more intellectual and lengthy review of *Less Than Nothing* was written by University of Chicago professor Robert Pippin, situating Žižek in the Hegelian philosophical field as "a serious attempt to re-animate or re-actualize Hegel." Pippin, "Back to Hegel?," 7.
24 Jonathan Rée, "Less Than Nothing by Slavoj Žižek—Review," *The Guardian*, June 27, 2012, https://www.theguardian.com/books/2012/jun/27/less-than-nothing-slavoj-zizek-review.
25 Rée, "Less Than Nothing."
26 Rée, "Less Than Nothing."
27 John Gray, "The Violent Visions of Slavoj Žižek," *New York Review of Books*, July 12, 2012, https://www.nybooks.com/articles/2012/07/12/violent-visions-slavoj-zizek/.
28 Gray, "Violent Visions of Slavoj Žižek."
29 Gray, "Violent Visions of Slavoj Žižek."
30 Besides his book *Violence* from 2008, see Žižek's foreword, "The Dark Matter of Violence, or, Putting Terror in Perspective," in Sophie Wahnich, *In Defence of the Terror: Liberty or Death in the French Revolution* (London: Verso, 2012), xi–xxx.
31 Gray, "Violent Visions of Slavoj Žižek."
32 Gray, "Violent Visions of Slavoj Žižek."
33 For another kind of performative superpositioning of fact and fiction, see Žižek's 2016 experimental cinematic intervention, *Houston, We Have a Problem* (directed by Žiga Virc). In this docufiction or mockumentary, the story (or myth) of the Yugoslav space program is told in a way that blurs both extremes of a factual documented tale and an imagined fictional novel. In one of the movie's later scenes, Žižek is portrayed as a CIA spy working on America's behalf to topple the Yugoslav regime.
34 Jacobs and Townsley, *Media Intellectuals*, 10.
35 Paul A. Taylor, "Žižek's Reception: Fifty Shades of Gray Ideology," in *Žižek and Media Studies: A Reader*, ed. Matthew Flisfeder and Louis Willis (London: Palgrave Macmillan, 2014), 17. See also his "Žižek's Brand of Philosophical Excess and the Treason of the Intellectuals: Wagers of Sin, Ugly Ducklings, and Mythical Swans," *International Journal of Žižek Studies* 8, no. 2 (2014): http://www.zizekstudies.org/index.php/IJZS/article/view/829/834.
36 Taylor, "Žižek's Reception." See also Peter Thompson, "The Slavoj Žižek v. Noam Chomsky Spat Is Worth a Ringside Seat," *The Guardian*, July 19,

2013, https://www.theguardian.com/commentisfree/2013/jul/19/noam-chomsky-slavoj-zizek-ding-dong; Sohrab Ahmari, "'Chomsky vs. 'Elvis' in a Left-Wing Cage Fight," *Wall Street Journal*, July 28, 2013, https://www.wsj.com/articles/SB10001424127887324328904578622190386123344.

37 In first place there was "violence," followed by "philosopher," "Chomsky," "Trump," and "Hegel." Source: "Žižek's Top 5 Related Search Items, 2004–2019," Google Trends, accessed August 19, 2018.

38 See Brain Leiter, "Chomsky Slams the Empty 'Posturing' of Zizek and Derrida," June 25, 2013, https://leiterreports.typepad.com/blog/2013/06/chomsky-slams-the-empty-posturing-of-zizek-and-derrida.html.

39 See Josh Jones, "Slavoj Žižek Publishes a Very Clearly Written Essay-Length Response to Chomsky's 'Brutal' Criticisms," July 27, 2013, https://www.openculture.com/2013/07/slavoj-zizek-publishes-a-very-clearly-written-essay-length-response-to-chomskys-brutal-criticisms.html.

40 This particular opposition to theory has its own intellectual history: the first big public intellectual debate in this context was between Noam Chomsky and Lacan in 1966. As Guéguen recalls, "From time to time, a few misunderstandings arise; Chomsky would have been offended when Lacan asserts that 'he thinks with his feet.'" See Pierre-Gilles Guéguen, "Lacan, American," *The Symptom* 13 (2012): http://www.lacan.com/symptom13/lacan-american.html. The second occurrence of that lineage is the Dutch-televised Chomsky-Foucault debate of 1971, where Chomsky defended the position of concrete human creative nature against Foucault's abstract discursive critique of it.

41 For an analysis of the changing "lecture performance," see Lucia Rainer, *On the Threshold of Knowing* (Bielefeld, Germany: Transcript, 2017).

42 Chomsky's intervention also follows the model of intellectual intervention, from past events to present matters and to future readings, yet, as by the time of the debate with Žižek, and unlike Žižek, Chomsky was no longer an active linguist, he maintained his professional credibility and scientific legitimacy. See Noam Chomsky, "The Responsibility of Intellectuals," *New York Review of Books*, February 23, 1967.

43 For example, Donald Rumsfeld's "theory of knowledge" was an opportunity for Žižek to link Aristotle's semiotic square (as a reference figure from the past), the Iraq War (pressing issue from the present), and the unconscious (which may lead to new future): Western leaders knew there were no "weapons of mass destruction" in Iraq, but to achieve their military intervention (for economic, oil-related reasons), they had to publicly pretend as if they did not know it. Žižek explained: "To unearth these 'unknown knowns' is the task of an intellectual." See Slavoj Žižek, "What Rumsfeld Doesn't Know That He Knows about Abu Ghraib," *In These Times*, May 21, 2004; Žižek, "The Empty Wheelbarrow," *The Guardian*, February 19, 2005, https://www.theguardian.com/comment/story/0,3604,1417982,00.html.

44 Incidentally, the fetishized position of facts is found not only in the political

left, as with Chomsky or Gray, but also on the right, with Ben Shapiro's recent motto—"facts don't care about your feelings."
45   So, for another common example, we all know that smoking is factually harmful, yet some choose to smoke and act, truly fictitiously, as if it were not.
46   Chomsky in Taylor, "Žižek's Reception," 17.
47   Slavoj Žižek, "Some Bewildered Clarifications," *International Journal of Žižek Studies* 7, no. 2 (2013): http://www.zizekstudies.org/index.php/IJZS/article/view/725; Žižek, "Some Bewildered Clarifications: A Response to Noam Chomsky by Slavoj Žižek," *Verso Blog*, July 25, 2013, https://www.versobooks.com/blogs/1365-some-bewildered-clarifications-a-response-to-noam-chomsky-by-slavoj-zizek.
48   Taylor, "Žižek's Reception," 19. See also Ralf Dahrendorf, "The Intellectual and Society: The Societal Function of the 'Fool' in the Twentieth Century," in *On Intellectuals*, ed. Rieff Philip (New York: Doubleday & Co., 1969), 49–52; Eliran Bar-El and Patrick Baert, "'The Fool' Revisited: The Making of Žižek as Sacrificial Public Intellectual," *Cultural Sociology* 15, no. 4 (December 2021): 539–57.
49   Taylor, "Žižek's Reception," 20.
50   Taylor, 20.
51   Taylor, 19.
52   Taylor, 21.
53   Taylor, 21.
54   Taylor, 23.
55   Luke Massey, "Slavoj Žižek: 'Most of the Idiots I Know Are Academics,'" New Statesman, October 8, 2013, https://www.newstatesman.com/ideas/2013/10/slavoj-zizek-most-idiots-i-know-are-academics.
56   Žižek in Massey, "Slavoj Žižek."
57   Žižek in Massey, "Slavoj Žižek."
58   Hamid Dabashi, "Can Non-Europeans think?" *Al Jazeera*, January 15, 2013, https://www.aljazeera.com/indepth/opinion/2013/01/2013114142638797542.html.
59   Incidentally, in another piece, Dabashi has positioned Chomsky and Žižek on the same side, claiming that both "are wrong on the US elections." See Hamid Dabashi, "Fuck You Žižek!," *Zed Books Blog*, July 26, 2016, https://medium.com/@ramman_erin/why-is-žižek-92ef5f8c7e4d.
60   Santiago Zabala, "Slavoj Žižek and the Role of the Philosopher," *Al Jazeera*, December 25, 2012, https://www.aljazeera.com/indepth/opinion/2012/12/20121224122215406939.html.
61   Zabala, "Slavoj Žižek."
62   See Walter D. Mignolo, "Yes, We Can: Non-European Thinkers and Philosophers," *Al Jazeera*, February 19, 2013, https://www.aljazeera.com/indepth/opinion/2013/02/20132672747320891.html.
63   Mignolo, "Yes, We Can."

64 Mignolo, "Yes, We Can."
65 See Hamid Dabashi, *Can Non-Europeans Think?* (Chicago: University of Chicago Press, 2015).
66 Slavoj Žižek, "A Reply to My Critics," *Philosophical Salon*, August 5, 2016, https://thephilosophicalsalon.com/a-reply-to-my-critics/; Žižek, "A Reply to My Critics: Part Two," *Philosophical Salon*, August 14, 2016, https://thephilosophicalsalon.com/reply-to-my-critics-part-two/.
67 Slavoj Žižek, *Agitating the Frame: Five Essays on Economy, Ideology, Sexuality and Cinema* (Delhi: Navayana, 2014), 14.
68 Bakke, *Likeness*, 109.
69 Bakke, 110.
70 See Jaap Bos, David W. Park, and Petteri Pietikainen, "Strategic Self-Marginalization: The Case of Psychoanalysis," *Journal of the History of the Behavioral Sciences* 41, no. 3 (June 2005): 207–24. Slavoj Žižek, "Am I a Philosopher?" (paper presented as keynote lecture for the International Žižek Studies Conference, 2016), https://zizek.uk/slavoj-zizek-am-i-a-philosopher/.
71 Žižek, "Am I a Philosopher?"
72 Alain Badiou in Žižek, "Am I a Philosopher?" Engaging in positioning even within his teams and networks, Žižek reported on his relations with Badiou in his article "Badiou: Notes from an Ongoing Debate," *International Journal of Žižek Studies* 1, no. 2 (2007): 28–43. Still in the French context, his intervention on Deleuze also positioned him as a relevant intellectual resonating with the growing theoretical interest in Deleuze's thought, as manifested in, for example, actor-network theory and assemblage theory. He also positioned himself with relation to Hardt and Negri's renewed communism. See Slavoj Žižek, *Organs without Bodies: Deleuze and Consequences* (London: Routledge, 2003); Žižek, "Have Michael Hardt and Antonio Negri Rewritten the Communist Manifesto for the Twenty-First Century?," *Rethinking Marxism* 13, nos. 3–4 (2001): 190–98.
73 Kenneth Reinhard, preface, in Alain Badiou, *Lacan: Anti-philosophy 3* (New York: Columbia University Press, 2018), xxiv, 232.
74 See Mladen Dolar, *A Voice and Nothing More* (Cambridge, MA: MIT Press, 2006); Alenka Zupančič, *Ethics of the Real: Kant, Lacan* (London: Verso, 2000); Zupančič, *The Shortest Shadow: Nietzsche's Philosophy of the Two* (Cambridge, MA: MIT Press, 2003); Zupančič, *What is Sex?* (Cambridge, MA: MIT Press, 2017).
75 Peter Engelmann, "Editor's Preface," in *Philosophy in the Present*, by Alain Badiou and Slavoj Žižek (Cambridge, UK: Polity Press, 2009), vii–x.
76 See Matt Warman, "Stephen Hawking Tells Google 'Philosophy Is Dead,'" *The Telegraph*, May 17, 2011, http://www.telegraph.co.uk/technology/google/8520033/Stephen-Hawking-tells-Google-philosophy-is-dead.html.
77 Reinhard in Badiou, *Lacan*, xxiv.
78 Reinhard in Badiou, *Lacan*, xxv. For Lacan's notion of subjective destitu-

tion, see his "proposition du 9 octobre 1967 sur le psychanalyste de l'École," "Discours a l'École freudienne de Paris," and "L'acte psychanalytique," all in Jacques Lacan, Autres écrits (Paris: Seuil, 2001).
79 Reinhard in Badiou, xxix.
80 Reinhard in Badiou, xxxvii.
81 See Henrik Jøker Bjerre and Brian Benjamin Hansen, "The Discourse of the Wild Analyst," in Repeating Žižek, ed. Agon Hamza (Durham, NC: Duke University Press, 2015), 146–58.
82 Alain Badiou, Lacan: Anti-philosophy 3 (New York: Columbia University Press, 2018), 109.
83 The editor's response could be found at "Who Is Zizek and Why Is He Corrupting My Son?" My Heart Will Go On (blog), November 2015, http://myheartwillgoonandsoonandsoon.blogspot.com/2015/11/who-is-zizek-and-why-is-he-corrupting.html. Incidentally, in one of Žižek's latest interventions he self-positioned himself with relation to the Socratic sacrificial task of philosophy: "From Socrates onward, the function of philosophy has been to corrupt the youth, to alienate (or, rather, estrange) them from the predominant ideologico-political order, to sow radical doubts and enable them to think autonomously." See Slavoj Žižek, Incontinence of the Void: Economico-Philosophical Spandrels (Cambridge, MA: MIT Press, 2017), 141.
84 See Claudia Breger, "The Leader's Two Bodies: Slavoj Žižek's Postmodern Political Theology," Diacritics 31, no. 1 (Spring 2001): 73–90.
85 Alenka Zupančič, personal interview by author, April 26, 2017, Slovenian Academy of Sciences and Arts, Ljubljana.
86 Alain Badiou, Lacan: Anti-philosophy 3 (New York: Columbia University Press, 2018), 165.
87 Badiou, Lacan, 165.
88 Badiou, 166.
89 Žižek frequently uses contemporary examples, from Coca-Cola to Starbucks Coffee and the Kinder Surprise Egg.
90 Kaitlyn Tucker Sorenson, "Experience as Device: Encountering Russian Formalism in the Ljubljana School," Slavic Review 79, no. 1 (Spring 2020): 91–114.
91 Badiou, Lacan, 168.
92 Badiou, 168–69.
93 Badiou, 169.
94 See Marcus Pound, Žižek: A (Very) Critical Introduction (Cambridge, UK: W. B. Eerdmans, 2008).
95 Rex Butler, ed., The Žižek Dictionary (Durham, UK: Acumen, 2014).
96 See Lucas Thorpe, The Kant Dictionary (London: Bloomsbury, 2014); Michael Inwood, Hegel Dictionary (Oxford, UK: Blackwell, 1992); Glenn A. Magee, The Hegel Dictionary (London: Continuum, 2010); Dylan Evans, An Introductory Dictionary of Lacanian Psychoanalysis (London: Routledge, 1996); Steven Corcoran, The Badiou Dictionary (Edinburgh: Edinburgh University Press, 2015).
97 Butler, Žižek Dictionary, xv.

98   Butler, xvi.
99   These books also show how superpositioning is used by Žižek not only in the content of his performances but also in their form itself, structuring his books as means to deploy a concept "in the sense of *figuerae veneris* in erotics: different positions or figurations" of it, or, for another instance, self-positioning the book as the filler of "the empty space that emerge in the interstices between philosophy, psychoanalysis, and the critique of political economy." See Slavoj Žižek, *Disparities* (London: Bloomsbury, 2016), 4; Žižek, *Incontinence of the Void: Economico-Philosophical Spandrels* (Cambridge, MA: MIT Press, 2017), xi.
100 See Christopher Kul-Want, *Introducing Žižek: A Graphic Guide* (London: Icon Books, 2011); Slavoj Žižek, *Event: Philosophy in Transit* (London: Penguin, 2014).
101 *Vice* is a popular Canadian American print and digital magazine founded in 1994, appealing mostly to the younger public. *Vice Meets Žižek* is a video interview conducted by Alex Miller in 2013 at Žižek's home, where they discussed, humorously, *The Pervert's Guide to Ideology* and other cultural and political issues (https://www.vice.com/en_uk/article/dpwzjj/slavoj-zizek). Being partly based in London made Žižek available to frequent news studios in person and make recurrent appearances on the BBC, for example. In this appearance, Žižek discussed Trump and Brexit while making common references to British culture such as T. S. Eliot and positioning his "radical left" in relation to other intellectuals such as Chomsky. See "Slavoj Zizek on Trump and Brexit," BBC News, January 17, 2017, 8:24 minutes, https://www.youtube.com/watch?v=2ZUCemb2plE.
102 See Eoin Higgins, "Left Forum Zizek Controversy: Activists & Organizers Speak Out," May 25, 2016, https://eoinhiggins.com/left-forum-zizek-controversy-activists-organizers-speak-out-a2d2d54b0500.
103 Slavoj Žižek, personal interview by author, April 25, 2017, Ljubljana. See also Ilan Kapoor, "Žižek, Antagonism and Politics Now: Three Recent Controversies," *International Journal of Žižek Studies* 12, no. 1 (2018): https://zizekstudies.org/index.php/IJZS/article/download/1041/1071.
104 See Slavoj Žižek and Srećko Horvat, *What Does Europe Want? The Union and Its Discontent* (Dorset, UK: Istros Books, 2013); Slavoj Žižek, *Trouble in Paradise: From the End of History to the End of Capitalism* (St. Ives, UK: Allan Lane, 2014); Žižek, *Against the Double Blackmail: Refugees, Terror and Other Troubles with Neighbors* (St. Ives, UK: Allan Lane, 2016); Žižek, *The Courage of Hopelessness: Chronicles of a Year of Acting Dangerously* (St. Ives, UK: Allan Lane, 2017); Jela Krečič, ed., *The Final Countdown: Europe, Refugees and the Left* (Ljubljana: Tiskarna Januš, 2017).
105 Slavoj Žižek, interview by author, 2017.
106 Geoff Boucher et al., eds., *Traversing the Fantasy: Critical Responses to Slavoj Žižek* (London: Routledge, 2005), xvi. See Robert S. Boynton, "Enjoy Your Žižek," *Lingua Franca* 8, no. 7 (October 1998): 1–10.

107 Razmig Keucheyan, *The Left Hemisphere: Mapping Critical Theory Today* (London: Verso, 2013), 62.
108 McKenzie Wark, *General Intellects: Twenty Five Thinkers for the 21st Century* (London: Verso, 2017).
109 Wark, *General Intellects*, 2.
110 Wark, 5.
111 Wark, 144.
112 Wark, 144.
113 Wark, 144.
114 Alenka Zupančič, personal interview by author, April 26, 2017, Slovenian Academy of Sciences and Arts, Ljubljana.
115 Alenka Zupančič, personal interview by author, April 26, 2017, Slovenian Academy of Sciences and Arts, Ljubljana.
116 Mladen Dolar, personal interview by author, April 24, 2017, Le Petit Café, Ljubljana.
117 Alenka Zupančič, personal interview by author, April 26, 2017, Slovenian Academy of Sciences and Arts, Ljubljana.
118 Mladen Dolar, personal interview by author, April 24, 2017, Le Petit Café, Ljubljana.
119 Slavoj Žižek, personal interview by author, April 25, 2017, Ljubljana.
120 Slavoj Žižek, personal interview by author, April 25, 2017, Ljubljana.
121 Slavoj Žižek, personal interview by author, April 25, 2017, Ljubljana.
122 A nonexhaustive list of Žižek's visiting professor positions is the Department of Psychoanalysis, Université Paris 8 (1982–83 and 1985–86); the Department of Comparative Literature, University of Minnesota, Minneapolis (1992); the Cardozo Law School, New York (1994); Columbia University, New York (1995); Princeton University (1996); the New School for Social Research, New York (1997); and the Kulturwissenschaftliches Institut, Essen (2000–2002).
123 See, for example, Tonglin Lu, ed., "The Chinese Perspective on Žižek and Žižek's Perspective on China," *Positions: East Asia Cultures Critique* 19, no. 3 (Winter 2011): 617–798.

CONCLUSION

1 G. W. F. Hegel, *Lectures on the History of Philosophy: Volume 1*, trans. E. S. Haldane (London: Routledge & Kegan Paul, 2016), 400. See also Mladen Dolar, *Fenomenologija duha I* (Ljubljana: Društvo za Teoretsko Psihoanalizo, 1990), 20.
2 G. W. F. Hegel, *Phenomenology of Spirit* (Oxford: Oxford University Press, 1977), 492.
3 David P. Marshall and Cassandra Atherton, "Situating Public Intellectuals," *Media International Australia* 156, no. 1 (August 2015): 73, https://doi.org/10.1177/1329878X1515600109.

4   Marshall and Atherton, 69.
5   Paul A. Taylor, "Žižek's Reception: Fifty Shades of Gray Ideology," in *Žižek and Media Studies: A Reader*, ed. Matthew Flisfeder and Louis Willis (London: Palgrave Macmillan, 2014), 16.
6   See Richard A. Posner, *Public Intellectuals: A Study of Decline* (Cambridge, MA: Harvard University Press, 2001).
7   Noah Berlatsky, "Death to the Public Intellectual," *New Republic*, February 18, 2015, https://newrepublic.com/article/121086/death-public-intellectual-what-mark-greif-essays-gets-wrong.
8   Slavoj Žižek, *Like a Thief in Broad Daylight: Power in the Era of Post-Humanity* (St. Ives, UK: Allan Lane, 2018).
9   Trawny, in Žižek, *Like a Thief*, 2.
10 Žižek, *Like a Thief*, 4.
11 Žižek, 4.
12 Žižek, 4.
13 See "Slavoj Žižek: 'I Would Vote Trump,'" November 3, 2016, *Channel 4 News*, https://www.facebook.com/watch/?v=10154211377601939.
14 Mike Crumplar, "Žižek Was Right in 2016," *Mcrumps*, https://mcrumps.com/2018/12/07/zizek-was-right-in-2016/.
15 Mike Crumplar, "Slipping Slavoj," *Jacobite*, May 2, 2018, https://jacobitemag.com/2018/05/02/slipping-slavoj/.
16 Crumplar, "Žižek Was Right in 2016."
17 Žižek, *Like a Thief*, 81.
18 Žižek, 81.
19 Crumplar, "Žižek Was Right in 2016," emphases in original.
20 Crumplar, "Žižek Was Right in 2016."
21 Bakke, *Likeness*, 123.
22 Ben Burgis, *Canceling Comedians While the World Burns: A Critique of the Contemporary Left* (Winchester, UK: Zero Books, 2021), 81, emphasis in original. Although Žižek is not a comedian, he was identified as a "theory-comedian." See Lauren Berlant and Jordan Greenwald, "Affect in the End Times: A Conversation with Lauren Berlant," *Qui Parle* 20, no. 2 (Spring–Summer 2012): 85.
23 Burgis, *Canceling Comedians*, 102, emphasis in original.
24 See also Inge van de Vena and Ties van Gemert, "Filter Bubbles and Guru Effects: Jordan B. Peterson as a Public Intellectual in the Attention Economy," *Celebrity Studies* (2020): https://doi.org/0.1080/19392397.2020.1845966.
25 Stephen Marche, "The 'Debate of the Century': What Happened When Jordan Peterson Debated Slavoj Žižek," *The Guardian*, April 20, 2019.
26 Burgis, *Canceling Comedians*, 105.
27 Mark in Burgis, 106.
28 See, for example, Todd McGowan, *Universality and Identity Politics* (New York: Columbia University Press, 2020).
29 Pippa Norris, "Closed Minds? Is a 'Cancel Culture' Stifling Academic Free-

dom and Intellectual Debate in Political Science?," *HKS Working Paper No. RWP20-025* (August 3, 2020): http://dx.doi.org/10.2139/ssrn.3671026.

30   Slavoj Žižek, interviewed by Robert Rowland, "What Does the Future Hold?," *How To Academy*, https://www.youtube.com/watch?v=luSkpONb2d4&t=2552s.

31   Michel de Certeau, *The Practice of Everyday Life* (Berkeley: University of California Press, 1984), 7.

32   Alvin W. Gouldner, *The Future of Intellectuals and the Rise of the New Class* (London: Palgrave Macmillan, 1979), 28.

33   Anthony Giddens, *Social Theory and Modern Sociology* (Stanford, CA: Stanford University Press, 1987), 261.

34   Giddens, 261.

35   De Certeau, *Practice of Everyday Life*, xx–xxi.

36   De Certeau, xv.

37   See Alenka Zupančič, "You'd Have to Be Stupid Not to See That," *Parallax* 22, no. 4 (October 2016): 413–25.

38   See Adam Kotsko, "How to Read Žižek," *Los Angeles Review of Books*, September 2, 2012, https://lareviewofbooks.org/article/how-to-read-zizek/; Paul Bowman, "How to Not Read Žižek: A Reply to Johnson," *Global Discourse* 2, no. 1 (January 2011): 152–66.

39   De Certeau, *Practice of Everyday Life*, 169.

40   De Certeau, xxi.

41   Benjamin Noys, "Žižek's Reading Machine," in *Repeating Žižek*, ed. Agon Hamza (Durham, NC: Duke University Press, 2015), 73.

42   Noys, 75.

43   Noys, 80.

44   Noys, 82.

45   Noys, 81. See also Gabriel Tupinambá, "What Is a Party a Part Of?," *Crisis and Critique* 1, no. 1 (2014): 219–36; Gabriel Tupinambá and Yuan Yao, *Hegel, Lacan, Žižek* (New York: Atropos Press, 2013).

46   De Certeau, *Practice of Everyday Life*, 172.

47   De Certeau, 171.

48   De Certeau, 134.

49   Robert Pfaller, "Why Žižek? Interpassivity and Misdemeanours: The Analysis of Ideology and the Žižekian Toolbox," *International Journal of Žižek Studies* 1, no. 1 (2007): 33–50; Pfaller, *Interpassivity: The Aesthetics of Delegated Enjoyment* (Edinburgh: Edinburgh University Press, 2017).

50   Clint Burnham, *Does the Internet Have an Unconscious? Slavoj Žižek and Digital Culture* (London: Bloomsbury, 2018), 24.

51   Clint Burnham, "Slavoj Žižek as an Internet Philosopher," in *Žižek and the Media: A Reader*, ed. M. Flisfeder and L. P. Willis (Basingstoke, UK: Palgrave Macmillan, 2014), 201–10.

52   Burnham, 24.

53   Andy Beckett, "Accelerationism: How a Fringe Philosophy Predicted the Fu-

ture We Live In," *The Guardian*, May 11, 2017, https://www.theguardian.com/world/2017/may/11/accelerationism-how-a-fringe-philosophy-predicted-the-future-we-live-in.

54 Oltarzewska, "'So Much Depends on Circumstances,'" 54.

55 See Gary A. Olson and Lynn Worsham, "Slavoj Zizek: Philosopher, Cultural Critic, and Cyber-Communist," *JAC* 21, no. 2 (Spring 2001): 251–86. See also Jeffrey J. Williams, "The Rise of the Promotional Intellectual," *Chronicle of Higher Education*, August 5, 2018, https://www.chronicle.com/article/The-Rise-of-the-Promotional/244135.

56 David J. Gunkel, "Recombinant Thought: Slavoj Žižek and the Art and Science of the Mashup," in *International Journal of Žižek Studies* 6, no. 3 (2012): http://zizekstudies.org/index.php/IJZS/article/view/27/24.

57 Michael Heim, *Electric Language: A Philosophical Study of Word Processing* (New Haven, CT: Yale University Press, 1987), 210.

58 Leigh C. La Berge, "The Writing Cure: Slavoj Žižek, Analysand of Modernity," in *The Truth of Žižek*, ed. Paul Bowman and Richard Stamp (London: Continuum, 2007), 17.

59 La Berge, 24.

Index

Abercrombie & Fitch, 124, 148
academia: condition in, 158, 164; contemporary, 106; co-option of, 31; culture, 78; exclusion from, 45; generation, 72; influence in, 74, 132; judgment and, 13; relations in, 172–73; relevance and, 21, 24, 64, 74, 86, 99, 106–7, 121; social scientific, 81; trends in, 109, 181–82; Western, 98, 102. *See also* media-academia trade-off
Adorno, Theodor, 28, 40, 84, 95, 178, 202n23
Alexander, Jeffery, 5, 15, 114, 120, 142
Althusser, Louis, 40, 55, 61, 71–72, 79, 83–88, 95, 202n23
Analecta (journal), 43f, 66–67, 161
Arab Spring, 24, 103, 135, 139, 141–43, 169, 170f
Assange, Julian, 151, 173

Badiou, Alain, 69–70, 75, 143, 150, 161–65, 178, 227n72
Baert, Patrick, 54, 200n91
Bled congress (1960), 26f, 29
Bourdieu, Pierre, 10–16, 95, 107, 218n81
Bush, George W., 57, 116, 119, 136, 142, 181
Butler, Judith, 86, 111, 129, 133, 139, 212n82

Camic, Charles, 9–10, 16
capitalism, 3, 7, 25, 29, 33, 51, 62, 74, 95–99, 103, 117, 119, 137, 138, 153, 163, 178, 181
celebrity, 1, 12–15, 112, 133, 148, 153, 177, 180, 200n90; culture, 14, 112; intellectual, 1, 13–14
Chicago school of economics, 60
China, 2, 187
Chomsky, Noam, 24, 113–14, 152–59, 181, 225nn40–44, 229n101
Christianity, 92, 124, 127, 150
cinema, 2, 7, 52, 77, 81, 101, 112, 115, 126, 128–32, 139, 148, 151, 188–89, 224n33
civil society, 23, 26–27, 31, 46, 49, 51–54, 62–63
Collins, Randall, 10, 12, 16
communism, 3, 25, 29, 33, 51, 63, 74–75, 91, 117, 128, 139, 143, 159, 161, 227n72
Copjec, Joan, 75, 94, 173
Corbyn, Jeremy, 179
culture, 5, 7, 40, 44, 52, 55, 72, 86, 94, 100, 106, 113, 121, 123, 151, 153, 161, 173, 185, 229n101; academic, 15; alternative, 23, 26, 31, 46–48, 50, 53; American, 163; cancel, 181–82; celebrity, 14, 112; contemporary, 73, 102, 154–56; critical discourse of, 183; digital, 17, 105, 117, 187; industry, 78; internet, 174, 177; online, 115, 176; popular, 2, 11, 18–20, 64, 75, 89, 92–93, 96, 110, 120, 124, 148, 152, 157, 164, 184, 188; Slovenian, 51; socialist, 54; subculture, 49; Western, 62

cynicism, 30, 38–39, 48, 53–56, 88, 96–97, 138

Dabashi, Hamid, 152, 158–59, 226n59
Dean, Jodi, 7
de Certeau, Michel, 16, 146, 182–86
Deleuze, Gilles, 40, 70, 143, 202n23, 220n115, 227n72
democracy, 7, 30, 61–62, 79, 81, 84, 86–88, 91–92, 142–43, 163; democratization, 8, 57, 177
Derrida, Jacques, 1, 33, 36–37, 40, 44, 64, 70, 78, 83, 87, 96, 120, 131, 135, 143, 154, 178, 203n38, 204n61, 220n115, 222n148; critique, 120; deconstruction, 9, 42, 112, 131; and power, 146
digital public sphere, 2, 4, 6, 20, 23, 74, 145, 176, 181; digitalization, 3–4, 20, 105. *See also* media
Dissent (magazine), 13
Dolar, Mladen, 22, 28–32, 36, 39, 40–42, 47–49, 53–55, 62, 64, 66–68, 70, 95, 106, 161, 166, 171–73, 191, 203n38, 206n87, 207n123

Eastern bloc, 1, 27, 29, 33, 41, 45–46, 76, 105, 193n4
extraintellectual arena, 13, 17, 20–21, 103, 108, 114, 121, 133, 135, 144, 163, 179, 183
Eyal, Gil, 6, 15–16

Facebook, 22, 178
fake news, 154, 157
feminism, 77, 108
financial crisis (2008), 103, 135–40f
Foucault, Michel, 33, 40, 42, 70–71, 83–88, 96, 121, 128, 143, 154, 158, 196n44, 202n23, 204n61
France, 1–3, 10, 23, 28, 37, 41, 66–80, 106, 220n115
Frankfurt School, 21, 28–41, 67, 84, 108
French theory, 1, 3, 39, 69, 78–79, 112, 203n38, 220n115
Freud, Sigmund, 33, 52, 55, 57–58, 78, 83, 95, 110, 126, 129, 142, 152, 187, 189,

199n86, 202n23, 207n123, 213n98; field, 35, 97, 123; school, 47, 70
Fukuyama, Francis, 137

German idealism, 1, 40, 71, 97, 188
Google, 22, 119, 154, 169f, 187
Gray, John, 152–59, 225n44
Gross, Neil, 9–10, 16
Guardian, 2, 122, 131, 138–39, 142, 148, 151, 157, 169, 170f

Habermas, Jürgen, 21, 30, 34, 82–88, 99, 120–21, 158, 178, 204n61, 217n71
Hegel, G. W. F., 14, 28, 33, 36, 38, 40–46, 52, 61, 67, 71, 73, 75, 77, 79, 81, 83–88, 92, 94, 97, 108, 110, 113–16, 121, 123, 131, 150, 164, 179, 185, 203n53; dialectic, 38, 77, 133
Hegelacanese, 19, 23–26, 56, 66, 75–78, 82, 87, 89–103, 116, 121, 127, 129, 144, 147, 158, 162, 166, 175, 179, 186, 188
Heidegger, Martin, 1, 27, 31–44, 51, 59, 64, 71, 76, 79, 83, 96, 99, 108, 120, 150, 178, 202n23

ideology, 9, 30, 38–39, 48, 50, 56, 60–61, 68, 79, 82, 86, 88, 93–97, 112, 115–16, 123, 127, 129, 138, 146, 156, 162, 178; critique, 55, 57, 90; definition, 91, 155; and discourse analysis, 77; end of, 85; and utopia, 9
India, 2
individualization. *See* intellectual: individualization
intellectual: arena, 11, 16–17, 19, 21, 26, 35, 40, 42, 47, 66–67, 72, 87, 99, 107; authoritative, 6–7, 20, 22, 54, 66, 93, 96, 106, 109, 125, 127, 132, 137, 176; authority, 11, 183, 186, 195n18; celebrity, 1, 13, 200n90; expert, 5–6, 16, 20, 22, 71, 74, 92, 99, 102, 106, 127, 176, 182, 200n91; French, 16, 23, 69, 71, 102, 227n72; global, 2, 23, 25, 45–46, 63, 67, 69, 75, 77, 82, 99, 104, 106–9, 114, 117, 159, 188; individualization, 23, 33, 82, 122, 131; intervention, 2, 6,

17, 21, 24, 53, 57, 75–83, 87, 89–91, 99, 103, 106, 116, 121, 139, 142, 175–78, 183, 220n115, 222n148, 229n101; mapping, 34, 38; media, 7, 212n83; networks and teams, 18, 37, 218n81; performance, 107; persons, 15; product, 2, 3, 18; public, 3–7, 19–20, 23–26, 59, 66, 68, 75, 80–81, 84, 112, 120–24, 132, 135, 138–42, 148, 151, 153–58, 161, 167, 171, 173, 176–77, 180, 189, 200n91; sacrificial, 15, 20, 22, 24, 66, 93, 106, 126, 145, 155, 175–77, 180, 199n89; scientific, 47; Slovenian, 34–35, 37, 40, 42; study of, 9–18; tension, 27, 40, 225n40
internet, 6, 8, 68, 104, 119, 128, 133, 172, 184–88; age, 103, 132, 165, 175; culture, 174, 177; philosopher, 187; presence, 100
intraintellectual arena, 13–14, 16–17, 20, 68, 81–83, 87, 103, 108, 110, 114, 123, 133, 135, 146, 179, 183
Iron Curtain, 28–29, 45, 52

Jameson, Fredric, 94–95, 103, 123, 173

Kant, Immanuel, 52, 79, 94, 97, 166, 218n81; post-Kantian, 164
Kierkegaard, Søren, 8
Korčula, 30

Lacan, Jacques, 33, 36–37, 40–46, 52–65, 70–88, 92, 102, 111–13, 116, 121, 124, 129, 150–54, 165–67, 170, 172, 202n23, 204n61, 210n33, 217n71, 220n115, 225n40; Lacan.com, 189; Lacanian, 34, 38, 67, 90, 94–101, 106–10, 115, 122–23, 125–27, 158, 161–63, 173, 185, 211n59; movement, 51; "the Slovenian Lacan," 31
Laclau, Ernesto, 17, 23, 61, 66–67, 74–90, 106–11, 173, 212n82; and Mouffe, 74–75, 79, 87, 90, 107, 109
Laibach, 47, 50–51, 53–57, 97, 101
Lamont, Michèle, 9
Lenin, Vladimir, 122, 132, 143, 170
Less Than Nothing (Žižek), 148–52, 224n23

Ljubljana, 1, 26f, 30, 36, 47, 49–50, 92; School for Theoretical Psychoanalysis, 2, 23–28, 31, 35, 41–45, 51, 62, 64, 72, 79, 82, 165, 171, 173, 201n2, 203n38; University of, 32, 39, 67
London, 29, 76–77, 133, 137, 142, 149; School of Economics, 152
London Review of Books, 78, 110, 122–23, 136

Mannheim, Karl, 9, 11
Marx, Groucho, 125
Marx, Karl, 27, 33, 38–39, 44, 46, 62, 71, 73, 83–95, 124–25, 143, 150, 153, 155, 172, 199n86, 218n81; brother, 134; domination, concept of, 142; ideology, 9; Marxism, 23, 29–32, 35–36, 40–42, 55, 64, 67, 98–99, 137, 161, 171, 181; philosophy, 28, 34; post-Marxism, 17, 74–81; theory, 187
materialism, 29; dialectical, 32, 149; historical, 32, 118, 124
Matrix, The (film), 3, 100–101, 115
May 1968, 28, 32, 40, 63, 70, 73, 158
media, 2–3, 21–24, 49, 100, 105, 121, 126, 132–34, 153–54, 160, 179; access, 8, 177; alternative, 53; bias, 157; digital, 7, 119; mass, 6–7, 13, 82, 112, 180; mediatization, 14, 20; print, 22, 49, 71, 76, 105, 112, 144, 192, 229n101; public, 165, 169–70; social, 15, 128, 167, 176, 181–84; Western, 64. *See also* media-academia trade-off
media-academia trade-off, 20, 22, 148, 153, 162, 170, 175, 200n90
memes, 22, 128, 154, 178, 186, 188
Miller, Jacques-Alain, 37, 44, 64, 66–72, 79, 100, 138, 173, 202n23
Mladina (journal), 35, 50–51, 53, 80, 202n33
Mouffe, Chantal, 77, 83, 86; and Laclau, 74–75, 79, 87, 90, 107, 109
movement: collective, 46, 101; communist, 74; cultural, 52–53; ecological, 179; gay, 50; of ideas, 31, 185; of intervention, 20–21, 71, 79, 81, 114, 135;

movement (continued)
LGBTQ, 169; nationalist, 59; Non-Aligned, 27, 30; popular, 139; punk, 48, 54, 56–67, 163; right-wing, 38; scientific, 47, Slovenian, 60, social, 17, 51, 64, 138, 142; structuralist, 39; student, 32; women's, 169; of writing, 133

Neue Slowenische Kunst (NSK), 46–57, 64, 97, 101, 173, 206n85
New York Review of Books, 13, 155
New York Times, 129, 131, 152
9/11. *See* September 11
Nova Revija (journal), 32, 36, 50

Obama, Barack, 135, 141

Palestine, 2, 117
Paris, 11, 28–29, 41–44, 70–72, 77, 203n38
performance, 2, 13, 15, 19, 24, 50, 57, 67, 69, 74–75, 87, 95, 116, 129, 132, 138–39, 144, 146, 149–59, 166–78, 183–89, 218n81, 229n99; cinematic, 131; collaborative, 122; consistent, 147; dialectical, 193n6; digital, 65; experimental, 181; global, 142; innovative, 46–47; intellectual, 107; ironic, 22; Laibach, 56; NSK, 53, 97; performativity, 6, 15, 18, 22, 24, 26, 52, 54, 154, 184; provocative, 163; public, 16, 114, 137; relational, 35; repertoire, 20, 23, 38, 87–88, 100, 103, 116, 125–29, 136, 139, 143–44, 147, 158, 175, 178, 214n124, 219n106; repetitive, 23, 106, 133, 148, 162; rhetorical, 78; sacrificial, 102, 199n89
Peterson, Jordan, 181–82
philosophy, 1, 29, 32, 45, 53, 71, 76, 78, 83, 94, 100, 110, 121, 123–24, 129, 133, 148, 150–51, 154, 172, 178, 182–85, 228n83, 229n99; analytic, 10, 89; and antiphilosophy, 24, 145–46, 160–64; contemporary, 102; department, 36, 39, 70, 107; German, 97; Hegelian, 46; Marxist, 28, 34; public, 120; radical, 66; speculative, 177

Plato, 4, 11, 71, 79, 84, 94, 100, 139, 150, 195n18, 214n124
political correctness, 62, 169, 180, 182, 213n102
positioning, 26–27, 29, 32, 41, 44, 51–53, 59, 66–68, 71–74, 77–79, 82–90, 97, 103–7, 111, 117, 121–24, 136, 139–40, 152–53, 187, 204n61, 220n128, 227n72; canonical, 113; cost, 131; counterpositioning, 154; critical, 112; cultural, 31; diversified, 114; dominant, 109; global, 65; intellectual, 22–23, 38–39, 69, 108, 155; political, 37, 95, 137; process, 3, 8, 11, 61, 75; repositioning, 170; sacrificial, 127, 175, 185–86; self, 30, 60, 92–93, 96, 99, 199n89; superpositioning, 24, 33–34, 40, 42, 54–55, 63, 76, 80–81, 85, 91, 94, 98, 100, 110, 118, 125–29, 138, 143–51, 156–69, 171–73, 177–83, 188, 218n81, 224n33, 229nn99–101; theory, 6, 13, 15–21, 199n77
post-codex, 7, 24, 66, 133, 176, 178, 186
postmodernism: context, 20, 135; ideology, 57, 128, 156, 163; intellectual current of, 74, 94, 99, 112, 152, 204n61; reception, 109, 177; subjectivity, 97, 141; trap, 88–89
poststructuralism, 77, 83–84, 89, 210n33
Praxis (journal), 29–36, 40
Problemi (journal), 31–32, 36, 39, 42, 44–48, 54–55, 66–67, 166, 172, 201n2
psychoanalysis, 2, 19, 31, 42–44, 47, 52, 67, 73, 76, 82–83, 94, 98, 121, 162, 213n98, 229n99, 230n122; Freudian, 152; Lacanian, 71, 77, 79, 86, 95, 123, 127, 220n115; the Society for Theoretical, 25, 45, 92, 173, 201n2, 206n87; treatment, 124
punk, 31, 46–57, 97, 163

Rorty, Richard, 10, 16, 95
Russia, 2, 173
Russia Today, 167, 170f

Salecl, Renata, 51, 60, 64, 66, 173, 206n87
Sanders, Bernie, 179

INDEX   239

September 11, 19, 24, 103–4, 114–21, 135–39, 142, 163, 169, 170f
Slovenia, 1–4, 18, 22–23, 25–44, 47, 51–53, 57–60, 63–73, 80, 84, 93, 100–102, 159, 161, 193n4, 203n38
socialism, 25, 27, 29, 36, 39, 57, 74, 91, 98, 106
Socrates, 4, 11, 106, 124, 162, 175, 195n18, 228n83
Stalin, Joseph, 23, 26f, 27–32, 64, 74, 143; Stalinism, 27, 106, 129
structuralism, 31, 33–46, 52, 76–89. *See also* poststructuralism
Sublime Object of Ideology, The (Žižek), 17, 23, 31, 68, 74–75, 77, 79, 82, 91, 93, 110, 148, 158, 178

technology, 7, 182; digital, 100, 150
Tel Quel, 42–44
theology, 92, 121, 124; political, 67, 123, 128
Tito, Josip Broz, 23, 25–32, 46, 59, 57, 64, 206n85
trauma, 19, 23, 26, 33, 58, 60, 87, 90; collective, 63; cultural theory, 24, 103, 114–20, 135–36, 140–44
Trump, Donald, 135, 141f, 169, 170f, 179–81, 229n101
Twitter, 187; tweets, 7, 184, 186

unconscious, 16, 52, 85–86, 94, 98–99, 113, 115, 152, 156–57, 163, 186, 189, 213n98, 225n43
United Kingdom, 2, 65–66, 106, 179
United States, 2–3, 10, 57, 61, 65, 73, 77–78, 87, 89, 100, 105–6, 112, 114, 116, 117–18, 120, 126, 132, 141, 169, 172, 179, 181, 187, 197n49, 210n33, 215n14; American, 4, 10, 57, 61, 69, 94, 97, 101, 115–28, 136, 163, 182, 229n101

vouching, 23, 74, 77, 79, 82

Wikipedia, 7; WikiLeaks, 142
Wo Es War (series), 89, 95, 98, 161, 213n98

YouTube, 126, 128, 133, 181, 189
Yugoslavia, 1, 25–33, 37, 46, 50, 57–58, 60–64, 67, 92, 154, 168, 206n85; Socialist Federal Republic of, 23, 27, 193

Žižek, Slavoj: articles, 2, 22, 24, 30, 63, 75, 89, 99–100, 104, 121, 136, 156–59, 173, 184; birth, 1–2, 35f; books, 11, 31, 68–69f, 71, 75, 77, 82, 91, 93, 97–98, 107–8, 115, 117, 121–24, 136, 142, 147–50, 152, 161, 167, 178; corruption, 4, 163–64; elections, 23, 53, 59–61, 92, 141f, 169, 170f, 179, 181; emergence, 3, 4, 12, 19, 24–27, 31, 35, 37, 42, 46, 66–69, 72–77, 82, 106, 176; films, 2, 100–102, 129–32, 148–49, 151, 157; jokes, 20, 73, 88, 91, 94, 102, 107, 125, 132, 136, 144, 146–48, 151, 154, 175; journals, 31, 36, 39, 47, 63, 134, 166; MA thesis, 36, 39; pedagogy, 24, 77, 123, 145–46; performance, 2, 13–19, 22–24, 35, 46–47, 53, 67, 69, 74–75, 78, 87, 95, 102, 105, 107, 114, 116, 122, 129–44, 146–58, 161–70, 173–74, 176–77, 181, 184–89, 229n101; PhDs, 25, 36–37, 69–70, 193n1; phenomenon, 3, 11–12, 14–15, 22–23, 26, 66, 151, 166, 173, 188; popularization, 24, 120–21, 151, 184, 193n1; positioning, 16, 18, 20, 23, 29, 32–34, 44, 55, 66–67, 72, 78, 82, 85, 93, 102, 104, 108–9, 117–18, 127–29, 152–53, 159–66, 180, 199n89, 203n38, 227n72, 228n83, 229n99; publishing, 172–73; reception, 3, 24, 69, 73–78, 102, 104, 108–12, 119, 121, 133, 143, 150, 154, 157, 170–71, 177, 187; rejection, 3, 24, 69, 73–74, 104, 137, 141, 143, 157, 183; style, 19, 23, 72–74, 82, 102, 106–11, 115–23, 129, 131, 136, 139, 142, 145, 147, 151, 160, 178, 189
Zupančič, Alenka, 22, 53–54, 67, 95, 107, 161, 163, 166, 171–72, 191